THE INCARNATION

AND

COMMON LIFE.

THE INCARNATION

AND

COMMON LIFE

BY

BROOKE FOSS WESTCOTT, D.D., D.C.L.

PUBLISHERS
Eugene, Oregon

THERE CAN BE NEITHER JEW NOR GREEK, THERE CAN BE NEITHER BOND NOR FREE, THERE CAN BE NO MALE AND FEMALE; FOR YE ALL ARE ONE MAN IN CHRIST JESUS.

Gal. iii. 28.

IN HIM WE LIVE AND MOVE AND HAVE OUR BEING.

Acts xvii. 28.

Wipf and Stock Publishers
199 West 8th Avenue, Suite 3
Eugene, Oregon 97401

The Incarnation and Common Life
By Westcott, B.F.
ISBN: 1-59244-511-X
Publication date 1/29/2004
Previously published by Macmillan and Co., 1893

PREFACE.

It can very rarely happen that one who has spent long and busy years as student and teacher should be suddenly called at the close of life to the oversight of a Diocese in which the problems of modern life are presented in the most urgent and impressive form. Such a transition brings with it of necessity many strange experiences. It gives by its very unexpectedness a singular reality to earlier thoughts. The Faith which has been pondered in quiet must without preparation be brought into the market-place and vindicated as a power of action.

In the following pages I have endeavoured to express what I have felt from time to time when I have been called to consider some particular phase of our present life, and to mark, however imperfectly, the application of the Gospel to our own difficulties and sorrows and duties. The highest conceivable attestation of a divine revelation lies in its power to meet each new want of man as it arises, and to gain fresh force from the growth of human knowledge. The message of the Incarnation satisfies this criterion in unexpected ways, and our distresses enable us to feel its wider applications.

There is indeed a progress in the interpretation and practical apprehension of the Gospel, which, while it is not due to natural forces, is conditioned by them. There is such a progress within the limits of the New Testament. The apostolic teaching in the Epistle of St James remains within the range of the thoughts of the Synagogue, illuminated by the Coming of the Christ. In the Epistle to the Ephesians the noblest conceptions of Imperial Rome are used to give distinctness to the idea of the unity of the Church.

Scripture and History alike teach us that Christianity is not defined by the letter of the written Word. Every incident, every precept which the written Word contains, is a germ, fruitful in manifold developments which do not indeed add anything to the substance of the written Word, but witness to its life.

Preface.

This must be so if we believe that 'the Word 'became flesh and tabernacled among us...full of 'grace and truth.' In this central fact of the life of the world, which discloses the capacity and the destiny of man, and of the creation over which man is set as sovereign and representative, there is no change in the Person of the Word. He through Whom and unto Whom all things were created took humanity to Himself and lived a human life. In the fulness of time the Word became not a man as one man of many men, but 'flesh.' In Him humanity found its unity under the conditions of earth, and, if I may so speak, its personality. Such a fact is not a solitary fact though it is unique in the sense that experience cannot furnish any presumption against it, for it admits of no parallel. It is at once the crown and the foundation of a long spiritual growth. *The Word became* (not *was made*) *flesh* in due season according to the orderly unfolding of the divine purpose. The Creation and the Incarnation both answer to the timeless counsel of GOD, Who *appointed Him heir of all things, through Whom He also made the world* (τοὺς αἰῶνας). The manhood which was broken up into innumerable fragments was gathered essentially into Him. In Him, Who is unchangeably the Son of GOD, each man is enabled to find his true fulfilment as part of a whole; and the human race is enabled to realise the Divine Fatherhood in its Sinless Head, 'the last Adam,' not as a hope or an aspiration but as a fact. At the same time by the assumption of 'blood and flesh' (Heb. ii. 14), the Word has revealed to us that these material forms, which are transitory as far as the experience of sense goes, have a Divine affinity and therefore correspond with a spiritual being. What we see becomes a sacrament of the unseen.

These general thoughts underlie all that I have written; but it has not been my purpose to attempt to define in detail the doctrine of the Incarnation. It is enough for us to ponder the words of St John and give to each phrase its natural and full sense:

IN THE BEGINNING WAS THE WORD,
AND THE WORD WAS WITH GOD,
AND THE WORD WAS GOD,...
AND THE WORD BECAME FLESH,
    AND TABERNACLED AMONG US,...
    FULL OF GRACE AND TRUTH.

Here for a moment the eternal is disclosed and we see what *was* when time began: we see that 'flesh' is capable of union with GOD and has been assumed by 'GOD the only Son' ($\theta\epsilon\grave{o}s\ \mu o\nu o\gamma\epsilon\nu\acute{\eta}s$ John i. 18), and that His human life is a

Preface.

well-spring of Divine help and gives reality to our knowledge. Such a view of the world and of life, and the fact which gives it, are most truly natural. The aspirations, the movements, the achievements of men, are unintelligible except through the recognition of a vital relation between the Creator and the Creation. In Christ as men we can approach GOD. In Christ our human ways of thinking of GOD, limited as they must be and issuing in an antithesis on every side, are justified. In Christ we pray to the Father—His Father and our Father—and receive all that we require for our spiritual sustenance, through that which He has freely given and freely gives by His Spirit. In Christ all things—all things which belong to the consummation of manhood—are possible.

The proof of these lofty assertions must be given in deed. No one can confess more sorrowfully than he who holds most surely that 'the Word became flesh' that we have not as believers lived our Creed. But at least we have kept our ideal; and during the last three eventful years I seem to have seen that GOD is leading us to bring it with a transforming energy into our personal and social and national life.

For us the words of St Paul have the promise of fresh victories:

ALL THINGS ARE YOURS; AND YE ARE CHRIST'S; AND CHRIST IS GOD'S.

For us the words of the Lord in their breadth and their exclusiveness open the vision of a living unity to which we can bring every work and thought and effort, knowing that our labour is not vain:

I AM THE WAY AND THE TRUTH AND THE LIFE:

NO ONE COMETH TO THE FATHER BUT THROUGH ME.

B. F. D.

APPLETON-LE-MOOR,
   Aug. 26, 1893.

CONTENTS

PAGE

Fellowship in Intercession. 3
Durham Cathedral, Ascension Day, 1890

Social Obligations of the National Church. 19
Diocesan Conference, Oct. 29, 1891

The Incarnation a Revelation of Human Duties.
Durham, Nov. 17; *Auckland Castle*, Nov. 19, 1892 . 41

The Spirit sent in the Name of the Son. 109
York Minster, Feb. 8, 1893

The Aim and the Strength of Christian Action. 125
Chapel Royal, St James', Feb. 19, 1893

Ideals. 141
Mansion House, London, March 7, 1891

The Family. 161
St Hilda's, Hedgefield, July 30, 1892

The Consecration of the Teacher. 175
Durham Cathedral, Oct. 18, 1891

The Christian Idea of Almsgiving. 195
Durham Cathedral, Jan. 15, 1891

Our own Poor in India.
St James', Piccadilly, Sunday after Ascension, 1891 . 209

Socialism. 225
Church Congress, Hull, Oct. 1, 1890

Educational Value of Co-operation. 241
Tynemouth, Sept. 3, 1890

Contents.

	PAGE
The Method, the Aim, and the Sanction of Co-operation. *Blaydon-on-Tyne*, Nov. 13, 1891	259
The Manifold Revelation of Truth. *Newcastle-on-Tyne*, Aug. 1, 1893	277
A Gospel for the poor. *St Andrew's, Deptford*, Third Sunday in Advent, 1891	295
Sursum Corda. *Sherborne Minster*, June 22, 1893	311
A quiet life: its joy and power. *Auckland Castle*, March 30, 1891	327
Our duty to posterity. *Peterborough*, June 2, 1892	341

APPENDIX I.

I. Walking by Faith not by Sight. *St Mary's, Cambridge*, Ascension-Day, 1888	363
II. The Conditions of progressive Revelation. *Westminster Abbey*, 8th Sunday after Trinity, 1888	375

APPENDIX II.

I. Letter to the Archdeacons of the Diocese. Advent, 1890	387
II. Letter to the Clergy and Laity. Septuagesima, 1892	394
III. Letters to the Clergy. March—June, 1892	400
IV. Wearmouth Deanery of Church Workers. 1890, 1891	404
Notes	422

FELLOWSHIP IN INTERCESSION.

Brethren, pray for us.

1 Thess. v. 25.

CATHEDRAL, DURHAM.

ENTHRONEMENT.

Ascension Day, 1890.

FELLOWSHIP IN INTERCESSION.

WE are gathered here to-day, brethren, on an occasion which is in many aspects of unparalleled solemnity. Our thoughts are full of the past. We cannot but look back to the 15th of May, eleven years ago, when, speaking in this place, my predecessor laid open the secret of his life and work, the reverent fixing of his soul's eye upon the vision of the eternal presence, a vision of righteousness and grace and glory, which is for the believer a vision of purification and strength. And now, as we humbly hope, for him the vision of faith has become the vision of experience, and he "sees the face" of Him on whom he trusted.

We cannot but look back again to last Ascension Day, when the thanksgiving of the whole Diocese, as of one heart, found expression here, because he whom all loved was given for a time from death to life. And now his elder friend has been charged to take up, as strength may be given, his interrupted work—interrupted, indeed, yet crowned by the last wonderful summer of great words and great deeds, and not incomplete, if the fulness of service is in the perfectness of devotion acknowledged by universal reverence and affection.

We cannot but look back, and, if at first we are touched with natural sorrow in the retrospect, sorrow is soon turned into hope. We perceive, even with our feeble powers, that beneath all these vicissitudes one unchanging counsel of love goes forward to its accomplishment; that work and rest, effort and self-surrender, the stress of conflict and the silence of the grave, are facts of the one life whereby alone we live. What is lost to the eye rises transfigured in the soul, and we come to know that when the Lord said: "It is expedient for you that I go away," He revealed a divine law, by which each bereavement, each apparent loss, becomes through His grace the source of new spiritual blessing.

We cannot but look back, and we cannot but look forward. Looking back, then, in the spirit of devout gratitude to the example of him whom God has taken to Himself; and looking forward in the spirit of simplest obedience to the call which he has uttered, I say now with a full heart: "Brethren, pray for us."

But what is the prayer for which I ask? It is not the self-willed importunity of him who thinks that he shall be heard for his much speaking. It is not the opening to GOD of thoughts which His love has not anticipated. It is not the pleading of our personal wishes as isolated objects of Divine favour. Nay, rather, it is the humblest, tenderest, most unquestioning expression of our dependence; the confession of our wants and weaknesses, as we have felt them; the firmest resolution to rest in GOD'S will and to make His will our own; the energy of a spiritual communion by which we realise our own well-being in the well-being of others; the endeavour to quicken and chasten and hallow every prompting of duty by the light of Heaven.

In this sense, brethren, pray for us. Such prayer corresponds with our Christian fellowship, with our present needs, with our Divine assurance.

1. Such prayer, I say, corresponds with our Christian fellowship. We are not, we cannot be, alone. There is a larger life in which we are all bound to an irrevocable past and an immeasurable future; a life which we inherit; a life which we bequeath, weakened or purified by our own little labours. And there is also now a present life of the society in which we are all bound one to

another, a life of the city, of the diocese, of the nation; a life which in these different relations is completed in many parts and fulfilled through many offices; a life in which each member serves the whole body with his peculiar gifts; a life in which the rich harmony is marred by the silence of the feeblest voice; a life in which the greatest powers owe a debt of blessing to the humblest; a life in which each lives by all, through all, for all.

The reality of this vast social life, manifested through every man, and unexhausted, is an inexorable and an overwhelming fact. We are not, we cannot be, alone. In itself the fact is fitted to oppress us with the feeling of our powerlessness. But it can be transfigured. And to pray one for another is to transfigure it. So to pray as feeling burdens which are not laid directly upon us, is to know that by GOD'S most gracious dispensation we can lighten them. So to pray as thankfully recognising the variety of service by which we are sustained and enriched, is to multiply a thousandfold the energies of that sympathy which crowns our common intercourse with gladness. So to pray as laying ourselves, our plans, our hopes, our acquirements, our opportunities, in the sight of GOD for His use, is to learn the lesson of life, for—

> "Our life, with all it yields of joy and love,
> And hope and fear,
> Is just our chance o' the prize of learning love,
> How love might be, hath been, indeed, and is."

Such thoughts of the far-reaching consequences of our social dependence, of our social obligations, of our social opportunities, are in the air. They take shape in many strange and startling forms. Sometimes they stir the aspirations of heroic souls who feel the promise which lies still unfulfilled in our humanity. Sometimes they sharpen the cry of the lonely sufferer cast down in the fierce struggle of selfish competition. Sometimes they are made to furnish the watchwords of revolution. In whatever guise they come, they call out a response which grows deeper and fuller as the years go on, in spite of the errors by which they are disordered. But in our Christian faith, if only we have hearts to see, they meet us with absolute purity and absolute persuasiveness. When St Paul speaks of Christians being "in Christ," he has gathered up the Gospel in two syllables; he has proclaimed, as all may grasp it, the unfailing bond of fellowship, the adequate provision for effective ministry, the victorious sovereignty of redeeming love. "In Christ;" these words are the charter of Christian prayer. The one life by which the prayer is prompted is the force by which the prayer is fulfilled. In this sense, then, as united in one body, pledged to one service, quickened by one Head, " Brethren, pray for us."

2. Such prayer, as I have said, corresponds with Christian fellowship. It corresponds also with our present needs. Each age has its own problems, through which the reality, the intensity, the power of the vast life of which I have spoken, are revealed. And, as has been well said, the answer to these riddles of life and death is still, as in the old legend, "man"—man in some new aspect as he moves little by little towards his divine destiny—man in relation to nature, man in his personal freedom, man in his social connections. There can be no doubt as to the questions which we have to face in this generation. Within my own experience a silent revolution has been accomplished in England, and in a great part of Europe—more sure and more effective because it has been silent. The conditions of commerce and of production have been irrevocably transformed. The mass of the population has been slowly and surely concentrated in the large cities. The sovereign power in the State has passed from the few to the many. The treasures of literature and art and science have been opened with ever-increasing completeness to all classes. The re-

sponsibilities and the relations of nations have been seen under a new light. And whether we regard these movements with satisfaction or regret, with hope or fear, we must deal with the momentous issues to which they point.

How, then, we ask—often in sadness and perplexity—how shall we bring back to the intercourse of artisan and employer, to trade and manufacture, that sense of true human sympathy which gives dignity to labour and provides for the hallowing of great possessions? How shall we check the waste, the bitterness, the oppression, the anarchy of unlimited competition, and enable each worker to feel that he is bound with all his fellow-workers in one brotherhood of common service? How shall we arrest the threatened conflict of numbers and wealth and guard at once the worth of man as man and the splendid inheritances of the past which are entrusted for use to the administration of a few.

Or, again, how shall we bring to frail, enfeebled, stifled crowds in the thronged courts of our towns the freshness, the calm, the simplicity of natural life? How shall we temper and chasten the sense of power with the sense of responsibility and keep force from yielding to the dictates of selfish passion?

Or, again, how shall we secure that the influence of literature and art shall be pure and invigorating so as to stimulate with a generous enthusiasm and to refresh by healthy pleasure?

Or, yet once again, to glance at larger duties, how shall we each in our own little circle labour to realise that peoples, like men, must rejoice and suffer together; to check the proud assumption of our own superiority; to understand national trials which we have not suffered; to prepare for that which, as Emerson said sadly, has not yet been tried—a policy based upon the foundation of love.

Such questions are not matters for ingenious speculation only. They are of intense practical moment. They must be dealt with in some way by all of us. Our answers to them, or our refusals to answer them, in word or deed, conscious or unconscious, form the staple of our ordinary life, in the workshop and the study, in the home and the market, in the fields and in the council-chamber. And if I propose them to-day, it is not that I wish to discuss them in any way now. But I do wish, in my first words, to commend them to your most serious thought. I do wish to call again, as far as any influence is given to me, the energy and enterprise of our citizens from personal to civil duties. I do wish, speaking, as I believe, in the spirit of the great office in which

I desire to sink myself, to claim the whole of life, every human interest, every joy and every sorrow, every noble aspiration and every true thought, as falling within the domain of our faith. I do wish that we should agree together from the first that all the problems of modern life are in the end religious problems. For, if I am not prepared to answer in detail the questions which I have asked, I have no doubt as to the general character of the answer. The answer must be spiritual and not legal, from within and not from without. Better men, and better men only, will usher in the better age. For here also in this widest application the words are true that

> "Of the soul the body form doth take,
> For soul is form, and doth the body make."

Such reflections at the present day force themselves upon us everywhere. But here they are involved in the continuous traditions of the See. The coronet which still encircles the mitre has not lost its lesson because he whose symbol it is has been relieved from the exercise of civil power. At Durham, Castle and Cathedral stand side by side, not as rivals, but as sisters. By their foundation, by their growth, and by their remodelling, they witness to the same truth that life in its sharpest contrasts is still one, that the secular and religious are harmonised in a spiritual unity. The successor of Pudsey, of Bek, of Van Mildert, the tenant of Auckland, can never forget the breadth of his obligations, however the conditions of society are changed. He may, indeed, desire for himself that he were freed from the anxieties of a large household and from the administration of large means, but none the less he must believe that these cares can be made fertile in blessing if the trust is fulfilled faithfully with a single eye to the common good. Looking then, at the forces which are surely remoulding the forms of society, at the vast problems which already demand resolute study, at the responsibility which is laid upon a bishop to consider for Christ's sake the poor, the needy, and the stranger[1], and at the social characteristics of our own Diocese, I say yet a second time—"Brethren, pray for us."

3. And the prayer which is prompted by the sense of Christian fellowship, and which is deepened by the sense of our present needs, is sustained by the promises of the Gospel. Christianity deals with every social problem, not accidentally, but in virtue of its essence. Earthly duties (as we speak), earthly destinies, occupy the New Testament from the Sermon on the Mount to the Apocalypse. For us the Incarnation is the rule and the motive power of endeavours for

social improvement which no success can satisfy. The Passion is the revelation and the measure of human guilt and Divine love. The Resurrection is the sign of GOD'S purpose for all material and transitory things—the transfiguration of the completeness of human life. The Christian Church is, as we believe, the present organ of a living Spirit. We claim for it, in virtue of the assurance of the Lord, not simply the right of existence or the power of self-defence, but the certainty of conquest. Already, as we know, much has been done by the direct appeal to Christian principles for the cause of temperance and for the cause of purity. Much will be done in the near future, unless I am strangely mistaken, to overcome the passion for quick gain which threatens to defile and to debase all life with the spirit of gambling, to mitigate the evils of poverty and war, the inconsiderate selfishness of men and nations. The powers of the world to come are at our command. These times, also, are "times of Christ," for Christianity is of no age, and therefore it justifies itself in every age. But we, on our part, must match our thoughts and our efforts with our Creed. Yes, with our Creed. We shall not do our work by explaining away or minimising its central mystery, but by shewing that this mystery includes the realisation of the loftiest desires of man, while it interprets and satisfies the age-long prophecies of nature and life. We shall not do our work by anxiously narrowing the scope of the Gospel to the limits of our own conceptions, or measuring the value of our service by our own capacities. GOD works through us indeed, but He does work, and in His working He transcends our loftiest imaginations.

There is about us enough spiritual force and action to win the world, but it is dispersed, undisciplined, undirected, paralysed by unworthy suspicions, and dissipated by needless controversies. Meanwhile there are evils before us appalling in their magnitude and in their menaces. Let us frankly accept the readiness to assail them as so far a sign of fellowship, and the power to overcome them as so far a test of living faith. It is through the completeness of service, through the simplicity of devotion, that Christ will reveal His presence in us and in others, and let us not doubt that wisdom will be justified of all her children. So it will be, as I believe, that GOD will give to us in His good time the blessing for which eager hearts are waiting, and reveal the unity for which we have sought in vain. Where Christ is seen to be, there we shall recognise the presence of the one life; and where He is seen to be with the most perfect and harmonious energy of human service, there we shall recognise the power which is able to draw to itself every less effective form of vital religion.

To wait and watch for such a revelation is to feel the greatness of our call, the greatness of our faith. It is to bring to the trial of our own experience the belief which has been able to fashion through more than twelve centuries our northern people to the service of the Lord. It is to feel already that every scattered ray of light will hereafter be gathered into the glory of Christ, Creator, Redeemer, Fulfiller. It is to win for the ennobling of our common work, in its sadnesses and disappointments and failures, the lesson of the Ascension, in which we see the fulfilment of the destiny of man and the assurance of his sovereignty. Looking, then, at the all-embracing range of our Christian faith, at the victories which it has won, at the promises by which it is quickened, at the divisions by which its efficacy is hindered, at the Divine issue in which, as we most certainly believe, it will find its consummation, when GOD shall be all in all, yet once again I say, " Brethren, pray for us."

Pray for us. You know on what an inheritance of reverence and affection I am called to enter. You know how it was won. You know how alone it can be guarded and used. Help me then to forget every weakness, to banish every misgiving, to trust wholly to the commission which I have received, to stir up with glad remembrance the spirit which is given by GOD'S mercy to those who are charged with the government of souls, the spirit of power and love and discipline.

The teaching of Ascension Day, the teaching of prophet and psalmist, of evangelist and apostle, to which we have listened, meets every fear and enlarges every hope. It constrains us to look to Heaven and yet not away from earth. It confirms patience by the assurance of fresh power from on high while the time of labour lasts. It sustains infirmity by the vision of the Son of Man, throned at the right hand of the Father. It helps us to feel the Saviour's hands still lifted in blessing over those whom He has left only in bodily presence. It enables us to know, in spite of every spectacle of sin and sorrow, that He who is King of Glory is King over all the earth, and that He is preparing even now that universal dominion promised to men, which is indeed the dominion of GOD. It bids us offer every service of thought and word and work with this one petition in our hearts, "Be thou exalted, Lord, in thine own strength, so will we sing and praise Thy power."

With this great confidence, with this splendid hope, with this humble supplication, "Brethren, pray for us," even as I am pledged to bear you in my heart before GOD to my life's end.

SOCIAL OBLIGATIONS OF THE
NATIONAL CHURCH.

DIOCESAN CONFERENCE,
DARLINGTON.

INAUGURAL ADDRESS.
Oct. 29th, 1891.

SOCIAL OBLIGATIONS OF THE NATIONAL CHURCH.

THE thoughts of all in this Conference are naturally turned back to the corresponding meeting two years ago, when my predecessor, "called," as he said, "from death to life," addressed his last counsels to the Diocese which he had inspired with his own energy and devotion. That call from death was, as he added, "given for a purpose," not, indeed, such a purpose as we hoped and prayed for, but a purpose, as we trust, fertile in blessings. The brief space of renewed work which followed his return confirmed and consecrated with unique solemnity the lessons of ten years. It reaffirmed, with the assurance of one who had already looked on the realities of another order, the supremacy of service among the duties of man. It gave occasion for words of encouragement and warning which will live among us, even as he who uttered them still lives here with an influence not less powerful than that of his bodily presence.

At that memorable meeting Bishop Lightfoot proposed two subjects for special consideration, "The attitude of the Church towards the social and socialistic aspirations of the day," and "Home Reunion." The way to Home Reunion lies, I believe, through fellowship in the service of man, inspired and sustained by faith in Christ; so that under our present circumstances the social work of the Church is fitted to become at once the vindication of its spiritual power and the preparation for its restored unity. The two subjects are in fact one subject; and the traditions of the See animate us with unfaltering courage in the endeavour to pursue it.

A hundred years ago, when the fabric of European life was shaken to its foundations, Bishop Barrington stood forth as a pioneer of social reforms, and gathered round him in a "Society for bettering the condition and increasing the comforts of the poor" men like Mr Speaker Addington, W. Wilberforce, H. Hoare, Count Rumford, W. Pitt, Paley, H. Thornton, R. Burdon, T. Bernard, J. J. Angerstein, Sir G. Staunton, the Bishops of London, Lincoln, and St David's, the Earl of Winchelsea, Earl Spencer, the Marquis of Buckingham, the Marquis of Bute, the Marquis of

Hertford, who with generous and varied devotion applied themselves to the solution of the problems of poverty; and nowhere can we find a more just and hopeful vindication of the character of the masses of our countrymen, a wiser estimate of the principles to be followed in the administration of relief, a larger or more fruitful series of experiments in every form of philanthropic effort than in the Reports of the Society. Friendly societies workhouses, dwellings, and allotments; village mills, shops, kitchens, and public rooms; gaols and beggars; education and industrial schools; are discussed in them with practical illustrations. We can still learn much from the experience which was gained under conditions widely different from our own. At least we shall be unworthy of our fathers if we do not strive to accomplish in larger measure what they felt to be within reach as the outcome of the Christian Faith[2].

We cannot, indeed, directly copy their plans while we imitate their spirit. We have passed through two momentous revolutions in the last century—an industrial revolution, and a political revolution; and such changes, if they bring heavy responsibilities, bring also new hopes. The past, we can see, is no measure of the future. Earlier failures bring no condemnation to fresh endeavours. We can trace better than those who went before us the direction of popular movement. We can recognise at least the broad laws of social growth. We can acknowledge, even gladly, that modification is involved in the very nature of temporal existence; that stationariness or repetition is impossible in the forms of national life. Such general conceptions save us from many fruitless struggles, while they indicate in what way our labour may be most effective. The broad stream of events cannot be stayed or turned backward, but it can be guided along fertilising channels; it can be kept within just bounds; it can be made fit to bear all the treasures of past generations for the use of later ages. If the general direction of movement is found more and more to lie beyond human control, the circumstances of movement are found to be more and more modifiable by forces which are at length guided with wise design.

In the steady amelioration of life which thus becomes possible, the Church and the State, the spiritual and temporal powers, have each their proper work. Thinkers of every school are coming more and more to acknowledge that the State has a moral end: that the true ruler will seek unweariedly to secure conditions of labour in every case which shall be favourable, or at least not un-

National Church.   23

favourable, to the development of a noble character: to provide that all classes alike shall share in the fulness of the one life: to enforce by the sanction of law that which has been clearly proved to be for the common good; to organise protection for the weak; to aim at the well-being, and not only the material well-being, of every citizen. Meanwhile, it is the office of the Church, the spiritual power, to keep ever present to men, under all the changing conditions of action, the ideal which has been committed to its keeping: to enforce with unvarying energy the social destiny of all conduct and all endowments, of material wealth and intellectual power and personal influence: to bear witness to the larger fellowship by which class is bound to class, and nation to nation: to maintain and to vindicate the reality of "the powers of the age to come," the age which, in one sense, has come. It is not its office to discuss details or to prescribe rules. These belong to men who have a practical knowledge of affairs. But if the end is determined, there will not be wanting those who will give right counsel as to the way. It is, in a word, the office of the State to give effect to public opinion: it is the office of the Church to shape it. The Church educates and inspires society, which moulds the State. The State will always be a little behind public opinion, while it looks primarily to order. The Church will look primarily to progress, while it holds out in the Gospel an unattainable ideal for more and more complete embodiment. For the attainment of this end the Church proposes an adequate motive, it offers adequate strength, it possesses infinite patience. Motive, strength, patience, all alike lie in the fundamental message, "the Word became flesh."

The motive. However feebly we realise the fact, the truth, of the Incarnation, we find in it the inexhaustible spring of brotherhood. No difference which finds expression in terms of earth can stay it. In this sense also, "brothers are brothers evermore." We spell out the Divine message little by little in thought and in action, but the most rudimentary apprehension of its meaning brings home to us that man is bound to man, in virtue of his humanity, by that which is infinitely stronger than anything which tends to separate one from another: that in the reckoning of the great account the loss of one cannot be another's gain: that, as members of a body, we can only secure our own highest good by rendering most completely our social service: that no human action can be isolated, and no right action purely self-regarding: that looking to Him in whom we are, our working must be from within outward, from that which is permanent to that which is transitory: that we cannot knowingly acquiesce in a form of life lower than the Christian standard. We may be filled with shame and compunction for innumerable inconsistencies, failures, sins, but the motive which we have once felt loses nothing of its claim on our obedience. Christ— such is the formal confession of each one of us— took me to Himself when He took humanity to Himself, and I owe myself to those with whom He has united me.

The strength. The same great fact assures us that the union of GOD and man once accomplished is continuously effective: it assures us that through the bewildering conflicts on which we look a Divine counsel of righteousness and love moves surely to its accomplishment: it assures us that what we see in small and scattered fragments is on the Divine side "one act at once." In that assurance, disheartened as we often must be, perplexed, lost, we grow strong again. What we do not see is that by which we move and have our being. We look at each moment on a new world for which GOD has made provision in the order of time, new duties for which He offers corresponding gifts. The past cannot bind us. We strive in dependence on a living GOD. The appeal to the uniformities of Nature does not exclude the operation of new forces. We rely, and experience justifies the reliance, on the fact of a new birth.

The patience. Again the same fact brings impressively before us what we are forced to regard as the amazing slowness, the immeasurable long-suffering of the action of God. Untold æons prepared the earth for man—perhaps we may go further back and say our system for the earth—as it falls within our knowledge. Long ages prepared men for Christ. And now it has taken eighteen centuries for us to gain firm hold of so much of the power of His Person and Work as we have yet embodied. Such a vision of the ways of God brings us confidence in patient waiting. We measure with gratitude, limited only by our ignorance, the years, the labours, the treasures, which have gone to form our own heritage, to accumulate the generous traditions by which our hopes are kindled, and to quicken the life by which our endeavours are sustained; and we are contented to trust the issues of our short day to the loving wisdom which has wrought the past for our use. The end is not yet, but we know our position, our calling, our aim. It is enough.

The duty of bringing this motive, this strength, this patience into common life belongs to every Christian in virtue of the faith which he holds.

But the duty is laid upon the national Church with the obligation of unique responsibility. The national Church is the spiritual organ of the nation. It is set to welcome, to concentrate, to use every force and every grace for the good of the whole people. All that it holds is held for all. The one claim which it recognises is need.

But it will be said that it has failed in the past. It has, at least, never denied its obligations. For the rest, the confession of failure is a first step towards the exertion of new vigour; and nowhere, and at no time, would it be possible to point to greater, wider, more varied activity in any Christian society than that which has flowed from our re-awakened Church during the last sixty years. It has a breadth of sympathy, intellectual, social, spiritual, which appears to me to be unparalleled. It preserves a practical sense of the great sum of human interests of which religion is the harmony and the inspiration. It touches the extremes of our life, the highest and the lowest, simply and naturally, and binds them together. And if some of its representatives are charged with the administration of large resources it is that they may endeavour to shew how a great inheritance can be made to serve the well-being of the community.

To Christians, I say, and to the national

Church, the capacity and the charge are given to commend to our countrymen an ideal fitted to occupy the energies and meet the needs of our generation. Have we then, we ask sadly, delivered Christ's message to the world in intelligible language? Have we emphasised the duties which answer to the special circumstances of the time? In the middle ages the Faith disciplined and used the powers of feudalism: are we preparing with wise and wide foresight to discipline and use the powers of capitalism? Nay, rather, is there not fear lest the Church may take its character from the world? At the beginning of the century there was among us widespread indolence of quiet worldliness, and now there is the equally perilous restlessness of worldly excitement.

If, however, we look steadily on the facts of contemporary life, and on the essential lessons of the Gospel, we cannot fail to see the points to which we ought to turn our own thoughts and the thoughts of those who hear us—spirituality, simplicity, labour, service.

1. We need, I say, to insist on the spiritual basis of life. Materialism has invaded our philanthropy and our religion. We aim more continuously and more hopefully at changed circumstances than at changed men, at outward worship more than at secret fellowship, at com-

panionship in popular amusements more than communion in self-devotion. I do not underrate the importance of such efforts—I claim them as helps and accessories—but the experience of the early Church—to speak of that alone—shews that man moulds his environment more truly than the environment moulds the man, that "the soul makes the body," that we have access to powers of another order. If we can indeed believe that "there is a Holy Ghost" we shall be spared many of the anxieties of "much serving;" but is it not true that in our distresses we need to ask ourselves whether we do believe that "there is a Holy Ghost?"

2. We need again to dwell on the simplicity of the material conditions of the noblest manhood: on the austere side of the teaching of the New Testament: on the havoc wrought by luxury: on the moral value of the simplest acts of buying and selling. Facilities for imitation make example more effective than in former times, so that we are bound to regard the wide effects of our conduct with increased care. I will go further and dare to say that the sorrows, the temptations, the evils of the age, call for great sacrifices, in order that a truer standard of life may be established. When those who can command material indulgences shall be seen to lay

them aside freely, others who waste their energies in seeking them will learn that happiness is not dependent on the possession of superfluities. In old days the leaders of the nation justified their position by hazarding, and very commonly by laying down, their lives for the people. Their corresponding duty now is that they should live for the people, using or offering for the common good what their fathers have handed down to their keeping.

3. We need again to press home on all the necessity of resolute and measured labour. A life of amusement is not only wearisome: it is childish. Labour of head or hand must be the staple of every worthy career. Self-indulgence is no right end for man. Resources which we inherit, in intellect or wealth, are the opportunities of larger service. It is no less ignoble to live idly on the gifts of the past than to live idly on the alms of our contemporaries.

Labour is necessary; and every form of labour is fitted to become a school of character. The most mechanical labour gives occasion for observation and mental effort. We dishonour our craft if we treat it as a means of livelihood and not as a discipline of living. A factory or a mine is a little commonwealth, which gives scope for all the excellencies of civil life.

4. We need once more to enforce on every Churchman the obligation of personal service. Nothing can take the place of individual effort, and of the influence of soul on soul in natural intercourse. So only can the message of higher things be brought home to the mass of men. At present large organisations tend to make human relations formal. We have been trained through them to a truer sense of the whole, of the reality and power of corporate life. We require now to bring back the single man to his proper place in the great body: to recognise the worth of his peculiar part in the total effect: to reconcile the offices of the individual and of society in a fuller harmony. And if we hope for much in civil life from a higher estimate of municipal duties: if we rightly look to public feeling as a corrective for private self-will and caprice in the pursuit of political interests: there is room in Church life for the beneficent action of the same forces. A citizen who gives no thought to the service of the State is defective in that which is of the essence of his character, and so the Churchman who renders nothing of his own true self to the Church, but only an offering of his possessions, cannot be a sharer in its fulness. Joy comes through co-operation with our fellows; and it is by a vital participation in the manifold forces of the body

that we gain that feeling of vastness and proportion which tends at least to save us from the wastefulness of controversy.

By inculcating such obvious lessons as these, as following directly from the simple apprehension of the Gospel, the representatives of the national Church will prepare in the way of life for the solution of the urgent social problems which are pressing upon us. The work will be done, not by argument, or temporary adjustment, or compromise, but by striving patiently and resolutely for the gradual establishment of that relation between man and man which answers to what we believe to be the relation of man to GOD. The order for which we look is, as we hold, of GOD'S will, and not of our making. Our privilege is, as we may be enabled, to remove the obstacles which hinder its advent, and the veils which obscure its beauty.

There are veils, there are obstacles in our path; and it is one of the advantages of our position that we know better than our fathers could know in their day the facts of life with which we have to deal, their interdependence, their filiation on the past, the general extent and the direction in which they admit of modification. We know with fair completeness the evils with which we have to contend. If we have to face an arduous struggle, at least we do battle in the light. There is, for example, a general agreement that it is an evil—a national evil—that a large body of wage-earners should be in a position of permanent instability, both from the fluctuations in trade, and from the nature of their engagement: that it is an evil that there is a large class of workers ($11\frac{1}{2}$ per cent. in East London) who are industrially worse than useless, so that in the opinion of economists they might be swept away with advantage: an evil that in Liverpool a local Friendly Society refuses to enter as members the inhabitants of no less than 167 streets: an evil that about one-fourth of the deaths of adults in London takes place in workhouses or charitable institutions: an evil that in our habitual dealings one with another we make little or no account of the social effect of our actions.

These are evils, and it is our duty to face them. I am not indeed sanguine of obtaining a speedy remedy. Premature legislation is not only ineffective: it is demoralising. It brings the majesty of law into disregard. But I do ask all who are familiar with the circumstances of labour, and who have influence on public opinion, to regard these evils strenuously in the light of our common life. And above all I ask the teachers of our Church, who are called to the duty by the whole movement of the age, which is for them the voice of the Spirit, to turn with the energy of faith to the fundamental questions of national life. In the presence of the restlessness, the impatience, the arrogance, the despondency of improvisers, they have a message to deliver which, as I believe, is alone able to guide and sustain effort to its divine issue.

I know the attractions of the pursuit of speculative truth and of historical criticism, but these are wholly subsidiary to action, which is the characteristic of man. The Gospel which is committed to believers claims to have the power to deal with every practical question of human conduct for the manifestation of GOD's glory; and friends and foes alike have a right to demand that this claim should be vindicated on the broad fields of life.

To this end the quiet witness of faith will tell of faith in GOD and in man, as the child of GOD, to begin with; and, in all failures and disappointments and delays, of faith in Christ, as the complete revelation of the way, the truth, the life of GOD.

Faith in GOD, Whose counsel we seek to establish: faith in man, through whom the end must be reached: faith in Christ, in Whom both meet: can we need more to move the world?

The work proposed to us is not easy. It demands self-denial, resolution, clear sight; but loving means giving of ourselves; and, in the language of an early Christian, "the vision of GOD is the life of man."

The Gospel has, I believe, untried and unsuspected powers wherewith to meet social and national difficulties. The present crisis in our history gives occasion for their exercise. The urgency of social questions—questions of temperance, purity, peace, unity, concord, many forms of the one question of human brotherhood—is a challenge and an opportunity to the Church of Christ. Even statesmen recognise that self-surrender on a large scale is one of the forces of which account must be taken. Emerson has said with a tone of pathetic remonstrance that "the power of love as the basis of a State has never been tried." And have we Churchmen had as yet the courage of our Faith?

I feel that I have wandered very far from the common type of the addresses which are given at such meetings as these. Yet I could not but use the occasion to indicate thoughts which haunt me when I move among men, and to express the convictions which have steadily gained strength during my whole life.

The circumstances of my youth at Birmingham gave me a keen interest in the later stages of the Chartist movement. From that time forward I have followed as a Christian student the course of social theories, revolutions, growths, at home and abroad, and now, at the close of life, I am called to occupy a place where the questions which they raise profoundly affect the conduct of my work, so that as one who has spiritual oversight over a Diocese stirred from end to end by the fluctuations of industrial competition, who is pledged to be "merciful for Christ's sake to poor and needy people, and to all strangers destitute of help," who believes that Christ is the Light and the Life of the world, I must strive to the utmost of my power to press on those who share my faith the social obligations which it involves. If, indeed, we were inclined to forget our obligations, we should be quickly roused to remembrance. On every side the challenge is given to Christianity, and given most justly, to vindicate its claims. "Shew us your works," is the reply which rightly meets us when we declare our message; and though we may falter, the vindication is within our reach. The works are prepared for our hands. Looking back over the past, I can find no time when the message of the Faith would have received a readier welcome than now, or when it met more directly the sorrows and aspirations of men.

If we are confronted by discontent and dissatisfaction when the material conditions of the masses have improved, we need not feel discouraged. They simply shew that with the general growth of intelligence, a higher average of well-being is felt to be attainable than has been attained. The demand for justice, which is at present the popular plea, stands midway between the bestowal and acceptance of benevolence, which marked the philanthropy of the past, and the self-devotion of service, which will, as we trust, mark the Christian brotherhood of the future.

Our gathering together here, clergy and laity together, shews that we desire to take counsel, one with another, on the fulfilment of our duty. The Diocese offers, as far as I have yet been able to see, some singular advantages for social Christian work, both in its material conditions and in the spirit and relations of its people. Hereafter, if the opportunity be given me, I shall endeavour to work out more in detail some of the thoughts which I have indicated. For the present I have wished simply to insist on the general truth that we must, as Churchmen, not of one class but of all classes, make our Christian Faith the rule and the inspiration of our whole life, as men and citizens, keeping steadily before us the ideal of a corporate life in Christ, wherein there can be no gain which is not a common possession and no loss which is not a common injury.

It will be the duty of the clergy to keep before their people, without weariness and without impatience, the clear vision of the purpose of GOD for His creation. But the chief burden of action must lie upon the laity. They can embody little by little the truth on which they have looked, judging with practised foresight the worth of opportunities, and bringing a power of sympathy to ennoble the intercourse of men with men.

THE INCARNATION A REVELATION
OF HUMAN DUTIES.

THE CATHEDRAL, DURHAM.
November 17th.
Ps. cxxxvii.

THE CHAPEL, AUCKLAND CASTLE,
November 19th.
Ps. xcvii.

THE INCARNATION A REVELATION OF HUMAN DUTIES.

REVEREND BRETHREN,

Before I enter on the discussion of the special subject which I propose to suggest for your consideration, I must offer you my cordial thanks for the care and thought which, with one or two exceptions, you have bestowed on the questions which I proposed to you. The replies which you have returned combine to give a vivid and minute view of the circumstances and the problems of the Diocese which it would not have been possible to obtain in any other way; and the knowledge which I have thus gained will serve to encourage and to guide me in whatever work I may hereafter be allowed to do. On future occasions, if the opportunity is given me, I hope to deal at length with some of the points which have been brought into prominence; but I should not do justice to my feeling if I did not now acknowledge with deep thankfulness the abundant proofs which

I have received of the continued devotion and zeal of our Clergy and Lay-workers, and of the spirit of sympathy and fellowship by which their labours are supported. I do not however wish to dwell to-day on external signs of local or general progress in our Church, or even on fundamental questions of ecclesiastical organisation and politics. I wish rather at this season of most solemn reckoning to fix your attention and my own on the central point of our Faith, and to ask—in order that we may all ponder the thought in the presence of GOD— whether the fact of the Incarnation finds adequate expression in our opinions and in our conduct. The Incarnation, in proportion as we give a distinct meaning to the truth, must become to us a revelation of human duties, and it is in this light I invite you to regard it.

In approaching this overwhelming subject, I shall endeavour to fulfil a plan which I had already formed when I was called here, and which has been, as you know, present to my mind throughout my work in Durham. In the Diocesan Conference a year ago I touched upon the obligation which is laid upon the National Church, the spiritual organ of the Nation, to deal with the questions of common life in the light of the Christian Faith. I endeavoured to shew then that we have in the fact of the Incarnation, which it is

a Revelation of Human Duties. 43

our duty to proclaim, a motive adequate to stir us to resolute action, and strength adequate to support us in the face of difficulties apparently insuperable: that the vision of the patience of GOD is able to bring back confidence when we are disheartened by disappointments and delays: that as Christians, as Churchmen, we must strive unreservedly, clergy and laity alike, to make the Gospel the rule of our whole life in society and in the state, keeping before us the ideal of the one corporate life in Christ of which we have been made partakers: that we are bound not only to believe that 'Jesus is Lord' but to confess Him before men: that it is the characteristic office of the clergy to present principles in the light of fresh experience, and of the laity to embody them with practical wisdom.

I wish now to pursue these thoughts a little further. I wish to point out, in the hope that some here present will pursue the different lines of reflection into the details of ordinary work, that the Incarnation of the Word of GOD becomes to us, as we meditate on the fact, a growing revelation of duties personal, social, national: that it is able by its all-pervading influence to mould to noblest ends the character of men and classes and peoples: that the interpretation of it in its bearings upon conduct, with all that it brings of obligation and encouragement, is committed to us as ministers of the English Church with unique solemnity. For while we gladly recognise the services which other Communions render to the cause of righteousness, their labours cannot lessen our responsibility. They cannot, I repeat, lessen our responsibility, but they will, I trust, more and more help us to meet it.

The meaning of the Incarnation, the central event in the life of the world, the central truth in the experience of men, in which the seen and the unseen, the temporal and the eternal, the finite and the infinite, are brought together, is not obvious at once. The treasures of wisdom which the Incarnation includes will not be exhausted till humanity has reached its consummation. GOD sent forth His Son when the fulness of the time was come; and, from that date onward, the belief in the Word Incarnate has been a factor in human development, growing in power through further knowledge of life. For Christianity is not a speculation or a theory. It is historical in its preparation, in its essence, in its realisation: the record and the interpretation of man's experience. The revelation which it brings is in life and of life. The Faith, in which it is embodied and through which it acts, grows as humanity grows. Each age is bound to study afresh the central fact and to trace the broadening stream of its consequences. Each age has its special problems for which the Gospel has a special message. Men cannot recal the past and live by it. Nor again can they separate themselves from the past. What our fathers did makes our work possible and in part determines it. Under this aspect the work of each generation is disclosed by their circumstances, and we cannot mistake our own. We are required to prove our Faith in the wider fields of social life. The currency of the general conception of evolution enables us to understand much in the course of religious movements which was obscure before, and to foresee more clearly coming changes. Christianity, even when it is most individualistic, must affect Society, though it may be silently. But now, in England, social questions are definitely raised as never before, and they tend to become paramount. As this age has been an age of physical science so the next is likely to be an age of social science.

It is then of vital importance that we, as ministers of the Church, should approach social problems from a Christian point of sight. If we believe in the Fall and the Redemption and the Mission of the Spirit, the belief, so far as the belief is realised, must affect our judgments, our actions, our hopes. And we must vindicate our belief in deed; for as Christians we hold, and all experience goes to confirm our conviction, that we are not set on earth to contemplate passively an evolution wrought out about us and in us, but to be soldiers on a battle-field, charged to prepare and hasten the coming of the Lord. Further knowledge of the conditions by which our action is limited does not lessen the claims of duty but tends to guide us to more fruitful endeavours. A vivid perception of a purpose surely fulfilled according to our observation does not deprive us of childly trust in Him Who works before our eyes. The observed facts of evolution do not dispense with the thought of GOD. Nay rather, they postulate His action—to speak in the language of men—as the simplest hypothesis to explain, or more truly to describe intelligibly, the progress which they represent. But at the same time they suggest that something has impeded and marred the course of the progress which they establish. There is, when we regard events on a large scale, a growing order: that is a witness—to speak again in the language of men—to the wisdom and love of a Sovereign will. There is, when we look for the moment without us and within us, an unceasing conflict: that is the witness to man's self-assertion. Fixing our thoughts upon humanity, we see with increasing

a Revelation of Human Duties. 47

clearness, when we contemplate our powers, our aspirations, our failures, an ideal towards which we are made to strain; and experience shews that by ourselves we cannot reach it. None the less we persist in our effort; and the Gospel comes to encourage and to sustain us.

But that we may find and use the power of the Gospel, we must realise it in its whole essence and scope. We are not Theists. Our commission is not simply to call on men to believe in GOD, but to believe in GOD manifested in the flesh. By the Incarnation GOD is revealed to us as 'the Father,' so as to give validity to our human conceptions of His perfection. By the Incarnation He enters through His Son into the world of Nature and delivers us from the tyranny of materialism. By the Incarnation He makes known to us the spiritual basis of life in virtue of which man in the fulness of his nature is shewn to be capable of fellowship with GOD.

But while the Incarnation 'brings all heaven before our eyes,' it guards us from a dreamy mysticism. It hallows labour and our scene of labour. It claims the fullest offering of personal service. It embraces all men in the range of its greatest hope, and not only those who have reached a particular stage of culture. It enables us to reverence with a sublime faith, which experience has amply justified, men as men; for we believe that *Christ is the Saviour of the world* (St John iv. 42): that it is the will of GOD *that all men be saved and come to the knowledge of the truth* (1 Tim. ii. 4): that it was *His good pleasure to reconcile through Christ all things unto Himself having made peace through the blood of His cross, whether the things on the earth or the things in the heavens* (Col. i. 20).

All men and all being therefore come within the range of the Christian's hope; and our most frequent prayer— *Thy kingdom come*—reminds us that the Lord presents earth as the scene of our consummation. As His ambassadors we need to assert His claim to be creator and heir of the universe (Hebr. i. 2). The apostolic portraiture of the Master, as *He went about doing good, and healing all that were oppressed of the Devil* (Acts x. 38), must be the pattern of the disciples' labours. To us also, when we are lost in vain speculations on the mysteries of the Divine working, the words come: *Why stand ye gazing up into heaven?* (Acts i. 11).

We need this awakening summons to that which we may think secular work. It has happened now and again that our hesitation has prejudiced the popular estimate of our Faith. There is unhappily a true sense in which the common

a Revelation of Human Duties. 49

people have not heard us gladly. They think, however wrongly, that we are either ignorant of their trials or indifferent to them. In the mean time, while we have hung back, others have sought to bring expression and fulfilment to the generous desires of our race. Their work has been outwardly Christian in type, but they have lacked the spiritual foundation of the Christian Faith. Where they have failed, and all merely material reforms must fail, their ill-success has tended to discredit our efforts. It cannot but discredit them until we make our motive and our aim clear. This we can do and this we are bound to do. For us each amelioration of man's circumstances is the translation of a fragment of our Creed into action, and not the self-shaped effort of a kindly nature. It answers, as we believe, to the will of GOD; and the faith which quickened the purpose is sufficient to accomplish it. Our perfect exemplar exists already. Our citizenship —the type of every social privilege and duty— exists in heaven (Phil. iii. 20). That ideal underlies, limits, transfigures, our earthly citizenship. For us 'love' is no vague impulse, but the mature fruit of that 'love of the brethren,' which grows out of the common acknowledgment by Christians of their vital union with one Saviour (2 Pet. i. 7). The 'brother' in the Epistles of St John, whose language has been transferred to attractive if unsubstantial and ineffective common-places, is the fellow Christian and not the fellow-man. The truth which the Apostle emphasised is consequently in danger of being forgotten. We all need to recognise more fully than we have yet done the Divine fellowship of Christian with Christian before we can rightly discharge our wider duties.

For we all have wider duties. The capacity for influence is given to us, and we are charged to use it. Under three memorable images the Lord describes the office of Christians and of the Christian Church to men at large. *Ye are*, He said to His disciples gathered round Him, *the salt of the earth: Ye are the light of the world.* And again, *The kingdom of heaven is like to leaven which a woman took and hid in three measures of meal till the whole was leavened.*

Every phrase requires to be carefully weighed. In the ministry of the Gospel there is work for the individual; and there is work for the society. There is a work of preservation, of enlightenment, of transformation. Things in themselves corruptible and transitory receive from Christians in Christ that which brings to them soundness and permanence. Dark mysteries in society and nature are illuminated for believers, who are commissioned to spread the light which they welcome. The unordered mass of human energies is capable of transfiguration, and the Christian Society, so far as it is faithful to itself, silently and slowly extends on every side its quickening force. The Incarnation—to connect these duties with their source—carries with it all that is requisite for the fulfilment of the Divine counsel of creation: the power of the Resurrection, the glory of the Ascended Christ, the life which He breathed into His Church.

The fact, as I have already said, is slowly apprehended. The consequences are slowly realised. Yet there is a movement towards the divine goal. The conquests of the first three centuries—the successive conquests of the family, the schools, the empire—typify on the scene of the Old World the conquests which have to be won on a much larger scale in the New World. Something has been already done, but we have still much to learn in order that we may do our part.

Christian ideals have not yet taken a dominant place in our higher education; though I believe that it is becoming more and more clear that these alone satisfy the aspirations of the masters of ancient Greece and bring into life the theories which they formed apart from life.

In social action we are all tempted to acquiesce

in that which is 'lawful.' We consider what we may 'lawfully' do without incurring civil penalties and not what we ought to do. But civil law is no rule of positive duty. Its symbol is 'thou shalt not' and not 'thou shalt.' And for the inspiration of conduct we require to consider what a quickened sense of duty prompts us to aim at, rather than what a code forbids.

In international affairs a narrow 'patriotism' often hinders us from looking at the permanent issues of a policy suggested by present interests or pride.

We have then, I say, much to learn. The Christian Faith covers all life—the personal life, the life of the citizen and the life of the man. Each least and nearest interest gains in intensity as a wider interest is acknowledged. As Christians therefore we are bound ourselves to study and, as far as we may be able, to lead others to study the Christian ideal of our personal relations, of our class relations, of our national relations; and then to determine the next step which we can take in each direction towards it. This is the thought which I desire to master and to enforce. The Church of Christ has still the right, or rather the duty, of 'binding and loosing,' of declaring with authority what must and what must not be done. The commission given to the Apostles may have

a Revelation of Human Duties. 53

been allowed to fall into abeyance but it has never been revoked. It can be exercised in other ways and more effectively than by the decrees of Councils. That it should be exercised is a pressing need of an age when all men alike claim freedom of judgment and have equal political power. That we in our measure may be enabled to exercise it, we must seek anew the insight, the faith, the courage, which a vital acceptance of the Incarnation will bring to us.

I.

A modern writer commences a sombre essay on the prospects of humanity with these words: "A ruined temple, with its fallen columns and "broken arches, has often been taken as a sug- "gestive type of the transitory nature of all "human handiwork....Soon the building follows "the builder to an equal dust, and the universal "empire of Death alone survives over the tombs "of departed glory and greatness." In this view nothing is suggested beyond man's effort and man's failure. The same image is used by one of the greatest Puritans of the 17th century and made radiant with hope. "The stately ruins", Howe writes of the soul of man, "are visible to "every eye, that bear in their front, yet extant, "this doleful inscription: *Here GOD once dwelt*. "Enough appears of the admirable frame and "structure to show the Divine presence did some- "time reside in it....The lamps are extinct, the "altar overturned: the light and love are now "vanished, which did the one shine with so "heavenly brightness, the other burn with so "pious fervour." Perhaps we may think that even here the picture is too darkly painted; but, though it be so, Howe goes on to shew how GOD Who had designed that first temple completed through the Incarnate Word the work which He had begun. Thus we are raised above man both in the conception and in the consummation of his powers.

The two passages bring out vividly the contrast between the non-Christian and the Christian idea of humanity. For the non-Christian there can be no certainty of assurance in the prospect of the desolations of the world. For the Christian, the Incarnation proclaims that the Gospel of Creation has been fulfilled in fact and moves forward to a complete accomplishment. The first words which the Lord taught His disciples to use 'Father' (Lk. xi. 2) 'Our Father, which art in heaven' (Matt. vi. 9), express briefly what the Incarnation has wrought for us as men. They invest us with a privilege of divine sonship which

a Revelation of Human Duties.

finds no place in the Old Testament. The words are a prophecy, an interpretation, a promise. They point to a personal relation between GOD and man which each man is set to realise in life: they shew that we share this potentially with all other men; and the fact that Christ charges us to claim the double fellowship, fellowship with GOD ('Father') and fellowship with man in GOD ('*our* Father'), is an assurance that through His help we can obtain it. So then we face our work, sons of GOD, brothers of men; and this double master-thought—one thought in two aspects— will help us in dealing with our personal duties in regard to ourselves and in regard to others, as heirs of GOD's love and called to fulfil a human ministry.

It is indeed impossible to draw a sharp line between these two spheres of personal and social effort and action. It is impossible for anyone to confine the effects of what he does or leaves undone to himself alone. If he withdraws himself into a desert and spends his years in completest isolation, he defrauds his fellow-men of the fruits of the large heritage which he has received from the past. In the stir of action every man at every moment influences others, consciously or unconsciously, limiting and moulding them, scattering seeds of thought and deed which will be fruitful of good or evil while time lasts. If the solitary ascetic is to justify himself he must shew—and there are times perhaps when this would be possible—that his impressive protest against the spirit of his age is worth the cost at which it is made. If the man of affairs is to justify his life of restless enterprise, he must not appeal to material results but to the signs of character strengthened and purified. The responsibility of living might well appal us by its immeasurable issues, but as children we can rest gladly in our Father's will. This then is that which we are constrained to seek for in our personal relations through our faith in the Incarnation, a recognition of common Divine sonship and 'equal' spiritual brotherhood. It is a familiar claim; but perhaps it has lost much of its force because we have ceased to reflect upon it ourselves and to press it upon others. We assume that the claim is acknowledged, and we neglect to consider the fact by which it is established. For when seen in this light, as the application to men individually of the message that *the Word became flesh*, the assertion of the Divine sonship of each man, of the human brotherhood of all men in Christ, is fitted to chasten, to guide, to inspire us: to furnish at once a solid foundation and a touchstone for our theories of social intercourse. Just so soon and so far as we regard ourselves and others 'in Christ,' to use St Paul's phrase, according to the Divine counsel, we shall strive to secure for each man, as for ourselves, the opportunity of fulfilling his part in a Divine society, for developing a corresponding character, for attaining in his measure to the Divine likeness. The apostolic picture will be constantly before us as our charter and our law: *There is one Body and one Spirit, even as ye were called in one hope of your calling: one Lord, one Faith, one Baptism: one GOD and Father of all, Who is over all, and through all and in all* (Eph. iv. 4—6), ruling, uniting, sustaining.

The fundamental image of 'the body' guards us from many errors. The rich energy of the whole depends on the variety of the parts. There can be no physical or intellectual or moral equality among men as the members of the Body of Christ. Each man has his own peculiar function. Each man is heir of one past and has some unique heritage to administer and to hallow. The opportunity which we seek for him is not the opportunity of doing anything, but of doing that one thing which answers to his individuality and his place. As he does this he enters on the enjoyment of the fulness of the greater life to which he has contributed. Regarded under this

aspect—the aspect of our Christian Faith—life is
an opportunity for service. We are not our own.
We were not only redeemed by Christ: we were
bought by Him, and are His. The essence of
sin lies in selfishness, self-assertion ($\pi\lambda\epsilon o\nu\epsilon\xi i a$).
Brought to this test the great questions of tem-
perance and purity can be dealt with effectually.
The virtues are positive and not negative. They
are not personal but social. Any indulgence
which lessens our own efficiency, or brings injury
on another is sinful. St Paul has laid down the
principles: *If because of meat thy brother is
grieved, thou walkest no longer in love. Destroy
not with thy meat him for whom Christ died....
Overthrow not for meat's sake the work of* G<small>OD</small>
(Rom. xiv. 15, 20). And again: *Know ye not
that your bodies are members of Christ? shall I
then take away the members of Christ and make
them members of a harlot?* (1 Cor. vi. 15). Our
work will be permanently effective when we rest
on these fundamental thoughts. The most far-
reaching arguments, the highest motives, are the
most practical. No self-centred considerations
will shield a man in temptation. But the vision
of Christ will, for He will support the effort that
is made in acknowledgment of a duty which is
owed to Him.

False-dealing in trade and gambling can, I

a Revelation of Human Duties.   59

believe, only be overcome by the application of the same truth. They are offences against our fellowship in Christ. We must present them in this light. Nor will anyone think that such a view is exaggerated who has reflected on the reason which St Paul gives for truthfulness. *Speak ye truth*, he writes, *each one with his neighbour, because we are members one of another* (Eph. iv. 25).

I touch on these most obvious points for I think that we commonly shrink from bringing the great truths of our Faith to bear on the trials and duties of every day. Yet commonplace events make up the staple of our lives. Our ordinary occupations must form nine-tenths of our service —our service to GOD and to man—and if the power of our Faith is to be felt, we require not only private devotion but open confession (1 John iv. 3). The obligation lies on the layman no less than on the clergyman. Those who believe must act as believing and because they believe. If they do so, experience tells us that they will speedily influence public opinion; and at the same time they will themselves learn to trust more resolutely to the efficacy of spiritual forces. Life, I have said, is an opportunity for service. The way of the Master is the way of the disciple, and for the most part we are in a position in which the discipline and sense of service are natural. We have no difficulty in looking to our day's work, as it is given to us day by day, as something to be done for GOD's glory and man's welfare in our Father's presence and through His help. So it is with the bulk of our middle class. It is otherwise with the very rich and with the very poor. In this respect extremes meet, and it is hard to say whether superfluity or penury is more unfavourable to the realisation of the true idea of life. On the one side the pressure of conventional engagements and pleasures tends to crowd out the thought of service: on the other side the conditions of labour are such as to obscure the truth that this labour may be the service of a son.

Such contrasts, such hindrances to the Christian life, demand consideration. They raise problems which we are called to face. They involve perils against which we are bound to provide. They furnish tests of the sincerity and power of our faith. Has the parable of the manna no application here?

It is true that there can be no 'equal' participation in wealth or in any concrete 'good' consistent with due regard to the various capacities of men: true that the highest good of society as a whole, taking account of the future, depends

a Revelation of Human Duties. 61

on some measure of inequality in opportunities and means, corresponding to inequalities of power: true that wealth accumulated in private hands has unique power for conferring common benefits; true that a certain outward magnificence befits great offices: true that the adequate fulfilment of some duties requires exceptional provisions. But while we admit this to the full, there is a wide agreement that the present distribution of wealth in England is unfavourable to the highest general well-being of the country: that it is as perilous to the moral excellence of those who have in excess as to that of those who have not what they need: that it is unfavourable to healthy consumption by developing fictitious wants: that it establishes material wealth as the standard of success: that it tends to destroy the practical sense of the Divine sonship and the spiritual brotherhood of men. Such a judgment demands anxious consideration. It may not be possible to secure at present a better distribution of wealth among us. Violent changes, we have learnt from the past, would work no lasting good. But at least we can endeavour to determine the causes which have produced and are continuing to produce a dangerous inequality, and to ascertain how they can be modified.

In the mean time there is abundant scope for

private efforts on our part to secure a simpler type of living. We can habitually ask ourselves whether this or that exceptional indulgence is required for the efficiency of our service, and press the question upon others. We can at the same time endeavour to raise the standard of life among the poor. We can, using the lessons of our own experience, strive to bring back employers to live among their own people. We can multiply opportunities for sympathetic intercourse. We can perhaps do something to check the wastefulness of fashion which stimulates vanity and provokes imitation. We can help those who look only on the surface of things to understand something of the burden of great possessions. We can shew that we wish to use all whereby GOD has made us to differ from others not for the assertion of our superiority but for better service, *not saying that aught of the things which we possess is our own.*

Such duties lie upon us first. The clergy have exceptional knowledge of the circumstances of the poor, and, through that knowledge, exceptional motives for endeavouring to secure them a stable and honourable position. They have at the same time natural opportunities for meeting the wealthy. These opportunities they are bound to use for the accomplishment of their ministry.

a Revelation of Human Duties. 63

At the same time they are under no obligation which is not equally binding on the laity, and they need at every point lay counsel and cooperation. Such sympathy and help they must claim in the interest of all alike.

It is a commonplace that Christianity has recognised the dignity of manual labour, as true service of children of GOD. But can we shew that we have carried the conviction into life? Can we shew—I do not say that the influence of our Faith in drawing Christians together is stronger, with a simple and natural dominance, than the influences of class and education and taste in separating them but—that the acknowledgment of brotherhood in Christ leads the mass of our countrymen to inquire into the conditions under which the majority of those whom they call brethren actually live? How few, for example, realise the moral and physical dangers of different kinds of employments. How few take account of the cost at which their necessary wants are satisfied, or their amusements provided. How few pause to estimate the loss of life in many occupations which might be prevented if only attention were fixed upon the facts, and the resources of science patiently brought to bear upon the problems which they suggest. An American writer ventured to say that railways are laid on men for sleepers. Even this exaggeration will repay reflection.

For it is to the simplest and the broadest aspects of the life of the poor and not to accessories that attention ought to be directed, to the hours of work rather than to the hours of recreation.

A man's daily labour is the chief element in determining his character. It is by this he serves, and by this he grows. It is substantially his life, to be begun and ended, day by day, in the name of GOD. Thus the labour question is in the fullest sense a religious question. The workman is commonly said to offer his work in the market as a commodity. In fact he offers himself. If then the conditions of labour are not such as to make a true human life possible for the labourer, if he receives as the price of his toil a mutilated and impoverished manhood, there can be no lasting peace: there can be no prevailing Christian Faith. For a true human life the essential external requisites are adequate food, shelter, leisure and provision for incapacity or old age. Are we English Churchmen—clergy and laity alike— satisfied that, speaking generally, these are found among our poorer artisans? Nay rather, is it not too plain that they are not found? It is stated on good authority that only one third of our popula-

a Revelation of Human Duties. 65

tion are able to live in decent comfort. It is certain that great numbers have no reserve of means, and are unable to make adequate provision for incapacity or old age.

I have no wish to exaggerate the shadows of modern life. 'There are two ways,' it has been most wisely said, 'of looking even at mere figures....' It may 'with some show of reason be 'regarded as not so very bad that a tenth of the 'population should be reckoned as very poor in 'a district so confessedly poverty-stricken as East 'London; but when we count up the 100,000 'individuals, the 20,000 families, who lead so 'pinched a life among the population described, 'and remember that there are in addition double 'that number, who if not actually pressed by want, 'yet have nothing to spare, we shrink aghast 'from the picture.' Still we must calmly face it; and we have yet to learn how far it represents the condition of our own great towns, of Sunderland and Gateshead, of Shields and Hartlepool, of Darlington and Stockton. To contemplate such a state of things even afar off is surely to be constrained to leave nothing undone to amend it, relying on GOD'S will for His people, and the unexhausted and untried resources of the Gospel.

There was a time when Economists would have said that such an effort was hopeless. Wider experience has taught us another lesson. The institutions of society and the motives of men which determine the facts summarily described as 'economic laws' are liable to alteration. Forms of inheritance, of land-tenure, of cultivation, of industrial processes and remuneration, influence the distribution of wealth. These have been changed in the past, and are still liable to change. On the other hand men are stirred to energetic action by other impulses than the hope of gain. And these may be called hereafter into wider play. The power of love, the power of the Incarnation, has hitherto hardly been invoked as the sovereign principle of Christian action.

We are bound, as teachers, to consider social problems in their largest range, but our own peculiar duties lie within a definite region. And however widespread the evils may be with which we have to contend, our part can best be done by dealing with them locally as they are found among us, by patient personal intercourse, guided by intelligent sympathy. At present our strength and the strength of our fellow-workers is dissipated in fragmentary and spasmodic and ill-proportioned efforts. The first requisite for steady and continuous work is full knowledge of the facts; and I trust that some combined endeavour will be made, with as little delay as possible, to

a Revelation of Human Duties. 67

ascertain in detail the facts as to the housing of the poor in the Diocese of Durham—and in this I would include the provision on shipboard for our seafaring people—their methods of purchase, their hours of labour, their provision for old age: how far existing laws are known or enforced: how far existing helps are used. I do not ask the clergy to undertake these wide enquiries. They are already overburdened. But I ask that they invite the laity to undertake them. Every parish can help. Many who are not of our own Communion will, I believe, heartily cooperate in a work in which all Englishmen are alike interested. And when the facts are known, I believe that those who differ on many points will find ways opened for hearty fellowship in solving the problems which they suggest.

In seeking your help, your help as ministers of Christ, for obtaining this exact knowledge of the material condition of those who are committed to your charge, as the basis for necessary reforms, I do not confound the external conditions of good with good. I do not suppose that material improvements can regenerate men or that outward well-being can satisfy them. But I do say that we cannot realise what our Faith is, or teach others to realise it, unless we strive according to our opportunities to secure for those whom we acknowledge to be children of GOD and members of Christ opportunities of self-development and service corresponding to our own. I do say that it is the office of those to whom the message of the Gospel is entrusted to make it known in its apostolic breadth and power. I do say that certain outward conditions must be satisfied before a true life can be enjoyed: that our life is one and that each part affects the whole: that, if the conditions of labour for the young are such as to tend necessarily to destroy the effects of a brief and crowded education, if the energies of men are exhausted by a precarious struggle for food and shelter, if there is no quiet leisure for thought, if the near future is clouded, as often as thought is turned to it, it is vain to look for a vital welcome of the Faith which deals with the future through the present, and claims the life that now is as well as that which is to come. The teaching of the Lord on spiritual reformation, like the teaching of the prophets, was accompanied by active solicitude for the external bettering of the multitudes *distressed and scattered as sheep not having a shepherd* (Matt. ix. 36). At the same time the Gospel must be preached in its spiritual simplicity and directness and power. Sin must be shewn to be the spring of sorrows and the sting of death. He to whom we appeal as a child of GOD,

a Revelation of Human Duties. 69

must be led to look to his Father: he whom we claim as a brother, must be taught to look to Christ, through whose Life and Death and Resurrection validity has been given to the title. The power to which we appeal is a Divine kinship. Till this is acknowledged with its corresponding duties our work is not done.

So far I have spoken only of single workers—of the relation of man to man, as sons of GOD and brethren, but the family and not the man is the unit of humanity; and it is a significant fact that the first converts in Europe were families, 'Lydia and her household,' 'the jailer and all his.' In our schemes of reform the family has too often been forgotten; though we need, I think above all things, to labour for the restoration or development of simple family life. Legislative changes have tended to weaken the sense of home responsibility. Many popular institutions break up the fellowship of the hearth. If it be said that such fellowship is impossible, I can only answer that if it be so, our state is condemned. It is in the family that the future of a people is shaped. Each true home is a kingdom, a school, a sanctuary. The thirty years of silent unnoticed labour at Nazareth teach us, if we ponder over the meaning, what the home may be and in GOD's counsel is.

The lessons and the duties of the family belong to the rich in some sense even more than to the poor. But indeed every thought on which I have touched concerns, if it be in different ways, rich and poor alike. Every question which I have raised claims an answer from every Christian first in the silence of the soul and then in the market-place and in the council-chamber. The equal dignity, the equal destiny of man as man is a thought due to the Gospel which each generation has to master in dealing with its own problems. Differences of culture or place or wealth are opportunities for characteristic service. They exist only for the welfare of the body, for the fulness of the life in which every member shares. Among Christians *there can be,* St Paul tells us in comprehensive language which covers the great types of distinction among us, race, social condition, sex, *neither Jew nor Greek, there can be neither bond nor free, there can be no male and female: for ye are all one man in Christ Jesus* (Gal. iii. 28).

II.

Hitherto I have considered only our personal relations one to another under the necessary conditions of life. We are at our birth severally members of a family. We are to the end citizens of a state. No seclusion can free us from the responsibility of influence. Our life is from first to last social. As Christians we are 'one man in Christ Jesus,' and in this fellowship we gain the unity which is prepared for all.

Recognising this larger life I have endeavoured to shew that our Faith constrains us to strive after the realisation of our brotherhood with our fellows and to secure our own highest good by using our special endowments for the general welfare: to seek for others as for ourselves the opportunity of most effective service: to endeavour to understand truly the circumstances and feelings of those who depend on us and on whom we depend: to recognise that we are 'our brothers' keepers.'

But if we regard society at large we see that groups of men are differenced no less than individuals; and the fundamental harmonies of the home lead us to expect that these differences will be permanent. As it is, the nation consists not only of citizens and families, but also of classes. These are shaped and bound together by a common history, by common traditions, interests, duties; and they represent permanent types of service. Philosophers who have framed ideal commonwealths have recognised that the coexistence of distinct classes is necessary for the general well-being. Early rulers stereotyped them and fenced them round with impassable barriers, though it is a lesson of hope that in the oldest and most permanent Empire in the world free passage from class to class has always been allowed. Going back then to the image of the body, we can truly say that as the nation is one body, so, on this larger scale, the different classes are members of it. That which holds good of the whole Church, holds good of the Christian nation: *all the body fitly framed and knit together, through that which every joint supplieth, according to the working in due measure of each several part, maketh the increase of the body unto the building up of itself in love.*

Here then again as Christians we are bound to seek for the greatest human efficiency of each class as of each man: to seek that each class shall fulfil its office under conditions which are favourable not only to life but to good life. In the Christian state every group of workers ought to be able to take a recognised and honourable place in the whole body. So the social aspect of work will bring to all work equal dignity.

It has been said that states grow rich only by labour, even as character is rightly shaped by it. The statement is true in the material sense if we take account of the past no less than of the

a Revelation of Human Duties. 73

present; of intellectual, moral and spiritual labour no less than of manual labour. But the individual workman becomes less and less able to claim any result as his own according as society becomes more and more complex. All work depends on fellowship and serves to support it. If we look to the essential relations of things, the material reward of work is the provision that it may be done: the end of work is the general welfare. The true wealth of states is men and not merchandise. The true function of government is to watch over the growth of good citizens. Material wealth exists for the development of man not man for the acquisition of property. This principle has in fact hitherto ruled our social legislation, which has been influenced more by moral than by economic considerations. Our legislation has been, in other words, essentially if unconsciously Christian; and now our aim as believers in the Divine life of the nation must be to secure, as far as possible, that our national inheritance shall be made fruitful as it is distributed in many parts throughout the people, and that each worker shall be able to thank GOD for the joy of his own task and the share which he has in the common life. To this end we shall not seek to equalise material riches but to hallow large means by the sense of large responsibility: not to palliate the effects of poverty but to remove the causes of it: not to dispense with strenuous and even painful effort but to provide that labour in every form may be made the discipline of noble character.

If we look around we must confess that we have hardly faced the problem which is thus set before us. We have just emerged from an industrial revolution. Old ties have been removed. The new ties have not yet been shaped. The spirit of individualism is still invoked to justify boundless self-assertion; and even self-interest is insufficient to restrain ruinous competition. Such anarchy can only last for a brief space. Already we welcome on every side generous if impatient efforts to establish among us a social order more conformable to the facts of Divine sonship and human brotherhood. Nor need we be disheartened if discontent increases at the time when there is a growing desire to remove the evils by which it is aroused. Education cannot but stir new wants by awakening new capacities; and if these take a material form at first, it is because we have not shewn that the highest and most satisfying pleasures are independent of great possessions.

What then shall we do as ministers of Christ —this is the question which we have to ask— to hasten the advent of the better order? How

a Revelation of Human Duties. 75

shall we in the exercise of our office prepare the ready acceptance of new duties answering to the new conditions of capital and labour, of owners employers and artisans?

The first and the most obvious answer is that we shall use our unique power for promoting mutual understanding between different classes. We touch, as I have said, each extreme in the social scale. We have the opportunity of knowing directly with what disastrous issues, words, motives, feelings, are misinterpreted on this side and that. Our greatest industrial danger lies in the want of mutual confidence between employers and employed. Confidence is of slow growth. It comes most surely through equal intercourse. This in some forms we can further. We are above the suspicion of partisanship. We can encourage the fullest expression of opinion from the advocates of rival causes. We can sometimes invite an interchange of conflicting views.

But it is through fellowship in the highest work that we learn best how much those have in common who seem to be most widely separated by circumstances. And after thirty-five years I look with growing trust for the formation of little bands of Christian workers in every Diocese or even in every Rural Deanery united for common service—'brethren and sisters of the common hope'—taken from every class, who by fellowship in aim and labour and devotion shall bring together many hearts.

Such associations, growing out of our own circumstances and needs and aspirations, not artificial imitations of brotherhoods framed to meet the conditions of earlier times, would, I believe, interpret the Faith with a new power and reveal believers to themselves. They belong no less to a highly developed than to a primitive form of Christian society. They belong especially to periods of great change and bring satisfaction to the spirit of sacrifice and the spirit of devotion which these tend to awaken. If the leader arise among us, followers will not be wanting.

Everything seems to be ready for the new beginning. Meanwhile we shall use—or endeavour to use—every opportunity which is offered to us in ordinary life for learning the feelings and aims of employers and employed, and for bringing both classes together on the ground of the common Faith.

Free and habitual intercourse between them, both personally and through their accredited representatives, will prepare the way for a satisfactory and lasting settlement of the relative claims of capital and labour on the profits of industry. It is needless to speculate on the form

a Revelation of Human Duties. 77

which it is likely to take. But already a great change has taken place in the provision of capital for industrial enterprises, which, since it brings special dangers and opportunities, requires to be noticed. The largest businesses are more and more falling into the hands of Joint Stock Companies. It is said that these already engross one third of the commerce of England. In this sense very many of us are capitalists, not as lenders of money merely, but as partners in some industrial undertaking, sharing its fortunes and responsibilities, though we are not directly engaged in it.

The position is one which calls for serious consideration. A divided responsibility is in all cases difficult to discharge, but in this case the responsibility is so widely spread that it is practically forgotten. Shares in great companies are regarded simply as investments (like loans) without any duties of proprietorship. The whole business, with its complicated human relationships, tends to become a profit-making machine. The discussions at the Annual Meetings turn mainly upon the dividend. Expenditure which is not directly remunerative is viewed with suspicion or disfavour.

Here then it rests with us to apprehend ourselves and to enforce, as far as we are able, a juster view of the obligations of shareholders.

We can feel the temptation, and we can feel the opportunity. The share in a business, small as it may be, carries with it not only responsibility for the capital as property but also responsibility for the administration of it. The holder is both a trustee in regard to the sum which the shares represent, and an agent in regard to the end for which it is employed. It is his duty to satisfy himself that his money will be put to a good use, and so made to contribute to ends which are materially and morally desirable. He is bound, that is, to consider both the object of the enterprise to which he contributes and the manner in which it is conducted: to consider, in other words, the character and the conditions of the work, and even the more remote results which it may produce. The amount of the dividend, irrespective of the way in which it is earned, cannot justify his choice of the investment. He is required, as one who knows that he has received all for the common good, not only to offer duly of that which he receives but also to be assured in his own mind that what he has is rightly employed.

The influence of a single shareholder may be slight, but even one who supports the Directorate in endeavouring to improve the conditions of labour and give those who serve an interest in the prosperity which they help to create, will di-

a Revelation of Human Duties. 79

rect attention to a principle and call out sympathetic support. A wide proprietorship ought to secure steady and generous consideration for workmen, and provide in due time for those larger forms of cooperation in which many see the best hope for the future.

On the other hand the common indifference of shareholders to the conduct of that which is their own business, if only it is financially successful, and their personal ignorance of the work by which they profit, gives plausibility to the popular charge that the capitalist uses the artisan for his own gain.

These considerations are, I repeat, of great and far-reaching importance; and we need to weigh them both for the guidance of our own action and for the wise counselling of those who seek our advice.

It may be urged that I am pleading to a large extent for a sentiment: that the Directorates of our greatest Companies are alive to their duties and that skilled labour is able to maintain its own cause successfully. Yet sentiment has a dominant effect on life and character; and it makes a difference whether a result is obtained by conflict or by concert. There are also larger possibilities in the administration of great Companies to which I have pointed as deserving attention;

and there is even among skilled artisans a proportion of partially unemployed whose case is peculiarly sad. But at the same time I readily admit that the most pressing social difficulty now lies in the condition of irregular and unskilled labourers. To them we naturally turn our thoughts chiefly, for they most need help. They have suffered most acutely from the industrial revolution. They have the least capacity for combination, and the least opportunity for combining. They seem to be as yet unable to rise to a higher standard of life by their own efforts. They do not even aspire to it. Education has not stirred in them a generous discontent. They suffer in moral force from labour which is uncertain and unnaturally protracted, and the value of their labour is seriously lessened. As far as I can yet judge they require some extended legislative protection, and, I will venture to add, some legislative coercion. There are classes which are still children, and in their case the Government must not shrink from discipline. It cannot rightly leave uncorrected and unrestrained masses of men whose low type of life spreads corruption. It treats attempted suicide as a crime: it ought to treat 'the slow suicide of idleness' as a crime no less.

Labour refuges and labour colonies, both at home and abroad, may be of good service. The

a Revelation of Human Duties. 81

experiments in Holland and Germany give warnings and encouragements. But we have yet much to learn. We have to determine particularly the right limits of public and private efforts, of coercive discipline and personal influence. And without advocating at present any special solution of the problem, I plead that we should seriously study it. England brought the problem upon us, and England must solve it. For us Durham is our school. And it will be possible, I trust, to form groups of laymen, who will patiently study its lessons: who will inquire and consult and teach: who will ascertain the number and the descent and the distribution of the skilled and unskilled: who will determine the extent and the causes of the rapid shifting of the population in some places: who will investigate in detail the causes of the pauperism which exists in the Diocese: who will trace for us in the history of the last fifty years the great lines of improvement along which we can move further with the confidence of faith.

I fully recognise the difficulties of bringing class to class in harmonious fellowship, and above all of finding a worthy place in the social body for the lowest class; but here the Gospel sustains us. For the most desolate Christ died. They too are part of the world which GOD loved. That devotion to the common good through which alone men as men can be bound together in widest and closest communion is necessarily included in the Christian Faith. And what we look for, work for, pray for, as believers, is a nation where class shall be bound to class by the fullest participation in the treasures of the one life: where the members of each group of workers shall find in their work the development of their character and the consecration of their powers: where the highest ambition of men shall be to be leaders of their own class, so using their special powers without waste and following the common traditions to nobler issues: where each citizen shall know, and be strengthened by the knowledge, that he labours not for himself only, nor for his family, nor for his country, but for GOD.

Such a nation 'framed and fitly joined together by that which every joint supplieth,' rising out of the past, new at once and yet old, would rightly embody the social spirit of Christ and prepare the Advent of the Kingdom of GOD.

Is it not worth working for? And will not the splendid vision, as we work, cheer us and lead us forward?

III.

We must carry our thoughts of the body and the members yet farther. Man, we believe, was broken into men that in every variety of relation he might work out his separate powers before all were summed up in the Christ. As the nation is a whole made up of classes, so the race is a whole made up of nations. This conception is at last coming into prominence in the fulness of time. The unity of the race offers the same problems, the same difficulties, the same hopes as the unity of the nation, though on a vaster scale. We can see that the several nations, in virtue of their character, their circumstances, their history, contribute towards the completeness of humanity. The glory of a nation, like the glory of a citizen or of a class, lies not in supremacy but in service. A nation is great when it fulfils its office, and enables other nations to fulfil theirs. There is need of the same self-repressive, and yet self-ennobling, devotion among peoples as among men for their highest development. Here also there are those who seem unable to aspire towards a worthy ideal of human life: those whose energies appear to be exhausted in self-aggrandisement. But wherever we look the promise rises before us:

I, if I be lifted up from the earth, will draw all men unto me.

We must then as Christians, as believers in this great unity of life, strive that other nations, no less than our own, may be enabled to gain their full development and cooperate with us for the widest good. As Churchmen we pray for this blessing in the Litany in comprehensive words, which bring out each aspect of its fulfilment, when we beseech the Lord that He will be pleased 'to 'give to all nations unity, peace, and concord,' unity, that they may severally command for use without internal distraction all the forces entrusted to their care; peace, that they may be free from the disasters of foreign conflict; concord, that they may combine together in generous endeavours to extend the general well-being of men. The petition in its completeness is, as far as I know, unique; and it is illustrated by a question in the service for the Consecration of Bishops. For while the Candidate for the Priesthood is asked whether he will 'maintain and set forward... 'quietness, peace, and love, among all Christian 'people,' he who is to be consecrated Bishop, seeing that in virtue of his office he must take a wider view of things and bear a heavier responsibility, is required to 'maintain and set forward... 'quietness, love and peace among all men.'

a Revelation of Human Duties. 85

In obedience to this charge I ask you now therefore to consider the question of international peace which, if in its accomplishment it concerns a distant future, is a searching test of the scope and vitality of our own faith. If we believe the Gospel to be what it claims to be, the fellowship of nations is included in its promised victories. The final issue may be remote, but the belief that universal peace lies in the counsel of GOD for mankind will influence our present conduct. In this respect the language of the prophets and of the Apocalypse expresses the truth which is involved in the Incarnation. And now at length we can see, in a long retrospect, that in spite of checks and delays the whole movement of life is towards a federation of civilised nations, preparatory to the civilisation and federation of all.

Such a consummation, however visionary it may seem to be, corresponds, I say, with the course of the development both of human association and of moral ideas which we can trace in the past. As we look back, we cannot fail to notice that the social instinct which belongs to man as man has found satisfaction from time to time in widening circles, in the family, the tribe, the nation. The largest sphere of fellowship still remains to be occupied, the race. And when at last the different elements of society were harmoniously combined in the city, as it was organised in the West by the power of one life, there was a foreshadowing of this crowning fellowship of nations.

In the last century two continental revolutions have marked stages in the progress towards this largest communion of men. In the revolution of 1789 individualism found its final expression. The inheritance from the past was lightly swept aside. Men were regarded as equal units, and a vague cosmopolitanism was taken to represent the feeling of the brotherhood of mankind. In such impoverishment of our powers and our endowments there could be no lasting satisfaction; and in 1848 there was the beginning of a prolonged effort to secure for each people the possession of its full treasure with a view to rendering its full service. The movement was essentially a movement of nationalities, and modern Europe is the result.

Now we are reaching out to yet another change, through which the nations of Western Europe will, as I believe, be united in a close confederation, and combine to bring all the resources which they have gathered through their history to the service of the race. We understand and acknowledge as never before that nations no less than men and classes, in spite of all the dis-

a Revelation of Human Duties. 87

turbances of selfish ambition, must suffer together and rejoice together: that each nation has its unique endowment and establishes its greatness by the fulfilment of its mission: that each is debtor to all, alike by what it has received and by what it owes: that the end for which we look will then be reached when *the kings of the earth*, with a common devotion, *bring their glory into the city of* GOD.

I know the difficulties which stand in the way of such a Confederation, the temptations of pride and rivalry which distract popular feeling, the inheritance of past errors and crimes which perplexes the policy of statesmen. But if Christendom is filled with one desire, I cannot but believe that GOD will fulfil the purpose which He inspires. The object of sincere aspiration in one generation becomes the sure possession of the next. If the thought of international concord is welcomed, the most powerful nations will recognise, as calm students recognise, that there is true strength and glory in generosity; and then, when they have put aside traditional jealousies through the stronger sense of a common duty, we shall see them islanded by neutral zones in untroubled security.

For Englishmen there is an object which is still nearer. Recent experience seems to shew that a general Arbitration treaty with America is within a measurable distance. There are hopes, like prophecies, which fulfil themselves. Such a hope as this we are bound as Christians to cherish. We can all at least take care, that within the range of our influence no idle or hasty or petulant word, no ungenerous judgment, shall mar it. The stable friendship of the English-speaking peoples would go far to assure the peace of the world.

The development of moral ideas, as I have said already, encourages us, no less than the progress of society, to look for the extinction of war. Little by little men have extended ever farther the claims of just consideration. A stranger is no longer an enemy. We have ceased to wish that other peoples should be like ourselves, and we honour their differences. Wars of conquest are universally condemned. The decalogue is held to have a national application. As men have been gathered in wider fellowship, sympathy has grown to match.

But it is said that the discipline which comes through military service, and the sacrifices which are required for a campaign, bring vigour to nations not unworthy of the price; and that the sufferings of war are preferable to the torpor of cowardly and selfish indulgence. But torpor is not peace. Peace calls for sacrifices as great as war, and offers fields for equal heroism. Peace

a Revelation of Human Duties.

demands courage of body and soul for the accomplishment of its works and kindles enthusiasm by the prospect of new victories. Perhaps our social evils are still unvanquished because we have not yet approached them with forces marshalled on a comprehensive plan, and stirred by the ardour of a common service. The very fact that the fulfilment of Christian duty is described under martial images helps us to feel that the conflict with evil offers scope for every virtue which ennobles war. A patient analysis of the qualities which win our admiration in the soldier proves that the horrors of active service are not required for their development. A great modern writer has taken the problem in an extreme form, and shewn that all that permanently attracts us in a character like Wallenstein is essentially Christian.

It is said again that, if we substitute arbitration for war, arbitration may miscarry. It is enough to reply that we have no security that an appeal to arms will establish a just claim. There is indeed no more reason to suppose that right as right will triumph in war than in a wager of battle. Moreover in a national controversy the question of right is rarely of easy decision. It is certainly not likely to be decided justly by 'the crude, cold, cruel arbitrament' of war. And when once the contest is begun, our own experience will tell us that we think more of the establishment of our own will, than of the determination of the merits of the controversy. We pray for victory and not for the victory of righteousness. We resolve, it may be, to be generous if we succeed, but we must first establish our superiority by success. Generosity in such a temper is a tribute to self-assertion and not to justice. If justice is indeed the supreme aim of those who engage in a national dispute, the most imperfect tribunal, which has to give its decision in the face of the world after open discussion, is more likely to secure it than contending armies. Meanwhile public opinion grows more and more powerful; and, when there is time for reflection, it is substantially fair. Time brings redress for wrong; and, if we look a little forward, we shall be able to discern that a nation which has submitted to what it holds to be an unjust judgment, will find ample compensation in the increase of moral strength. Even our own recent history teaches us that there are losses which after a time come to be regarded with greater satisfaction than successes which simply witness to strength.

If then a policy of peace clearly answers to the teaching of the Gospel: if it is presented to us as preparing the last stage in the progress of human fellowship: if it is, even at the present

a Revelation of Human Duties. 91

time, more likely to establish justice than war; what can we do to advance it?

We can avoid and discourage all language in regard to other nations which is in any way inconsistent with the respect due to their position.

We can endeavour to understand their feelings, difficulties, temptations, and not to measure them even unconsciously by the standard established for us by our traditions and beliefs.

We can adopt as the rule for our own temper the memorable clause in Penn's Treaty with the Indians which bound the contracting parties 'not to believe evil reports of one another'.

We can labour with patient and resolute effort to gain judicial impartiality if we are required to act as judges in our own cause where arbitration is inadmissible.

We can keep our eyes steadily fixed upon the goal of our Faith, and move towards it, in quietness and confidence, whenever the way is opened.

We can do all this while we shew that we are resolved to guard to the uttermost the heritage which we have received in trust for the race.

The enforcement of such duties becomes more important as popular power increases; and at the same time the increase of popular power brings fresh hope. Nations are not only generous, but also, as I have said before, in great crises they respond to the claims of justice if the facts are set out clearly. I can never forget the attitude of the masses of Englishmen during the suspense in the affair of the 'Trent', and when it was decided. Every one then must have thanked GOD that He had still kept the heart of the people whole in simple devotion to right. So it is that many popular leaders now, who do not avowedly hold the Christian Faith, have stood out boldly as champions of international peace. Their zeal may well awaken us to a sense of our duty and our power, our duty when we recal the words which, as we believe, heralded the Nativity: our power when we reflect on the Divine destiny of man. For nothing less than the conviction that *the Word became flesh* can sustain us in efforts which assume an essential equality in all who share our nature. No arguments based on material well-being are adequate to bear the strain of sacrifice. But the Gospel is. We can appeal to a Fact which gives present and permanent validity to universal instincts. If we do not appeal to it: if we do not trust it: so far we disparage it. If on the other hand we do, even with faltering, self-accusing lips, confess it, and strive through all failures to make it the rule of our conduct and our aspirations, GOD Himself will use our weakness for the accomplishment of His will.

a Revelation of Human Duties. 93

The position of England among the nations imposes upon us a peculiar responsibility in regard to the problem of peace. Our national freedom, gained through an uninterrupted period of self-development, demands some corresponding service. Our immunity from the local rivalries and temptations which trouble continental powers enables us to judge fairly, and (is it too much to hope?) to plead effectually.

The greatness of a nation is measured, I have said, not by its material triumphs but by the fulfilment of its office for humanity. The office of England is, if I interpret our history rightly, the harmonising of classes and of peoples. The result will be secured slowly. If we have the promise that we shall win our own souls by patience, there can be no other way for winning the souls of others. We know our aim and, keeping our eyes fixed upon it, we can work and wait for the abolition of war, as earlier generations worked and waited for the abolition of slavery.

The end must come by the gift of GOD, and therefore I will conclude what I have to say on this subject with one practical suggestion. I think we shall do well, if on some stated day— may I name the Sunday before Christmas?—we combine to turn the thoughts of our people to this largest earthly hope of peace and good-will, and lead them to offer to Him with one heart and soul and voice the familiar supplication that 'He will be pleased to give to all nations unity, peace and concord,' even as on that day we pray 'that He will come among us and with great might succour us,' 'sore let and hindered' as we are 'in running the race that is set before us.' The prayer will bring us near to those for whom we pray, near in spiritual fellowship.

The brotherhood of men, of classes, of nations: humanity fitly framed together by the ministry of every part for the realisation and enjoyment of one harmonious life: the prevailing power of devotion to a common cause: do the phrases seem visionary and unpractical? Does then, I ask, the phrase *the Word became flesh* mean less? Is that unpractical? If I am a Christian, I must hold that GOD wills for men the highest which we can imagine. If I am a Christian, I must for my own part acknowledge the widest issues of the Incarnation and strive to establish them. I shall not be in haste or impatient; but I shall watch the general direction of the movement of life and find in that the guidance which I need in my own labours.

At present we are beginning to recognise the

a Revelation of Human Duties. 95

influence of great ideals. They are in a true sense prophecies. Even if concrete changes are made in fact under the pressure of local and special circumstances, they are then most truly beneficent and lasting when they are made in relation to a recognised ideal. And the Christian ideal is unique in scope and power. It provides for developing and harmonising all the elements of life, and all life. It offers to us the highest which we can conceive for man in his whole nature, and for man in the widest range. It corresponds with our loftiest hopes; and while there is no anticipation of the central Fact in which it is summed up, men have shewn in fragments through the teaching of præ-Christian religions for what they were born. Are we then to suppose that the Christian ideal is unpractical? Are we to believe that these earlier indications of natural desires are not witnessings to the will of GOD, of which social evolution is the imperfect and slow expression? The thought of Providence alone makes the thought of progress intelligible.

It will be urged that men are swayed by motives which are measurable: that the conclusions which are deduced from the spirit of selfishness and competition have universal validity, as long as human nature remains the same. But are we to count only on the average motives and forces which we observe at present? The revolutions of history disprove such a conclusion. It is an exceptional thing that money—material wealth—should have the value which it has now. This value is due to the dominance of luxury, and will sink as material indulgence loses its power. Other motives may again prevail among men to guide the use of inherited possessions and the creation of new riches. This man may set himself to study—no simple problem—how he can best make his means serve the commonwealth. That man (to take actual examples) may choose to receive less than 'market value' for the superintendence of a great business. Another may decline, for a time or permanently, to receive interest for the capital which he advances. And all these, if they are able to describe their experience, will probably move others to follow their examples. If great wealth is used not simply in almsgiving but in the spirit of sonship and brotherhood through the thoughtful ministry of love, it will be used more effectually than in any other way for the amelioration of industrial life in both extremes of need and superfluity.

Religious movements have in all ages brought into play exceptional forces. The social movement which is stirred about us is essentially religious. For us it is avowedly religious, religious in its inspiration, in its strength, in its end. We also live in an age of revelation. There is still spiritual power available for us if we 'believe in the Holy Ghost.' We have still 'the prophetic word,' not an antique record hard of interpretation but a living voice speaking in the events of life, *till the day dawn and the daystar arise in our hearts.* The clergy are still a truly representative body, in touch with every class; moved by the largest variety of interests and opinions which are harmonised by one devotion; trained in full fellowship with the foremost workers in the state and above the divisions of party.

It is our part then to shew that the Church—the National Church—has a message to the Nation: that we bring with fresh conviction the fact of the Incarnation, unlimited in its application, to bear upon the problems of the time: that we believe in the victorious advance of the Christian Society (Matt. xvi. 18): that we have learnt in the family, and make it our business to proclaim the lesson, that social conduct is not ruled by the letter of the law, or by the decisions of 'justice,' or by the dictates of 'self-interest:' that the human, as distinct from the personal, element must enter into the dealings of man with man: that love must interpret and supplement the verdict of exact judgment.

Men cannot, even with a shew of reason, press their 'rights' to the uttermost. They ask for forgiveness as they have forgiven—forgiven that is real wrongs—foregone just claims. We have indeed 'no rights but duties;' and these can never be discharged in full. In strictness of account we must remain debtors to the end; and through the obligations of our Faith we are debtors to all who need us.

The social changes then for which we look must be reached not by premature legislation (that is finally by force) in advance of public opinion, but through common feeling. This feeling it is our office to quicken by the exhibition of the Faith. Conduct depends upon what we believe, not indeed upon intellectual formulas, but upon our living views of man, the world, and GOD. In this respect the Church moulds opinion. It has by Divine appointment, as I have already said, the power 'to bind and to loose,' to pronounce that this is of obligation and that not: to lay down the great lines of moral duty, not negatively only but positively, in accordance with the movement of life. This she does even unconsciously. And all can assist in deepening and extending the influence by pressing quietly and persistently the duty of looking to the Faith, its motives, its restraints, its supports, in everyday conduct. Public opinion, the popular idea of right, represents the minimum (so to speak) of Christian opinion. It registers the progress of personal conviction. It finally prevails in shaping government and industry and conduct. It finds expression in effectual legislation within the sphere of law; and outside the sphere of law it exercises a controlling force, so that things (for example) which were common a hundred or fifty years ago are now practically impossible, and corresponding changes are still silently in progress.

In order to extend the range of these effective judgments, we shall strive to concentrate and give consistency to the generous aspirations which rise on many sides towards righteousness and purity and temperance and fellowship. We shall reflect what we can ourselves do to shew our sincerity in advocating reforms which we believe to be needful. Some of us may be able to study special questions: we shall at least spare no pains to provide that they may be studied in order that we may apply to them wisely the teachings of Christ.

And I lay great stress on the need of patient study. Our chief danger at present is from the haste of impetuous generosity. We require not only right desires but wise counsels: careful investigation, and then resolute effort. Partial and premature remedies for evils are directly mischievous and bring discouragement afterwards. We must regard each question from many sides and then at last speak what we know. Above all we must confess unwaveringly, as I have said, that the solution of our problems is to be religious. We shall welcome cooperation in our endeavours after the practical embodiment of Christian principles from whatever quarter it is given, but we shall not at any cost dissemble our own conviction that our Faith is our inspiration. The results at which we aim finally are spiritual, and these can only be reached, as we hold, by spiritual forces.

There is, I believe, good hope of a wide response to an appeal for social service. The course of the last century and of the last generation is rich in promise. Simple life is greater than we know with 'joy in widest commonalty spread.' Even in things of sense it is only within a narrow range that 'companionship is one with loss.' Men are beginning to understand that 'everything that is supremely precious is common,' that labour is the bringer of all dignity and love the healer of all sorrow. 'The main con-'ditions of human happiness,' writes one whose knowledge of the poor is intimate and wide, 'I 'believe to be work and affection, and he who *a Revelation of Human Duties.* 101

'works for those he love fulfils these conditions 'most easily.' Nor would the quickening of interest in our own home problems lessen the interest of Christians in the distant work required of them in heathen countries. The more vivid and practical apprehension of the constraining power of the love of Christ in one field must of necessity increase the sense of obligation in every direction.

For the impulse, the encouragement, the strength, which our Faith offers to us, so far as they are felt, are felt to be unlimited in their application. GOD, we believe, has taken humanity to Himself, and man redeemed in Christ is called to work out his destiny in reliance on the Holy Spirit. In this Gospel lies the assurance, under the circumstances of human life, that that for which we long is within our reach. We do not make the ideal: we recognise it; and in striving for its establishment we are fellow-workers with GOD. In such labours the thought of the Communion of Saints comforts doubting hearts. This brings home to us naturally our Communion with GOD. It may well be that we shrink from the responsibility of influence while we cling to our private judgments: that we are disheartened by our failures and divisions; and then, when we ponder the Incarnation not only in its essence but in its circumstances, we come to realise that the Incarnation of the Son of GOD adds to authority the grace of sacrifice, to obedience the joy of Divine Fellowship, to the energy of service the endurance of love, while it offers the sense of the presence of GOD as the present pledge of unity.

It may be said that these are vague words. Even so they are not vain. This is not the place for discussing details of work. Details must be dealt with in close and familiar debate. But if the Gospel in its widest range is once acknowledged, the application will follow. It will become the inspiration of personal zeal which cannot want an object. It will encourage each worker to shew his love to his friend by claiming from him the active devotion in which he finds his own joy. And it is to indefinitely increased personal devotion, to individual ministries of love and faith, to watchful efforts of wise sympathy, we must look for the fulfilment of the work of the Spirit through the Christian Society. Every believer has his own function in the Body of Christ, and in virtue of that he is an Evangelist. The office and the shop and the factory and the ship-yard and the pit, the municipal council-chamber and the board-room of 'the Union,' are meeting-places with GOD where He can be honoured, if those whose duty lies there enter them as having welcomed the message of the Incarnation.

For if the message of the Incarnation necessarily transcends our thoughts in its fulness, none the less it comes within the range of our experience as far as our thoughts can reach. It touches life at every point, and we are bound to consider what it means for us, for our fellow-men and for the world. It is not enough to hold it as an article of our Creed: we must openly and in secret prove its efficacy in action. By our reticence, by our habitual reserve in dealing with it as the master-power in shaping and sustaining our thoughts, our purposes, our deeds, we encourage a feeling of secret mistrust as to the validity of the Faith.

In order then that we may master our message so as to deliver it with the persuasiveness of undoubting confidence, we have need of leisure, of quiet, of reflection. The strain of life is painfully intense in every direction. Impatience and excitement bring at last the languor of indifference. The restless engagements of external religion threaten to usurp the place of spiritual worship, and traditions of living faith. Multiplied and stately services may crowd out the exercises of calm and thoughtful devotion. The outward manifestations of spiritual life may exhaust its force. In this respect the pathetic warnings of Jeremiah speak to the heart of our nation and of our Church. GOD grant that we may heed them while there is yet time for both to fulfil their office.

History repeats itself in its warnings and opportunities and hopes. The great hope of the first age, which burns through the New Testament, has been deferred, because the love of the first age grew cold and its faith grew feeble. Perhaps we can see that the delay was necessary because the discipline of men was not complete. In eighteen centuries we have learnt much, and the Divine promise remains unchanged and unchangeable in the Incarnation. In spite of innumerable failures the Incarnation has established on a sure foundation the trust of natural optimism. In this confidence we labour on, knowing that *He Who began will perfect.*

During the last two years I have had occasion twice to study afresh the work and the spirit of each of the greatest spiritual leaders of our Northern Church, Columba, Aidan, Hilda. And it has been an encouragement to me to notice how each under different circumstances commends as the last lesson of varied experience peace and fellowship.

a Revelation of Human Duties. 105

'These, my little children,' said Columba, 'are my last words. I charge you to keep unfeigned love one with another. If you do so after the pattern of the fathers, GOD, the champion of the good, will help you....' Having said this he passed away the same night, while he made silently the sign of blessing.

Of Aidan we know that he was chosen for the Northumbrian Mission because he shewed by unpremeditated words that he was endowed with 'the grace of discretion, which is the mother of virtues': a man, as Bede writes, 'with a passion for peace and charity, and true priestly authority to reprove the proud and powerful, to comfort the weak and cheer the poor and uphold clemency.'

When Hilda, after bearing, it is said, with thanksgiving the discipline of severe sickness, found that her end was come, she summoned her nuns and charged them to keep 'the peace of the Gospel' one with another and with all men, and so 'passed from death to life[3].'

Thus our ancestors tell us with one voice that the brotherhood for which we look, the brotherhood of men, of classes, of nations, will come through spiritual fellowship. When we ponder their words, can we not feel that even now the Communion of Saints—the truth of which this glorious Chapel is a witness and a herald—is a reality? We cannot, as Christians, accept the phrase 'the struggle for life' as describing the true view of existence for men who are made to gain the likeness of God. In proportion as we become fit to enjoy, earth is found to be fuller of treasures, and the treasures of earth are seen to be capable of a wider distribution. In proportion as we understand the Gospel better—the Gospel which we are commissioned to proclaim in the language of our own generation—we shall see righteousness, joy, peace as the basis and the fruit of the Christian Society (Rom. xiv. 17) in place of self-assertion, excitement, competition.

The time is short: the issue is momentous: the hope is great: the promise of God cannot fail. We know that the Son of God hath come: we look for His coming (1 John iv. 2 f.; 2 John 7)[4].

My last word must be the first word which I spoke when I came among you, of which I have known the power: *Brethren pray for us.*

THE SPIRIT SENT IN THE NAME OF THE SON.

The Holy Spirit, whom the Father will send in My Name, He shall teach you all things.

St John xiv. 26.

YORK MINSTER.

Feb. 8th, 1893.

THE SPIRIT SENT IN THE NAME OF THE SON.

AN illustrious leader of our Church, Bishop Thirlwall, whose language was always severely guarded from exaggeration, said nearly twenty-five years ago: "The great intellectual and religious struggle of our day turns mainly on this question, Whether there is a Holy Ghost?" I will venture to define this statement more closely and say that the struggle turns on our belief in a Holy Ghost sent in the Name of Jesus Christ according to His own most emphatic promise. The significance of the addition will be felt if we recal the words in which the Lord described His own mission. "*I am come,*" He said, "*in My Father's Name;*" and looking back upon His accomplished work He summed up its fulfilment in these sentences: "*Father, I glorified Thee on the earth*" .... "*I manifested Thy Name unto the men whom Thou gavest Me out of the world*" ....

"*I made known unto them Thy Name, and I will make it known; that Thy love wherewith Thou lovedst Me may be in them, and I in them.*"

Our experience is a commentary on the words. By His Life and Death and Resurrection and Ascension the Incarnate Son revealed GOD as Father, and taught us what the Father is,—His Father and our Father,—in the sovereignty of His infinite power, in the righteousness of His infinite wisdom, in the tenderness of His infinite love. He brought home to us the truth of Divine Fatherhood in the terms of human knowledge, and taught each man to say, looking to heaven with a new confidence, not "our Father" only, but 'Father,' 'my Father.'

Even so the Spirit sent in Christ's Name teaches us, in lessons not less momentous and far-reaching, lessons slowly learnt, what the Son is—Son of GOD and Son of Man—Who has borne humanity to the Father's throne: teaches us the promises and the powers of the Incarnation: teaches us to bring to the interpretation of life in its whole range and of our lives in their individual value, the virtue of Christ's life, the life not of a man but of man, in which all life and every life finds its consummation. From stage to stage through silence and temptation and suffering Christ remained in perfect harmony with the will of GOD, offering Himself from first to last by the eternal Spirit a perfect sacrifice of victorious obedience available for the redemption of the whole world. And when He said upon the Cross "*It is finished,*" then 'man was made.' By that overthrow of the powers of evil the threefold lifting up from the earth was begun; and in Him man reached his destiny.

Man, I say, was made, and the work of creation reached its goal, when the Son in Whom it was the Father's good pleasure to sum up all things, committed Himself in absolute self-surrender to the Father's care, and lived through death. In His victory we find, while time lasts, our unfailing assurance. We are not called to enter on a doubtful conflict: He has conquered. Our highest hopes are not hopes only but faint apprehensions of that which He has already gained.

We can thus dimly understand how it was expedient that Christ should go away, in order that the faith of disciples, transcending the limitations of sense, might realise the boundless significance of His Person.

We can dimly understand how, when raised up the vanquisher of death, He breathed new life, by a creative act, into His Church; and how, exalted by the right hand of GOD, He poured forth upon it the Holy Spirit, as a new gift, and clothed it with power.

We can dimly understand how *all the Days* till the end when *GOD shall be all in all*, the Spirit will take of that which is the Son's and declare it to His people for their continuous growth.

We can dimly understand how He, before His Passion and Ascension, left uncompleted that sentence which we are now allowed to complete, and so to say with reverent adoration: *No one knoweth the Son save the Father*, and he to whomsoever the Spirit willeth to reveal Him.

For while "man was made" when Christ was glorified, men are being made still, as each is slowly fashioned into conformity with his Head, through the action of the Spirit, as He ever brings forth more of the treasures of wisdom and knowledge contained in Him Who is *the mystery*, the revelation, *of GOD, even Christ*, through which the ends and ways of life are shewn more clearly.

Here then is our trial, our strength, our work. The belief in the Holy Spirit sent in Christ's Name—sent to make Him known in the fulness of His being, truly GOD and truly man—is decisive of our intellectual and moral struggle. It gives validity to human knowledge, in all its variety and range, as answering to the conditions of a nature which has been taken into fellowship with GOD. It supplies to Christians a motive and a power sufficient to overcome every temptation of indolence and despondency.

This belief we are charged to master and to proclaim. We are standing even now in the presence of a Divine activity. We are called to listen to a voice from heaven: the voice of the Holy Spirit sent to us in Christ's Name,—the voice of "*the Spirit of Jesus.*"

"The Spirit of Jesus." It is a memorable title, and it is brought before us on a memorable occasion. When St Paul had passed through the great cities of Asia Minor, he "assayed to go into Bithynia; but the Spirit of Jesus suffered him not[5]." Yielding to that gentle guidance he crossed over into Europe, and the Gospel was brought to a new world.

"The Spirit of Jesus." It is a title to be pondered. We rightly shrink from endeavouring to define Divine relations by human language. Yet as we feel the vital importance of the truth which the Western Church desires to guard by affirming the procession of the Spirit from the Father and the Son, we feel no less surely that relatively to us the activity of the Spirit proceeding "from" the Son, for Whom the Incarnation is not potential only but realised, Who has taken up into Himself, as He is seated at the right hand of the Father, the fulness of humanity, is other than it was, to use the language of time, before He came down on earth. After the Ascension the gift of the Spirit, as the Spirit of 'Jesus the Son of GOD, Who has passed through the heavens,' is different, not only in degree but in kind from that which was before, separating by the whole breadth of human life the Old from the New.

Thus the Spirit sent in Christ's Name, the Spirit sent to us to-day, is characteristically the Spirit of the Son of man. He speaks to us, with infinite tenderness and compassion, so that we with our feeble powers can grasp the Truth which He interprets. He reveals to us slowly in the course of ages, as we are enabled to bear the message, the lessons of the Lord's humanity—a new thing upon the earth—apart from the inevitable restrictions which belong to our present form of existence. He illuminates through the thought of His glorified manhood the ideas of knowledge and love and fellowship. The union of believers 'in Christ' opens the way for His action in each least member. And from believers flow forth streams of living waters, to refresh and fertilise and purify the souls of men. The sense of need is a promise of help. No want and weakness is unconsidered by Him 'to whom all things lie open.' The difficulties of an age are signs of the direction of His movement. In His fulness there is relief for our distress; and while we are apt to lose ourselves in vain regrets for something which has passed away, the Spirit takes of that which is Christ's—some new treasure hidden deeper in His Person or His work—and declares it unto us for our instruction and strengthening.

We all know the trials which wider knowledge, larger aspirations, more general intercourse bring to our generation. Out of these comes for us fuller light. There are few, I fancy, who look upon the depths of the starry sky without repeating the old question, with more than the Psalmist's perplexity—"*O Lord, what is man that thou art mindful of him?*" The wonders of that which is to our senses infinitely great, and of that which is infinitely small, alike overwhelm the beholder. Our hearts fail us when we attempt to measure now that which once seemed to be a dominion not disproportionate to man's powers. We shrink from presumptuously claiming that one planet, out of one system in countless galaxies of systems, should have been the home of the Son of GOD. "What is man?" we cry, awe-stricken by our littleness in the face of the immensities of time and space. Then the Spirit opens to us a view of Christ's work which anticipates our misgivings. The Incarnation accomplished on earth—and every historical fact must be localised—reaches, we learn, in its effects to the utmost bounds of finite being. All things in heaven and in earth are summed up in Him who is their heir as He was their creator, and through Him find reconciliation and peace. *All creation*—there is no limit—bound together in the unity of the Divine thought—*waiteth for the revealing of the sons of* GOD, destined to find in their joy the answer to present pain, and in their consummation the fruit of present travail.

We are cast down by the daily record of sorrows which appear to admit no earthly assuagement and evils which, as far as we can see, must produce a progeny like themselves. Then again the Spirit takes of that which is Christ's, and shews us that these sorrows and these evils are not of the essence of human life: shews us that the Incarnate Lord has transfigured every sorrow and overcome every evil: shews us in the victory of the Cross what He has prepared for the world which he made: shews us in the revelation of Jesus,—the Son of man—Priest and King, the fulness of atonement and the certainty of triumph.

We are divided intellectually, personally, socially, one from another by barriers which belong to the very framework of our constitution. Still the Spirit takes of that which is Christ's, and opens to us something deeper, surer, more enduring than the phenomena which meet the eye, or the imaginations which can be shaped by thought. In the Word become flesh all in virtue of which each man is man, finds its place, and the presence of all humanity in Him becomes for all men a pledge of brotherhood. We can move about in common intercourse as called to be Saints among those who share our calling, striving to see ourselves and others as GOD sees us and watches over us in the tender patience of His eternal love, strong to bid our fellows strive towards the ideal which they acknowledge as their true aim.

Nation rises against nation in jealous distrust and selfish rivalry. Wars and rumours of wars stir passions which are the more perilous because they appeal to feelings of gratitude and devotion and self-surrender. Even here the Spirit takes of that which is Christ's, and holds before us, in the silent progress of the ages, the clear prospect that the peoples are slowly moving, through checks and losses and reverses, towards that City which is itself a Holy of Holies, and in the light of which the nations shall walk at last, when the kings of the earth bring their glory into it.

Earth draws us with multitudinous charms, which we cannot refuse to recognise except by the sacrifice of eye and hand. We yield to them, and find that, if we are not weakened by the indulgence, we are left unsatisfied. Once more the Spirit takes of that which is Christ's, and interprets our discontent and hallows our instinct. Looking to Him, who is the Truth and the Life, we see that all that art shews that is lovely, is lovely not as separate and self-subsistent, not as apart from Him, but as a fragment of the Truth which He is, a fragment in which He must be recognised if it is to bring lasting joy. Looking to Him *in whom all things consist*, we discern with adoring thankfulness that the Incarnation is the perfect revelation of the poetry of nature and of life, the revelation to the eye of faith of the 'world as GOD has made it.' Seen in Christ and in the light of His saving work, 'all is beauty, and knowing this is love, and love is duty.'

These glorious visions are called up, I say, by our difficulties, and they meet our wants. On many sides men are telling us—and it is a pathetic confession—that we are in danger of losing the heroic force of manhood in the general diffusion of an average culture; that there is a dissipation of spiritual energy as there is of physical energy; that there lies before us as the future of our civilization a dull monotony hardly distinguishable from death. Such a prophecy would be well-founded if the sum of spiritual force were constant. But there is opened for us a fountain of new life. Humanity is placed in vital connexion with the Godhead. The Spirit takes—takes according to our necessities—of the things of Christ and declares them unto us.

His taking, His declaring, however, is not enough. In order that we may receive the teaching, we ourselves need to wait in still patience. As it is, the restlessness, the busy hurry, the intensity of modern life keep us occupied with what has been well called 'the idolatry of work.' The outward and material fills our thoughts, and for a time satisfies our feelings. Worship tends to become a series of observances, and even doctrine to degenerate into scholastic speculations. Then in some 'hour of insight' we recognise the weakness of our powers, and the transitoriness of our own creations. We grow fearful and anxious, timorously seeking for some ancient precedent to support our Creed or our practice. But our justification must lie at last in the present. And we can find it here. GOD is with us. He has a blessing for our labours. He speaks to us through our experience, our history, our circumstances. We justly rejoice in our ancestry and in our inheritance.

> If we tried
> To sink the past beneath our feet, be sure
> The future would not stand.

But we do not serve the dead. We are not bound by the tradition of our fathers. The life and movement by which they were strong are ours also, if we on our part assert our privilege. For we must be active and not passive only, even in dealing with the things of GOD. We must—in the Lord's words—*take* the gift of the Holy Spirit (λάβετε πνεῦμα ἅγιον) and not merely receive it. We must trust with a whole heart GOD Who has given us our commission. Our English Church need not look on this side or that with timid glances for qualified recognition. It is its own witness through the fruitfulness of its activity. It has in itself the vindication of its position. It offers, as I believe, a natural meeting-place for Christians. But we cannot hasten the advent of that unity for which we labour and pray by condoning 'errors and superstitions which we have rightly and solemnly abjured,' or by sacrificing any part of the Apostolic Faith which has been committed to our keeping[6].

The strength of a man, of a class, of a nation, lies in its religious faith. Our Faith covers all life and the whole of man. Every truth contributes something to its more complete expression under the form of present human thought. The power which it brings answers to the claims which it makes. The Christian law is matched by corresponding grace. The Gospel brings the Beatitudes within our reach. To him that believeth all things are possible.

But to make this possibility a fact, we need, and we all know sadly that we need, the fresh conviction of a Spiritual Presence in our troubled world, and spiritual fellowship with the unseen realised through the fulness of our humanity. Many seek it in strange, unhallowed ways, and all the while the blessing is offered to us by the Spirit sent in Christ's Name, who is disclosing to souls opened to Him fresh mysteries of the Incarnation.

Brethren, may GOD Who has laid on us the heavy burden of interpreting His Gospel enable us to read and to proclaim His message to our own generation, the message of a Gospel for the universe, of sin overcome and sorrow transformed, of unity whereby we are *all one man in Christ*, of the fellowship of nations, of the new heaven and new earth rising out of the old.

We shall join directly in prayer that 'the Holy Spirit who was present at the first gathering of the Apostles, may be present also at ours now, to guide us into all the truth.' GOD grant that the prayer may be to us the glad confession, made one to another and to GOD, of a living faith, the solemn claim of our Divine endowment, the pledge of power corresponding to our wants and sufficient for our weakness, so that humbly trusting to the help of the Spirit sent in Christ's Name and acting in the power of our belief, we may fulfil His will without fear, and hand down to those who will continue our work an inheritance enriched by the treasures which He offers for our welcome.

THE AIM AND THE STRENGTH
OF CHRISTIAN ACTION.

Whatsoever ye do, do all to the glory of God.
1 Cor. x. 31.

Whatsoever ye do, in word or in deed, do all in the name of the Lord Jesus.
Col. iii. 17.

CHAPEL ROYAL, ST JAMES'S.
First Sunday in Lent, 1893.

THE AIM AND THE STRENGTH OF CHRISTIAN ACTION.

THE day carries our thoughts at once backwards and forwards. The memories of Christmas and Epiphany are still fresh ; and we are preparing to ponder again the lessons of Holy Week and Easter.

It is natural therefore that we should pause for a short space to dwell upon the simplest, the broadest, the most practical aspects of our Faith : to ask ourselves what place the mysteries—the revelations—of Bethlehem, of Calvary, of Olivet, have in our rule of conduct: to consider how we can bring the truths which we hold by intellectual conviction to bear more continuously and more effectively upon common life, how we can prove their power in action.

I assume that we are Christians, that we hold with whatever inevitable weakness of apprehension, that the Son of GOD came down from Heaven and took our nature upon Him, and lived our life and bore humanity in His Person to the Father's Throne. Such a belief is charged with vital power. The least reflection will shew that it is a revelation of the true glory of nature and life as they answer to the will of GOD : that it affirms a Divine purpose and presence to be looked for and recognised everywhere : that it transforms the simplest powers and opportunities which are given to us into means for making GOD better known : that the Christian has a motive and a strength for social service essentially different from those which avail for unbelievers. His motive is universal; for the Christian sees in his fellow-men sharers with him of a nature which his Lord has glorified. His strength is as his day; for the Christian knows that the Spirit sent in the Name of the Son takes of the things of Christ, and meets the needs of each age by fresh treasures of wisdom and knowledge included in His Person and Work.

Such conclusions if they are distinctly realised change our whole view of life. So it is that when we think of life in the light of the Incarnation, we are startled at the contrast between the ideal and the fact. It is indeed easy to pass sentence in general terms on the failures and the sins of man. It is supposed to be the preacher's office to

of Christian Action. 127

do so; and he is judged according to the skill with which he fulfils his part. But at the same time it is taken for granted that his verdicts, his appeals, his claims, belong to a region far remote from the working world. The French Court listens with interest or even with admiration to Bossuet, or Bourdaloue, or Massillon, and goes on to prepare a revolution by its unfeeling licentiousness, for it does not take their words seriously.

Perhaps we who are set to teach give occasion to this grievous misconception of the Gospel by our own inconsistencies. We have not the courage of our faith. We are ashamed of Christ in society. The falling away of a friend hardly seems to sadden us. But even if the knowledge is our own condemnation we do know that our message is intensely practical. Our aim is not to construct a theory of life for an imaginary commonwealth, but to enforce their duties on citizens of the Kingdom of GOD: to create a quiet, sober, resolute, conviction of the sovereign authority of the law of Christ: to call out a clear, calm, humble, confession of duty: to persuade those who have acknowledged Christ to meditate, silently, patiently, courageously, as in the sight of GOD and man, on life and death, on the meaning, the obligations, the gifts, of the Creed which they hold.

And one thing at least is clear that as knowledge increases the range of our Faith is found to extend in the same degree. If life is now seen to be more complex and more dependent than it was formerly held to be, reaching before and behind, fashioned by things above and things below, our Faith prevents and follows it, emphasising our sense of limitless responsibility and opening doors of hope.

This is the message of the Faith which we are commissioned to deliver, which we desire to deliver: this message of unlimited scope, of unlimited power is our Gospel. For Christianity is not a sum of isolated observances. It is the hallowing of all human interests and occupations alike. Worship is a very small fragment of devotion. The Christian does not offer to GOD part of his life or of his endowments in order that he may be at liberty to use the rest according to his own caprice. All life, all endowments, are equally owed to our Lord, and equally claimed by Him. Every human office in every part is holy. Our conduct—our whole conduct—is a continuous revelation of what we are. At each moment we are springs of influence. Virtue goes out of us also— or weakness. Our silence speaks. We who profess to be Christians must from day to day either confirm or disparage our Creed. Our faith—our

of Christian Action. 129

want of faith—must shew itself. It is finally the soul which acts. The body is but its instrument.

Under this aspect it is evident that the voice of conscience repeats in our hearts the words of St Paul : *Whether ye eat or drink, or whatever ye do, do all to the glory of GOD.* Do all, that is, so as to make the purpose and the will of GOD—His love and righteousness, His compassion and grace—better known and more inwardly prevailing. For we can, if we realise what the Gospel of the Word Incarnate is, aim at nothing less. And the conception which we form of our duty is of more importance than our first most imperfect performance. The days of most of us are filled by routine, but routine may be elevated if we look through it and beyond it to a great ideal. The ideal, if it is cherished, becomes an inspiration, and leads us through failures and sadnesses to forget ourselves and rest only on GOD.

Can we then say, when the question rises before us, that we do desire with whatever sorrowful confession of inconsistency and weakness, to offer ourselves—our souls and bodies—a living sacrifice to GOD, and to do all things to His glory ? or do we surrender ourselves—without any definite purpose at all—to the influence of each day as it comes, and drift with the changing currents of circumstance ? or seek only our own ends of pleasure or interest, satisfied to make the average conduct of those about us the standard of our own endeavours, and the average tradition of popular opinions the measure of our own belief?

If we regard the alternative calmly, in full view of the issues at stake, we cannot hesitate as to the answer which we should wish to make. We know for what we were made, and through what alone we can find rest in the solitude of self-questioning. And if we are awed by the overwhelming solemnity of life, seen as it truly is, our Faith illuminates the vision. St Paul, who fixes the aim of all action, when he says, Do all to the glory of GOD, reveals also the secret of guidance and support in the effort to reach towards it, when he says in another place, *Whatsoever ye do, in word or in deed, do all in the Name of the Lord Jesus.* Thus the aim and the rule of the Christian life are plainly set before us. We are charged to realise, as we may be enabled, and to shew the Divine presence even in the commonest things. We are taught that we shall obtain our end by calling to remembrance in every action the truth of the Incarnation. This truth, this fact, adds an element of infinity to all that is of earth; and it brings "the power of an indissoluble life" to sustain us in view of the startling contrasts and conflicts of human interests.

of Christian Action. 131

'In the name of the Lord Jesus.' To invoke that name is to recognise the fellowship of Heaven and Earth. It is to affirm the brotherhood of men in Him who has taken to Himself our common nature, and the Fatherhood of GOD through Him who is our common Lord. It is to confess that we are debtors to all, holding every advantage which has been given to us, as a trust for those through whom we live.

'A trust for those through whom we live.' Yes. If we believe in the Incarnation we must hold this conviction as the master-law of our conduct. In theory indeed no one will dispute the fact of our social stewardship: no one will maintain that we can confine the influence of any action to ourselves: no one will undertake to shew that we can rightly call anything 'our own': no one will deny that we must give some account of all that has been committed to us. But practically we relegate the reckoning to some incalculable future. We are tempted to think that because we are not accountable to an immediate task-master we can blamelessly deal at our will with our leisure and our means. We lack the imagination which would enable us to trace the bitter stream of consequences which flow from a light word, or an inconsiderate indulgence, or an act of wilful self-assertion. We forget—and it is a thought which we cannot press upon ourselves too persistently—that responsibility is measured by opportunity. Stewardship is indeed difficult for those who have much to administer. If our time, our fortune, our acquirements are at our own disposal, the heavy burden is laid upon us—and he knows the weight who on rare occasions has endeavoured to bear it—of bringing all to GOD as a reasonable and willing service. Such a sacrifice cannot be made at random or improvised in some moment of enthusiasm. It requires the vision of the glory of GOD that it may be prepared with resolute and patient care. It requires the appeal to the name of the Lord Jesus that it may be hallowed by one final act of self-surrender. Eighteen centuries have not modified the pathetic judgment : *How hardly shall they that have riches enter into the Kingdom of GOD*—they that have wealth of gold, or land, or intellect, or time, or power, or place, which tempts the possessor to think that he is independent, which flatters and deceives him by the prospect of personal delights.

But, thanks be to GOD, difficulty is the call to lofty enterprise. Great possessions may become great blessings to him who matches them with great counsels. And on every side there is now sore need of the utmost help of such as have most. Not for themselves, but for those who have no reserve, men hold the accumulated fruits of earlier industry. Not for themselves, but for those who are bound by daily toil, they hold the perilous gift of leisure. Not for themselves, but for those who trust the culture which they have not, they hold the treasures of learning and art. Not for themselves, but for those who respond to generous sympathy, they hold the great traditions of birth and rank. We may misapply, or waste, or neglect our resources, whatever they are: we may leave our work unfulfilled. But there is a benediction prepared for the discipline of anxious cares. If we fail to win it, our failure will come not from the largeness of the Divine bounty, but because in the contemplation of our endowments we neglected to look to the glory of GOD, and in our use of them we neglected to act in the name of the Lord Jesus.

The simplest, the homeliest, the most universal application of these general reflections is to our personal expenditure. Our Faith emphasises and hallows social differences. It bases the most sacred obligations of service upon them. We are all members of a body, and not units in an aggregate. We are not taught to obliterate the rich varieties of function among men in a colourless uniformity. But our several offices are fulfilled in the unity of one life. The gifts by which we are distinguished one from another are designed for the fulfilment of special duties. They are not to be used according to personal caprice or for private ends but in effective ministry.

A life spent in the pursuit of personal enjoyment, cannot justly claim to be a human, still less a Christian life. Every exceptional indulgence in amusement or living which we admit, every use which we make of money or leisure for rest, for travel, for the accumulation of works of art or literature, must satisfy two tests before it can be approved by an awakened conscience. It must be found to contribute directly or indirectly its full value to the efficiency of our work; and it must not be such as to cause even the weak to offend by a perilous example. In each respect we are bound to weigh carefully the results of our conduct as it affects the discharge of our appointed task, and as it affects those whom we naturally influence. Our expenditure as Christians from first to last must be directed not to private gratification but to the good of the whole body, and it is in this good we find our own highest satisfaction. There is need of sparing, of self-control, of reserve, for the possession of enduring joy no less than for the noblest exercise of genius.

That, therefore, is a culpable luxury for an individual which costs more either in money or time, or vital energy, than it contributes to his power of service. That is culpable self-assertion which makes a man neglectful or regardless of the remoter consequences of actions reasonable for himself. Nothing which tends to waste labour or force ; nothing which tends to stimulate vanity or nourish pride ; nothing which tends to lead astray by provoking frivolous or blame-worthy imitation ; nothing which tends to exaggerate the importance of material wealth or to encourage ostentation, can be done or enjoyed to the glory of GOD or in the Name of Christ.

Tried by such a standard—and the standard is final for the Christian—there is much in modern life, in popular fashions of dress and entertainment and recreation, which stands condemned beyond appeal : much which continues among us simply, I believe, by the unquestioning toleration of custom, because no one thinks the subject a matter for serious reflection.

And meanwhile as characters are marred, so also the resources are wasted which GOD has prepared for the renovation of the world, resources which lie far more in ourselves than in our material wealth: the influence of great place which might commend the dignity of a simple life and shew that human happiness is won—won only—by 'labour and love'': the sympathy of culture which might bring grace into the sordid homes of the poor and open the eyes of the blind to the beauties of earth and sky: the tenderness of personal intercourse which might spread a true banquet for the desolate and outcast: the authority of self-restraint which might shew the capacities of the humblest means: the energy of faith which might claim all alike as fellow-heirs of the riches of Christ. Can we not all see how opportunities and calls for service, as manifold as human endowments, offer themselves on this side and that? But thick, earthborn, clouds rise between us and the glory of GOD. The babble of innumerable voices drowns the name of the Lord Jesus when it is sounded in our ears. None the less life, with all it brings, is given us that we may receive and reflect that glory, that we may welcome and proclaim that name.

I have only indicated principles but they are luminous for our guidance. If they are accepted they are capable of transforming our whole life, little by little, to a divine pattern. They appear to me to be involved in the central fact of our Creed. We cannot, as far as I can judge, believe the Incarnation without acknowledging them to be of sovereign authority. The circumstances of our own time interpret them with growing clearness. They have a direct bearing upon present

of Christian Action. 137

and urgent problems. I ask then that at least they may be considered: that we may try ourselves by the standard which they set up: that we may settle in our own hearts what is our aim in life, what is our strength.

Our best hope for the future, and it is a hope which, as I believe, is rising upon us with fuller promise, lies in giving reality, as we can give, to the thought of our relations one to another as sharers in one nature which Christ has taken to Himself, and redeemed by His Life and Death, as members of one body in which He is the Head. This conception, this vital application of the Gospel has power to discipline, to unite, to inspire: to discipline those who are tempted by their circumstances to self-assertion: to unite those who are kept asunder by the temporary conflict of national interests: to inspire with fresh confidences those whose hearts fail them in the prospect of evils to which they can bring no remedy.

So may we, turning our Faith into act, *do all things for the glory of* GOD, which glory we have seen in the revelation of a Father's love: *do all things in the Name of the Lord Jesus,* which Name we have read in the records of a Son's self-sacrifice.

Philip saith unto Him, Lord, shew us the Father, and it sufficeth us.

Jesus saith unto him, Have I been so long time with you, and dost thou not know Me, Philip? he that hath seen Me hath seen the Father.

Verily, verily, I say unto you, He that believeth on Me, the works that I do shall he do also; and greater works than these shall he do; because I go unto the Father. And whatsoever ye shall ask in My name, that will I do, that the Father may be glorified in the Son. If ye shall ask Me anything in My name that will I do. (St John xiv, 8, 9, 12—14).

ps.

IDEALS.

See that thou make all things according to the pattern that was shewed thee in the mount.

HEBR. viii. 5.

MANSION HOUSE, LONDON.

March 7th, 1891.

Annual Address to the Students of the London University Extension Society.

IDEALS.

MANY of us remember the splendid myth in which Plato connects the position of men in their earthly life with their experience in an earlier existence. There are, he says, festivals in Heaven, when Zeus, followed by the Divine hosts, goes forth to the outer boundary of the universe, and, during its revolution, gazes on the supramundane realms of absolute being. The spectacle is the food of the heavenly nature, and gods and heroes fill themselves with it to the full in serene and untroubled tranquility. Other unembodied souls follow in the celestial train, struggling to share the life-giving vision. Some with grievous effort catch more or less transitory glimpses of righteousness and beauty and moral order, and so retain for another period their lofty state. Others, baffled and beaten down, fail to gain the glorious sight, and falling to earth, are forthwith confined in mortal frames. But since they still remember something of the truth which they have formerly seen, they cannot on their first embodiment sink below the state of man, and their place among men is determined by the measure of their remembrance. He who has seen and remembered most is born a philosopher. He who has seen and remembers least is born a despot.

Now, without discussing in detail the remarkable hierarchy of classes which Plato sketches between these extremes, or entering on any philosophical speculation, we can notice two central thoughts, two central truths, I will venture to call them, vividly expressed in this great picture. That which makes us men is the capacity for regarding the eternal. That which fixes our position in the scale of humanity is the energy of the eternal within and upon us, by which we are freed more or less from the dominion of material and selfish aims. Or, to express the teaching in popular language, man is a being who fashions ideals, and the worth of man in relation to his fellows depends upon the ideals which he cherishes.

Man partly is and wholly hopes to be.

I wish, then, to say a few words now, necessarily most fragmentary and imperfect, upon ideals regarded in this aspect. I wish to shew,

Ideals. 143

if there is need to shew it, that ideals are the very soul of life; that the characteristic spirit of University teaching, which this Society desires to bring within the reach of all, tends to quicken, to sustain, to perfect the loftiest ideals; that the circumstances of the time give peculiar importance to this aspect of the work of University Extension.

Ideals are, I say, the soul of life. The simplest human act is directed to an end; and life, a series of unnumbered acts, must answer to some end, some ideal mean or generous, seen by the eye of the heart and pursued consciously or often unconsciously, which gives a unity and a clue to the bewildering mazes of human conduct. The word progress is unmeaning without reference to an ideal. And I would say of ideals that which was said here of abstract thoughts by a distinguished scholar and statesman, that they 'are the meat and drink of life.' They support us, and still more, they rule us.

It is, then, momentous that we should pause from time to time to regard our ideals. They exercise their influence upon us insensibly. We grow like the object of our desire perhaps before we have distinctly realised its true nature; and so we may find ourselves like some of the souls at the close of Plato's Republic, involved in unexpected calamities through a heedless choice. At the same time, the effort to give distinctness to our ideals brings with it a purifying power. For, after all, there is but one ideal in which we can find rest—that which answers to the truth of things. To this alone the name ideal properly belongs. It remains when all illusions pass away. By us 'who are but parts' it is seen in parts, but it is one. It exists already. And we were born to seek it, to find it, to recognise it, to shew it. 'It is not,' as has been nobly said, 'the creation, but the gradual discovery of the human intellect.' Yes; the best will be done; is on the Divine side done now. There is an order in which all fragments will find their due place.

On the earth the broken arcs: in the heaven a perfect round.

This conviction that there is an order in things which we do not make, but can discern and interpret, is the inspiration of the man of science and of the artist, no less than of the man of affairs. The man of science dimly perceives that after which he is feeling. Phenomena speak to him with a voice which others cannot hear, because he has known in some degree their vital coherence, and he trusts to the perfection of the harmony of which he has found the first promise. To the artist outward things are signs rather than

Ideals.

copies. He uses them to suggest to others what he discerns behind them. His work is not an end in itself, but a revelation of that which is beyond. And for the statesmen ideals are the adequate support of resolute and unwearied patience.

It was said, I think, of Michael Angelo that he often hewed the marble before him without a model, as one who was setting free a figure imprisoned in the block, clear to his artist eye. The image is a just representation of the work of life. Our work in life is to set free from manifold encumbrances that which is present about us, good and true and lovely. But we must first see the ideal which we desire to bring to view, and the vigour of action depends upon the clearness of our sight, and such clearness comes through discipline. Every prospect on which we look is for us as we are. The phenomena are the material which are offered to us to use and interpret, and as the quickened soul realises their meaning and their relations, seeing becomes beholding, and the partial apprehension of the ideal by which and towards which we have been guided.

So to keep the ideal before us in the midst of our common occupations, to guard the conviction that there is an ideal, is to preserve the first freshness of our early impressions of the mysterious beauty of the world. Poets tell us that in the pilgrimage of life we shall watch the glory fade away from the things of earth. But if it be so, the fault lies with us. It will be because with the growth of things we have not grown to match. The halo still encircles the bush in the wilderness when we have learnt to study the material elements by themselves, only it is found to come by the gift of heaven. The sunshine which floods the whole landscape at mid-day is the same as that which was seen as a star of dawn when it lighted the solitary mountain peak, only it is infinitely vaster and therefore harder to comprehend in its fulness.

But while this is so, the conditions of living tempt or constrain us more and more to regard phenomena in relation to our own needs, and we come to forget their larger meaning. I have somewhere seen that an American writer has recorded how, when he was engaged as a Pilot on the Mississippi, he was at first filled with adoring wonder at the magnificence of the sunsets, and then in the course of his work came to regard them as useful weather signs. But while we welcome the utilitarian interpretation we need not acquiesce in it. This itself points to something greater by emphasising one of the harmonies of creation. Here, as elsewhere, the part enables us to rise to a fuller conception of the whole, if only the thought of the whole is present with us. So, moving from fragment to fragment, we learn to give distinctness to our ideal and to feel the unity and grandeur of the sum of being through our own experience. If the past shews no attainment it shews many advances and points to the hoped-for end. Tracing by intelligible marks how things have come to be, as far as they fall within the range of our powers, we look forward with a prophetic trust. We make the power of poetry our own, which a poet has defined to be "the feeling of a former world and of a future one." We come into contact with what has been truly called "the collective thought," and are kindled by the spirit of humanity, that humanity which is "a man that lives and learns for ever[8]." Exceptional occurrences, oppositions in thought, material phenomena, transcending all conception in their necessary conditions, take their place in our view as indications of a larger order. Man, society, nature, are seen to be instinct with one life, and regarded, even as we can now regard them, inspire the spectator with patience at once and hope.

Such a temper, which answers to the highest ideal of man and of his dwelling-place, is intensely practical. It is not for intellectual indulgence; it is a spur to action. It enforces a thought—a fragment of the ideal—till the thought is recognised as a principle and in due course the principle is embodied as a fact. Thoreau has said well 'If you have built castles in the air your labour need not be lost; that is where they should be. Now put the foundations under them.'

The temper is practical and it is attainable. I am inclined to say it is necessary for every human life. The average man, the man of business, the artisan, the miner, require the vision of the ideal, and they are capable of it. The vision of the ideal guards monotony of work from becoming monotony of life. The simplest home finds a place for it. And no problem is pressed upon now with more continuous urgency than how that place shall be rightly filled. The University Extension Movement is one important help towards the solution of the problem.

University teaching tends, I believe, with ever accumulating force and directness to quicken and to sustain ideals. It is characteristically structural, catholic, equalising, chastening, historical, personal, spiritual. Let me, in the fewest possible words, endeavour to explain and justify this formidable list of epithets. To every University man each word will, I think, recall a debt which must grow with the growth of life.

Ideals.

University teaching is, I say, structural. It aims, I mean, at giving a sense of the whole and preserving the proportion of the parts. It insists on a general training and a special training. It brings intelligent sympathy with all studies and guides to the mastery of some one. It provides that the physical student shall understand the aims, the resources, the achievements of literature; and that the scholar shall understand the methods and the limitations of physical science.

It is catholic. A University is strong enough to prevent the overpowering dominance of a popular pursuit. It is hospitable alike to the enthusiasm which proclaims new thoughts and to the reverence which lingers over the thoughts of a past age. It is tolerant of all things except onesided arrogance. No specialist can move among bands of fellow-students preoccupied with other interests without feeling the amplitude of knowledge and of life, and the manifold relations in which his own subject stands to others on which he cannot enter. The common search for truth and right brings mutual respect; and the teacher who has felt the subtle influence of the University must himself in turn diffuse its spirit.

It is equalising. Nowhere is fellowship more complete among representatives of every class than at a University. There poverty is no reproach, and wealth is no title to superiority. The foremost students are bound, perhaps unconsciously, in a brotherhood of heart through which comes the power of penetrating to the noblest in each man. The teacher who has learnt his lessons under such social conditions will be eager to bring the best to the humblest as a fellow-heir with him of the wealth of humanity; and he will not accept as permanent, conditions of life which exclude any class or any man from access to his birthright.

It is chastening. The University teacher cannot forget that his office is not to supersede labour, but to stimulate it. He will not entertain the vulgar notion that we can bestow on others our thoughts as we can bestow on them our money, so that they can employ them rightly before they have made them their own. He will bear in mind the pregnant saying of an old divine, "We have ourselves as we use ourselves." He will make it clear that great books can only be read in the spirit in which they were written, as serious work and not as indolent amusement. He will, therefore, claim from his hearers the difficult service of thinking, as one who knows that the true teacher, like Nature, gives nothing but materials and opportunities and impulse.

It is historical. A University is not a bureau. It is a living body, a complex result of life and not an official provision for carrying into effect a formal scheme. The teaching which answers to it is, as a necessary consequence, vital and not intellectual only. It bears the impress of many associations, old and new. It is flexible, in the largest sense human, of the past at once and of the present. A Cambridge man might find it hard to analyse or to estimate the effect which has been produced upon him by the great libraries, by the old buildings wedded to new, by the chapels of Trinity or King's, yet he will know that they have in many undefined ways given him breadth and sympathy and tenderness which will colour his own work.

It is personal. The method of learning is, I believe, of scarcely less moment than the matter. The student who has mastered a subject by the help of a text-book occupies a very different position intellectually and morally from one who has gained his knowledge in continuous contact with a teacher. The frank questioning, the interchange of thought, the influence of personal enthusiasm, the inspiring power of living words, which come in the free intercourse of the classroom, give a force and meaning to facts and theories which the book cannot convey.

It is spiritual. The end of the teacher whose work we strive to follow is not fixed by the communication of his special lesson. He will seek, indeed, to do this as perfectly as possible, but he will at the same time suggest the vast fields which lie unexplored even in his own department; he will make clear the limitations and assumptions under which his results are obtained; he will add, if I may so express the truth, the symbol of infinity to the provisional statements which represent the actual attainments of man; he will use the most effective technical education as the vehicle of wider culture. Literature, art, science will be for him partial revelations of a boundless life; and it will be his object to make the life felt through the least part with which he deals.

If, then, this is the general character of University teaching, however imperfectly it may be realised by the individual teacher, we may rightly maintain that it does, as I have said, tend to quicken and sustain ideals, to bring into view the loftiest aspects of man and nature, to assure to thought and action that liberal freedom which corresponds with the sense of absolute law, to keep open a free course for aspirations and endeavours which rise beyond the conventional standard of custom.

Ideals.

Hitherto the Universities have fulfilled their teaching office for a few. Now they are endeavouring to extend it to every town and village, and to make it effective even for those who are busily engaged in various industries. The movement corresponds in many respects with that out of which the old Universities themselves arose. It is still experimental, but the results already obtained have far more than satisfied the hopes of those who watched the beginning of the movement not without anxiety. They have won a distinct academic recognition at Cambridge, and they have contributed, I believe, in no small degree to create the desire for a teaching University in London. For, however important the test of an examination may be for fixing the value of acquirements, the discipline of learning is yet more important for character; and this discipline the Extension system offers in a form equally attractive and stimulating.

Such a system, fitted to bring many-sided liberal culture to every condition of life, to enlarge common interests, to deepen fellowship, to create simplicity through refinement, and to check the passion for excitement by the force of purer interests, would be welcome at any time.

But it is of singular importance now, when we are in danger of losing the true conceptions of nature, humanity, and life, and the calm vigour of action is failing us. The inspiration of great ideals seems to be alone able to meet the intellectual distraction, the materialism, the critical indifferentism, and the consequent enfeebling of will which appear to be the dominant perils of our age.

On the one side our attention is concentrated on isolated subjects. We are absorbed in the study of fragments. We are fascinated by minute details. We unconsciously treat our little domain as the whole. On the other side, in the eager hurry of life, every one is expected to possess a ready acquaintance with all that can be known. In this way genuine labour and superficial borrowing of opinions become equally destructive of broad and balanced judgment. But the contemplation of a great ideal of nature will bring proportion to special enquiries and justly discredit the affectation of an impossible omniscience. The worth of our own little service will be seen to be fixed by the grandeur of the cause to which it is rendered, and the worth of our knowledge by the help which it brings to others.

Again: as long as our aims, our methods, our sanctions, are material, there can be no equal fellowship, no enthusiasm of service, no stable peace. Wealth to be held irresponsibly as a

Ideals.

private possession is tacitly accepted as the standard of success. The skill which we labour to gain is regarded as a weapon to overcome a rival. The final appeal is to strong battalions. But the contemplation of a great ideal of humanity will constrain us to recognise as axioms that classes, nations, races rejoice and suffer together; that every possession, every power of a society or a people, is an instrument for wider service; that the accordant voices of history and conscience give a verdict which no force can arrest from final execution.

Yet, again, we are reminded at every turn that men who should be prophets and pioneers of a noble future are content to sink into expositors of the past or present. They devote themselves to making a survey, an analysis, a description. Life becomes a study without a moral, treated as equally interesting and equally transitory in all its forms, a drama provided for the amusement of those who are in a position to forget that the actors are men of like passions and like destiny with themselves. But as one of the most noble of modern political leaders said with his latest voice:—'Our world is not a spectacle; it is a field of battle upon which all who in their hearts love justice, beauty, and holiness are bound— whether as leaders or soldiers, conquerors or martyrs—to play their part.' And the contemplation of a great ideal of life will sustain the combatant in the struggle, and through every failure enable him to strive as knowing that, for States, as for men, the test of abiding greatness is the power of sacrifice.

Such an ideal will give back also, strengthened and purified, the true conviction of personal responsibility. At present we first shrink from forming a decision, and then we improvise one. We are first irresolute and then precipitate. It must be so till we fix our eyes upon an unchangeable goal and have faith to move towards it. As we do so, we may err in this step or that, but we shall never go wrong as to the line of our advance. Thus only can we do our work. An ideal is, we have seen, a condition of sustained action; and action is the mark of a man. He is born not to think, as regarding one element only of his constitution; not to be, as gathering into himself all the treasures which he can command; but to act, to consecrate to one supreme cause the fulness of his powers, as knowing that life is not a search for personal happiness or aggrandisement, not an effort after self-centred culture, but the accomplishment of a Divine service.

Such ideals of nature, humanity, life, are, I

Ideals. 157

repeat, intensely practical, even if they are unattainable. They are as sunlight upon our common ways. And the teachings which this Society is seeking to gain and to spread brings them into the very heart of our common business. It is on this that I wish to lay the utmost stress. We cannot all be scholars or philosophers or physicists, but we can all enter on the blessings of the larger heritage which it is the office of such explorers to gather. We can do our humblest tasks thoroughly and liberally, not as drudges, but as fellow-workers with saints and heroes; we can feel that we, too, in the lowest places, are servants of an illustrious commonwealth; we can find the opportunity for a generous career each in our narrow circles; we can pursue our peculiar work in the spirit which is common to us all as men, and enjoy the invigorating energy of a larger being; we can, if I may so use your motto, learn to convert that which is a means of livelihood into a means of life.

And it is, I believe by the help of these noblest ideals—ideals which belong to men as men, the ideals of our Christian faith—that purity and peace and freedom and dignity will be given to the masses of our countrymen. This conviction has brought me here to-day that I might plead once more for a work which I have watched with gratitude from its beginning. Only let those of us who have caught some distant glimpse of the beauty of creation as the thought of GOD, and of the obligation of labour as the lot of man, tell courageously what we have seen and known. All who share our nature are capable of our highest visions, and awakened reverence will do her perfect work. The ruined denes of Durham will then smile once more, and smoke-wrapped rows of huts will give place to homes of men. Ideals grow wider, and brighter, and nearer with our own years and with the years of the world. I see now that far more is within a measurable distance for nations and for men than seemed possible when I was first stirred by great hopes in my school days. Thoughts whispered then with bated breath have become commonplaces. We know our dangers; in part, we know our aims and resources. We stand on the edge of a new age. It is for the young to shape it. To them we commit without fear our ideals and our faith.

THE FAMILY.

I bow my knees unto the Father, from whom every family in heaven and on earth is named.

Eph. iii. 14 f.

CONSECRATION OF ST HILDA'S CHURCH, HEDGEFIELD, RYTON.

July 30*th*, 1892.

THE FAMILY.

IN the Epistle to the Ephesians St Paul lays open a vision of the spiritual origins and influences and issues of things temporal, and confirms the truth which lies in the bold surmise of the poet that earth is in some sense a shadow of heaven. Now he sees in the future of the material Temple with its 'wall of partition' a figure of the state of the world before the Advent, and then passes to the contemplation of its living antitype, built on the foundation of apostles and prophets with Christ for its head corner-stone. Now he traces in the organisation of the natural body the pattern of a glorious society fitly framed together by the ministries of every part, and guided by the animating energy of a Divine Head.

Now he shews how through the experience of the Church on earth the manifold wisdom of GOD is made known to the heavenly hierarchy.

Now he declares that marriage, in which the distinctive gifts and graces of divided humanity are brought together in harmonious fellowship is a sign, a sacrament in his own language, of that perfect union in which the Incarnate Word takes to Himself His Bride, the firstfruits of creation. And so in the paragraph where the text occurs he touches with thankful exultation on the universality of the Gospel, by which the many races of men Jews and Gentiles—the people and the nations—are reunited, and the purpose of GOD in the education of the world is at last made clear.

Not in one line but in many; not through a calm, uninterrupted growth but in sorrow and tribulation men were trained in the post—this is his thought—to receive the crowning truth and justified their training by their faith. By the help of that most signal example we can see how every ordered commonwealth, every bond of kinsmanship, owes its strength to a divine presence. From the One Father, every fatherhood, every family through which the grace of fatherhood is embodied, derives its essential virtue.

St Paul is thinking primarily of the larger families of men and spirits, but it is no straining of his words to apply them to the family of home. In this sense the family is the divine unit of mankind the unit of the Church as it is the unit of the nation. The forces of home come from GOD, and are supported by GOD, and are claimed for GOD.

I shall ask you then this afternoon at this glad and long-expected Festival to regard the family as a revelation to us of the Father's will, a revelation visible to the eyes of the heart, of authority, of discipline, of sheltering love.

The subject is of momentous importance at the present time. On the one hand an aggressive individualism assails more and more openly the social sanctities of the family. On the other hand the state is more and more pressed to take upon itself offices which in the past were left to private duty. And however highly we may rate the value of self-reliant independence, however justly we may seek physical and intellectual vigour, even these would be dearly purchased by the sacrifice of that reverence and tenderness and sense of responsibility by which the family lives its true life. All history proclaims that as the family is, so is the nation. And GOD, in His great mercy, has hitherto enabled Englishmen to guard the home and still commits it to our keeping.

The subject is also natural to-day. The family is the woman's realm. In the family, woman can use most beneficently her characteristic gifts of faith, of affection, of purity. And to-day we commemorate the first authentic mother of our Northern Church. Under the stern conditions of a rude and turbulent age Hilda fulfilled a true woman's work on a heroic scale. With Aidan and Bede she stands foremost among the founders of our civilisation. Firm in government, rich in counsel, tender in sympathy she moulded the elements of a wild age after a Christian type. Now in narrow limits, under a settled order, I claim that each mother should in her place be a Hilda.

The family is, as I have said, if we regard it rightly, a revelation of authority, of discipline, of sheltering love, realised through the happy fulfilment of ordinary duties. The family, in other words, is a kingdom, a school, a sanctuary and within its range the wife, the mother, is supreme.

1. The family is, I say, a kingdom. It is not of our design. It is not of our making. It is not of our choosing. It is not dependent on our pleasure for its continuance. When complete it includes each typical relation of society, the relation of command, of obedience, of fellowship. The members of a family in simple intercourse learn, however imperfectly, the duty of service.

The Family.

The feeling of the family conquers self. It is enough to appeal to the experience of home to refute the cynical assertion that personal interest is man's single or strongest motive. In the family the tenderest affection, the most watchful care, the largest forethought, are not lavished on the strongest or the most helpful but rather on the most helpless and weak who can make no measurable return to their comforters. In the family need is taken as the measure of help, and a principle is spontaneously acknowledged which in its widest application would be adequate to deal with the sorrows of the world.

To cultivate this principle, to give form and consistency to the spontaneous generosity of love, is the parents' and especially the mother's work. Their authority is divine. They have committed to them a sacred ministry. They are charged to exercise it 'to the praise and honour of GOD'; and in the exercise they will study their children: they will note differences between them: they will vary their methods: they will watch with delicate patience for opportunities of using authority. They will not judge of acts by the appearance, but distinguish here a weakness or an error, and there a real evil or a vice in the blood. They will not give commands, in the caprice of power, but weigh them wisely and then enforce them without fail, knowing the peril of arbitrary words, and the fatal irreverence which comes from the impunity of disobedience.

The lessons thus learnt—or it may be neglected—will have wide consequences. Well will it be for the nation and for the Church if the child finds the instructive respect with which he turned to those who were for him the first representatives of authority, grow through happy experience to sure and loyal devotion to a divine order, if the parent recognises in the answering love of the child the blessing of responsibility duly met. Well will it be if the kingdom of home brings to its members the joy of ruling and the joy of serving, two forms of the one joy of a corporate life, that they may with matured strength gladly fulfil their part in the kingdom of the world.

2. The family is a kingdom; and it is also a school, a school of character. The outer school cannot mould the whole of man's nature. Character is shaped by action and not by words. What has been learnt by memory must be tested and embodied by experience. Under one aspect the outer school stimulates new and importunate wants, while the home is fitted to bring that social discipline which checks the selfish endeavour to satisfy them. At the same time the

The Family. 167

school offers new interests which may brighten home. I never visit an Infant School without wishing that I had with me a company of mothers who might see on a large scale what simple resources avail to happily engage and occupy the youngest. I rarely hear a higher class read without thinking how effectively fathers might illustrate the lesson by what they have themselves seen and done. Thus the life without and the life within might be bound together, and out of the home would spring naturally the spirit of sympathy and of self-devotion. Out of the home too must spring the spirit of purity. For Home has its own proper warnings when the occasion comes. The knowledge of the elder may guard the innocent from falling; and the young have no better earthly safeguard than to carry with them the thought of mother or sister as the witness of all they do or say or think.

3. So the family which is a school becomes a sanctuary also. I do not forget the outward conditions under which some families are still forced to live. I can hear the indignant question: 'Do you call a crowded room a home'? and I answer that we need only to recall the conditions of the husbands and wives and children and slaves in Asia to whom St Paul wrote, in order to find that there is in Christianity a power of spiritual trans-

formation. It is more true that men make their circumstances than that circumstances make men. The splendour of palaces does not secure innocence and holiness within their walls, but a sense of the presence of GOD does. Where GOD is welcomed as a guest there an atmosphere of sanctity is diffused around. A witness whose experience is unsurpassed writes: 'I know numbers of the prettiest, happiest little homes which consist of a single room.' We ask then that His hallowing Presence should be habitually sought. We ask that 'daily bread' should be received with some simple words of blessing: that work and rest should be consecrated by some simple words of prayer and praise. In these observances there is nothing forced or unnatural: nothing which is not possible under the commonest outward circumstances: nothing which does not answer to the promptings of the human heart. And for the fulfilment of this desire we claim woman's help. There is a message even for the present age in the fact emphatically recorded by St John, that a woman was divinely charged to be the first herald of the Resurrection, the herald of the new life.

The need of England, the need of every land, is 'good mothers.' If they fail, it is not for lack of womanly endowments in those who are

The Family. 169

called to fulfil the duty. Poor and desolate outcasts, whom we are tempted to place lowest, are capable of every sacrifice to shield their children from bodily suffering or loss. .Let them only feel, and let mothers of every class feel, that there are sicknesses of the soul which require the ministries of wise and tender affection, spiritual perils which need to be guarded against by watchful forethought, desires of the heart which crave the fulness of more than human love, and we shall be brought near to the consummation of our daily prayer in the advent of the kingdom of GOD.

And in this respect Durham has one great advantage. There is very little work of married women among us. GOD grant that the leisure may be used for perfecting the ministries of home.

Do I seem to have proposed too high an aim, to have forgotten the conditions of ordinary life, in the pursuit of visionary fancies? Surely not so. My words have not gone beyond the counsels of GOD's love. The highest is for all. The highest, if only we will trust the voice within us stirred by His Spirit, is found to be the simplest: the commonest is found to be the most refreshing. We are all called to be saints, summoned and fitted for a consecrated life. We are all—let us ponder the truth with grateful awe—members of Christ, the children of GOD, heirs of the kingdom of heaven. This is God's will for us. These are His gifts to us, gifts which will then become blessings if we grow to match them in humble surrender to His guidance: gifts which severally disclose the divine foundation of social duties, the permanence of individual responsibility, the character which we must gain through our earthly training if we are to find in the open vision of God the consummation of our hope.

The family, as I have already said, offers scope for every type of human service, for the solemn exercise of command, for the glad response of obedience, for encouragement, for instruction, for sympathy. It is founded on love, it is disciplined by love, it is fertile in love. Every one can hear within that narrow circle the call which comes to him, and through God's Spirit he can obey it. For let us remember what our Faith is, not as a tradition but as a power. We too, and not the first disciples or the apostles only, work in the presence of a living and speaking Lord. And as we work in that transfiguring light a character is fashioned which will be fitted to meet the fulness of Christian duty.

The family—let me use what may seem to be a strong phrase, which I have weighed well—is, if we look at its essential form, a divine preparation for the Communion of Saints. In the family

The Family. 171

we all habitually recognise the influence of the absent. In the family we gratefully acknowledge the influence of the departed. In the family we feel without effort the presence of the unseen. And such fellowship is, we know, not for the future only, not for imagination only, but for the strengthening and the joy of life. The family is, at least the family may be, I repeat, a preparation, a foretaste, of the Communion of Saints.

Powers lie hidden in the soul of every man and woman which are able to sustain the loftiest devotion. In the revolution of 1848 a mob of outcasts guarded the royal treasure of France through the streets of Paris. In the American civil war the common people gave heroes to offer themselves gladly for the maintenance of a great idea, who would otherwise have died in obscurity. The powers are present, but they are checked and chilled by the burden of commonplace thoughts; we do not appeal as strongly as we ought to do to these more generous instincts. We may appeal to them, I believe, most effectively through the family.

Then the spirit of self-devotion once quickened at home will direct action in the wider relations of national life. So the kingdom of GOD will be brought near, not by any sudden revolution, but little by little, not by the earthquake or the storm or the fire, but by the still small voice which makes known to believers the greatness of their calling.

Meanwhile we can labour on without the despondency of hurry. GOD will hasten the end in its time. And beyond all that is dark we shall see the glory of one Face. In every imperfect representation of the Truth we shall discern the working of our Lord. In the sadnesses of misunderstandings and conflicts we shall win our souls in patience. We shall win our souls in patience, and, masters of ourselves in Christ and servants of all the brethren, we shall know the fulness of that peace—the peace of the Gospel—for which Hilda pleaded with her last words. So pleading she saw death, or rather as Bede writes, she passed from death to life.

'The peace of the Gospel'—that is Hilda's message to us to-day, and to this house—the peace which comes from the assurance that it is the good pleasure of GOD to sum up all things in Christ. And for this cause we can now *bow our knees unto the Father from Whom every family in heaven and on earth is named that He would grant* all who shall hereafter worship here *to know the love of Christ which passeth knowledge, that* they *may be filled unto all the fulness of GOD.*

THE CONSECRATION OF THE TEACHER.

Sanctify them in the Truth.

St John xvii. 17.

JUBILEE OF BEDE COLLEGE, DURHAM.
Oct. 18, 1891.

THE CONSECRATION OF THE TEACHER.

THE occasion of our meeting to-day must stir our hearts with thoughts of gratitude and self-questioning, of gratitude for the signal blessings which GOD has granted to those who have laboured for the religious education of the people during the last fifty years, of self-questioning when we regard the work which is now made ready for our accomplishment. If gratitude is real it must find expression in devotion. If we recognise aright what GOD has done for us, we shall consider seriously what we ourselves, in obedience to His voice, are waiting to do for Him as His Spirit moves us. The Christian teacher in School and in Church is required to-day to do his work under new conditions, conditions which I hold to be not less invigorating or less encouraging than those under which our fathers built up the inheritance on which we have entered. How are we preparing to meet them?

The Consecration of the Teacher.

It is of the Schoolmaster we think at present. I have spoken elsewhere on his Mission, on the limitations and the opportunities, the fruits and the hopes of his office. This morning I wish to speak on the spirit in which he will prepare himself for his Mission, and preparation most happily is as long as life. If it be true, as our experience must have taught us, that the scholar is a teacher: it is true also that the teacher is a scholar as long as he fulfils a living service. And for the guidance of our thoughts I have chosen words which he will ever keep in his heart, words which bring before us in the briefest form the inspiration and the hallowing of that student life which is the spring and the support of the Master's life.

Sanctify them in the Truth. The words form part, as you will remember, of the most solemn prayer ever offered upon earth of which any record has been preserved for us, of that Prayer which is emphatically the Lord's Prayer. They express the final sum of the spiritual endowment which the Lord desired for His disciples through their life-long,—their world-long—work. And the exact language is significant. *Sanctify them,* He says, *in the Truth: in* the Truth and not simply *through* the Truth: in *the* Truth and not in *Thy* Truth. The Truth is, as it were, the

The Consecration of the Teacher. 177

atmosphere, the element, in which believers are immersed and by which they are sustained: and we must think of the Truth, in the widest sense in which we can conceive of it. Such Truth, which Christ is, and which Christ reveals, is everywhere about us: it corresponds with the whole range of present experience: it is realised in a personal communion with its Source. Its function is not simply to support but to transfigure. Its issue is not knowledge but holiness.

Sanctify them in the Truth. We cannot, it is evident, limit the application of the petition to any particular age or class. The petition and the charge which the petition involves are for all times and for all believers. The action of the Truth is effective in due measure in every ministry of life. The Truth itself is progressive because it is living. No one, whatever may be his appointed duty, is excluded from a share in its purifying influence. No one can claim to have a monopoly in the pursuit of it. But at the same time the Lord's words do, I think, answer in a special manner to the calling of the Christian student. They regard in a peculiar sense the wants, the dangers, the hopes, the strength of teachers. They demand from us in our several works patient and devout attention. They reveal to us the aim to which we are bound to bend our efforts: they supply a test by which we may discern how far we fall away from it.

Sanctify them in the Truth. As we ponder the prayer, we shall see that the consecration to which the Lord points, is founded upon a complete and willing sacrifice on the part of man. It is consummated by a divine transformation. It is expressed in active service.

The Truth demands perfect self-devotion.

The Truth brings him who welcomes it into harmony with itself.

The Truth becomes through its servant a force victorious over the world.

Self-surrender, transformation, service, these three seem to be the chief moments of consecration in the Truth: these three are the characteristic marks of the student who is *made a disciple unto the kingdom of heaven,* made a disciple in order that he may convey to others the lessons which he has learnt.

1. The first mark of the Christian student is self-surrender: he offers himself wholly to the Truth. It is not only that he dedicates time, labour, thought, unsparingly to the search for it: it is not only that he postpones every personal advantage to the prosecution of his generous quest: it is not only that he tries all things with a sincerity as pure as his reverence. He does all

The Consecration of the Teacher.

this as in the Presence of Him of Whose perfect will Truth is the image. He recognises a Sovereign power without him, living and ruling, bringing into view at each hour new regions of fact and claiming for their proclamation the use of fresh powers. He knows that in the execution of his limited work perfect obedience is perfect freedom. He approaches his task as one who gladly gives all that he has and is for the furtherance of the cause to which he is dedicated. He has learnt that his 'individual difference' is just that which GOD requires of him in the fulfilment of his labour. He is equally far from exaggerating and from disparaging the importance of his own task. He aims not at a private conquest of some fragment of the universe of thought but at a vital sympathy with the whole of it. His end is not knowledge, it is not even wisdom: it is Truth, knowledge and wisdom regarded in their moral unity as the foundation of life.

Such whole-hearted devotion guards him from seductive errors. The partial is always claiming supremacy. But the true student is strong against the temptations. He knows that each fragmentary fulfilment of man's powers, it matters not essentially whether it be Art as the expression of emotion or Dogma as the expression of thought, when it claims to be exclusive and absolute becomes at once delusive and practically false. He therefore keeps before him a sense of the entire sum in the least part. His work, whatever it may be, calls out from the first the sympathetic activity of his whole nature. His will finds exercise no less than his understanding, his feeling no less than his reason.

To one who is inspired by such whole-hearted devotion the Truth does not appear as something to be mastered, confined, imprisoned, but loved, embraced, embodied by him who has been allowed to see it. Every detail, however minute it may be in itself is regarded as having a living connexion with the great order through which GOD is pleased to make Himself known to men. The past, with all its lessons of victory and failure, with all its voices of warning and instruction, is seen to enter into the present, and to speak to us in our own words and by our own experience, to speak through us to those who will continue our work and carry it forward to nobler results.

And here lies the severest test of the student's self-surrender. He has to learn a lesson which has been in one sense only given in part. He must hold communion, this is his trial and his strength, with the Spirit of the Living and True GOD. He must listen heedfully for the first whisperings of a new message: he must bear without complaining long intervals of silence: he must take to himself not only the sharp agony of the Passion and the abounding joy of the Rising again, but that space of unlighted, chilling, gloom by which they are separated. It may be that GOD is preparing for him through the pains of a troubled time, through the removal of that which can be shaken, some better thing, in which the tentative and partial thoughts which he has received from his fathers shall be fulfilled. It may be that he will have to endure to the last the stern discipline of questionings unanswered. But at least he will in anywise be sure of this, that he has not through wilful impatience or false reverence closed one avenue by which the Truth might have found access to his soul. He will have gained the spirit of the soldier, if he has not been allowed to gather the fruits of victory; and it happens not unfrequently that the nobility and assurance of faith are perfected not through brilliant achievements, but through much endurance.

Such unreservedness of self-surrender, the devotion of the student, is not easy of attainment. We are all sadly conscious of the difficulties by which it is beset. We are tempted to interpret facts prematurely in the interest of what we hold to be the Truth, to endeavour restlessly to round to completeness what is yet imperfectly disclosed, to seclude faithlessly from approach some region as holy ground on which GOD perhaps is waiting to reveal a fresh charge. And by yielding to such impulses we make progress impossible as far as lies in us. We dissemble or obscure those elements in the problem which point to a more general solution. We make ourselves or our interpretation of the past the measure of what must be. In such a case even a right anticipation of future lessons is dearly purchased at the cost of that simple trust in the divine order which alone gives harmony to life.

2. *Sanctify them in the Truth.* Self-surrender to the Truth is the first mark of the Christian student. Self-surrender is accompanied by transformation. GOD quickens and transfigures by illuminating. *The message which we have received is that GOD is light.* He manifests Himself to us in accordance with His nature, as we are able to bear His brightness; and we, on our part, are changed into His likeness by reflecting His glory. Or, as the thought is here brought before us, the effect of living in the Truth is holiness.

From this point of view we can understand how Christianity satisfies the old paradox that knowledge is virtue. In this sense the know-

The Consecration of the Teacher. 183

ledge of phenomena, which suggests the notions of distinctness, separation, distance, is not knowledge. But Christian knowledge is the welcoming of the Truth within us, the realisation of a fellowship with the spiritual and eternal of which the things that are seen are sacraments. And the Truth which takes shape in the soul cannot but have its work. Such efficacy lies indeed in the very character of the divine revelation. That what we can learn of GOD and of His work is suited to modify our affections and to bring the godlike nature within our reach. The living apprehension of the Truth is therefore necessarily effective as a motive and effective as an influence. It is a power within first and a power without afterwards. Here we are left in no doubt. It is through the Truth, not through any semblance or counterfeit of it, not through any vain shadow to which we force ourselves to render a half-sincere homage, that GOD makes us like unto His Son. It is through the Truth, communed with as a living guide and not guarded like an idol, that our way is made plain before us. It is through the Truth, held with undoubting guilelessness, that we are made strong to do our work.

This fact is one on which it is necessary to insist, for there is no aspect of the Christian Faith which is more commonly misunderstood or misrepresented. Our Christian Creed, the definite expression of the highest spiritual realities, is not a mere collection of abstract propositions which are an end in themselves, complete in their speculative exactness. Every article has a direct bearing upon life. It is so, it must be so, in every department of knowledge. A spiritual factor enters into the apprehension of the Truth: a spiritual process accompanies the possession of the Truth. There cannot be one fragment of Truth which is powerless for the inspiration or the guidance of action. For man, doing is the goal of thinking; and Holiness manifests itself in love. The Christian therefore so far as he is a Christian must be stronger and more active than other men, according as he knows what Christ has done for him and for the world: what Christ is and what the world is. If he is not: if his belief is no more than a series of dogmas which remain in the region of the intellect, he knows nothing as he ought to know.

Thus the consecration in the Truth which Christ has prepared for us is as deep and as long as our earthly work. He has made all things possible for us; and even through failure and difficulty, so long as we look to Him, we draw nearer to our goal. It is not a negative purity to which He calls us, but a positive holiness.

The Consecration of the Teacher.

'*Ye are clean*,' He said to His disciples; and the same night He added the prayer '*Sanctify them in the Truth.*'

3. *Sanctify them in the Truth.* St Bernard has summarised in well-known words five possible motives of the student. 'There are some,' he writes, 'who wish to know for the simple sake 'of knowing; and it is shameful curiosity. And 'there are some who wish to know that they may 'be known; and it is shameful vanity. And there 'are some who wish to know that they may sell 'their knowledge; and it is shameful greed. There 'are some too who wish to know that they may 'edify; and it is love: some who wish to know 'that they may be edified; and it is wise fore-'thought.' The last two ends are indeed identical. The experience of a fuller and freer life than Bernard was acquainted with has taught us that the perfection of the individual is the perfection of service. Self cannot be in any form the last aim in the search for Truth or in the possession of Truth. The moral destination of Truth is social and not personal. What is revealed to us is given not for hoarding but for using, as a means for wider ministry, and not as a pretext for isolation in the barren pleasures of self-culture. It follows therefore that the self-surrender of the student, the self-surrender which transforms, is

fruitful in service. We all acknowledge in general terms the obligation of service which is laid upon us by the opportunities of study and teaching which we have received. And still I think that we often fail to reflect how far the obligation reaches. For must we not confess that we are inclined to direct our work with a view to ruling rather than to serving: that in our passion for results we are apt to follow subjects and methods which promise them in a definite and telling shape to the neglect of those in which no successes can be tabulated? The temptation extends even to the highest regions of work. In these we see its full perils. The greatest and most urgent problems are often postponed to those which offer the prospect of a brilliant solution to short labour. In this way the very idea of Truth is narrowed and lowered; and we are in danger of making life less worth living, while we are more and more busy in learning how to extend the term of life and to multiply its instruments and its furniture.

But such miscalculated or uncalculated and wasteful activity falls far short of the consecration of the Christian student. His work, be it great or small, be it concentrated upon the discharge of routine duties or turned to the loftiest speculation, will never want the hallowing assurance

The Consecration of the Teacher. 187

that it is an attempt to meet a moral obligation, an obligation not personal but social. The Truth to which he has given himself in one, it may be the least, of its parts, the Truth by which he has been moulded to a nobler nature is the motive power by which he is inspired, and that which in turn he strives to bring home to his class or to the world. He has his appropriate share in the interpretation of the Truth and in the fulfilment of this office, without restlessness and without insincerity, he finds the exercise and the discipline of every power with which he has been entrusted for the service of the Christian Society, which is the Body of Christ: the one way in which he can acknowledge what he owes to those who have prepared in earlier times the methods and the materials of his labour.

Sanctify them in the Truth: Self-surrender, transformation, service: this is what Christ asked for us: this is what, by His intercession, He places within our reach. No one can deny our need of the blessing: no one can deny its power. The words which immediately follow the prayer seem to shew how it must be won.

Sanctify them in the Truth: Thy Word is Truth.

Thy Word is Truth: as long as the world lasts GOD still speaks. His Word written and unwritten, His Word in the Bible, in Nature, in History, has a message for every generation, an answer to every human cry. We dare not limit either the time or the manner of His utterance. Forms of thought, the organisation of the state, the relations of the sciences vary, and He meets our changing position with appropriate teaching. His message comes to each age and to each people as it came at Pentecost, in their own language. It comes to us through the struggles of the nations and the movements of society, through every fact which marks one least step in the method of creation or in the history of man. It is this message, given to us in our language, which we have to welcome and to interpret now. So only will our personal consecration be perfected: so only will our social office be fulfilled.

Do I seem, my friends, to have set too high a standard for the spirit of your preparation? to have claimed too lofty a devotion for the fulfilment of a work which is often held to be—and so may often become—commonplace or even mechanical? I can only say that I speak from my own experience. I know that nothing is harder, even as nothing is more fruitful, than elementary teaching. I know that consecration in the Truth, according to the measure of our weakness, is an essential condition of the service. I know that large views are necessary for the right interpretation of the simplest things. I know that we must see the whole in the least part if we are to gain and to convey a true conception of nature or man, of work or duty. I know that we are surrounded by divine mysteries which the humblest can feel, and that the sense of mystery is the spring of thoughtful reverence, and that reverence is the secret of unfailing strength.

The age seems to be moving towards great changes. The well-being, the healthy development, I will not say merely the safety, of society depends in the near future on the character of the masses of the people, and their character depends upon their teachers; and who among their teachers have greater opportunities or greater power than those who give the first impulse to thought, the first motive to ambition, the first vision of the range and variety of human interests? What we need at the present time above all things is to spiritualise the popular estimate of the resources and the aims of life. The teacher will do his part and can only do his part in securing this end if he is himself sanctified in the Truth.

Sanctify them in the Truth. If we think of

ourselves the prospect of this consecration in the Truth is overwhelming. But the thought of self is the ruin of every great work. He Who assigns the charge is ready to give the power to fulfil it. If we receive little, it is because we ask for little. We ask for little because we believe little. We measure our enterprises by a calculation of our own resources, and we forget the potency of a divine fellowship.

In any case, no doubt, we shall fall below, far below, the ideal towards which we aspire; but the aspiration is not therefore vain nor is the ideal illusory. We know in part and we prophesy in part. The Truth is disclosed to us in riddles and reflections. Every worthy life must be a series of approximations to the unattainable. But each baffled endeavour offers to the faithful aspirant some fresh if fleeting vision of the King in His beauty; and the Society is richer by the hope to which he has given shape. So it is that while we fall one by one and pass away, the whole body inherits our labours, and little by little realises the Truth towards which we have reached.

We may not be able to accomplish much, but we can all of us shew of what mind we are. We can shew that we do indeed offer ourselves body, soul, and spirit, not one part but all without reserve, for consecration in the Truth. We can shew that the progress for which others precariously look is pledged to us by the promise of GOD. We can shew that everything which is truly human is for that reason, in virtue of the Incarnation, potentially divine.

We can shew that it is possible to look on all the facts of the world without extenuating the consequences of sin or limiting the victorious power of the divine love.

We can shew the splendid possibilities of life which lie within the reach of every man, who shares even in his lowest estate the nature which Christ has borne to the Father's throne. In this way the simplest life can become through our labours the natural expression of a great faith: and for ourselves the routine of work can be made a ministry of consecration.

Quid ergo dicit modum sciendi (1 Cor. viii. 2)? *quid? nisi ut scias quo ordine, quo studio, quo fine quaeque nosse oporteat? Quo ordine; ut id prius quod maturius ad salutem: quo studio; ut id ardentius quod vehementius ad amorem: quo fine; ut non ad inanem gloriam aut curiositatem aut aliquid simile, sed tantum ad aedificationem tuam vel proximi. Sunt namque qui scire volunt eo fine tantum ut sciant: et turpis curiositas est. Et sunt qui scire volunt ut sciantur ipsi: et turpis vanitas est...Et sunt item qui scire volunt ut scientiam suam vendant, verbi causa pro pecunia, pro honoribus: et turpis quaestus est. Sed sunt quoque qui scire volunt ut aedificent: et caritas est. Et item qui scire volunt ut aedificentur: et prudentia est* (Bernard, *in Cant.* Serm. xxxvi, 3.).

THE CHRISTIAN IDEA OF ALMS-GIVING.

(Sermon on behalf of the Diocesan Society of the Sons of the Clergy.)

Not that I seek for the gift but I seek for the fruit that increaseth to your account.

PHIL. iv. 17.

DURHAM, *January* 15*th*, 1891.

THE CHRISTIAN IDEA OF ALMSGIVING.

I seek for the fruit that increaseth to your account. These words of St Paul suggest to us the essential idea and the enduring benediction of Christian benevolence. The act of generous bounty is not simply an isolated gift: it is a fruit, the result of a long growth. It is not a service transient and external, exhausted in the doing, but the sign of a vital force fertile in the future for him who has done it. The gift is, if I may so express the thought, more necessary and richer in blessing for him who bestows it than for him to whose need it ministers.

The context adds pathos and force to the apostle's language. St Paul was a prisoner, held back from his missionary wanderings, yet, while chained to the soldier who guarded him, he could recognise that his sufferings had tended to the advance of the Gospel. But at the same time, in the conflicts and turmoil of Rome, his heart went out to his first converts in Europe. He longed to see them with the yearnings of Christian affection. And therefore he dwells on the memory of their early devotion. It might have seemed for a moment that this zeal had been chilled. He notices the misgiving only to set it aside. It was not the spirit but the opportunity which had been wanting to them. And so in due time their love had burst forth again with fresh vigour and grace. It has been said that he only who loves can make a true gift. This Epistle illustrates the truth. It is the voice of the loved to the loving. No word of reproof mars the full current of grateful sympathy with which the prisoner of the Lord meets the Church which alone ministered to his wants at the beginning of the Gospel.

But in dwelling upon the past services of the Philippians, St Paul feels that he might expose himself to a misconception. It might seem that his gratitude was a veiled request. Therefore, he adds, to avert the possible suspicion: *not that I seek for the gift, but I do seek for the fruit that increaseth unto your account.* For himself he requires nothing. The very supplies which they sent were in his sight a sacrifice to GOD, and therefore most precious. He wanted not theirs, but them: not a tribute, a relief, but a sign of the continued spiritual progress of his disciples:

The Christian Idea of Almsgiving. 197

not something which he could use, but something which he could interpret: not that which they would wholly surrender, but that which would abide with them for blessing: not a gift, but fruit. *I seek,* he writes, *for the fruit that increaseth unto your account.* Fruit is an end and a beginning, the crown of one long process and the germ of another: fruit witnesses to what has been in a long time of preparation, and provides for that which shall be in due succession. It is a result and a promise. Almsgiving, the offering of Christian benevolence, is fruit in both aspects. As we ponder the image, we shall see in it, as I have already said, the idea of almsgiving and the benediction of almsgiving.

1. The idea of almsgiving. Almsgiving is the natural, the necessary expression of a healthy Christian character. The Christian cannot but be communicative of the goods which he has. Almsgiving is not a concession to importunity, by which we free ourselves from unwelcome petitioners: it is not a sacrifice to public opinion, by which we satisfy the claims popularly made upon our place or fortune: it is not an appeal for praise: it is not a self-complacent show of generosity: it is not, in a word, due to any external motive. It is the spontaneous outcome of life. What the life is, the fruit will be, in the highest

forms as in the lowest. Our thoughts have their fruits, and our thoughts themselves are fruits.

In this light we can feel the inexorable truth of the Lord's sentence: *By their fruits ye shall know them.* Nothing can take the place of the ripe result of life. There may be the swift response of a superficial sensibility: there may be the luxuriant growth of lofty intentions: but the blessing is only for him who brings forth fruit—fruit answering to the divine seed—in patience.

The actions of a Christian, then, are a fruit of the Christian character. As we give distinctness to the idea another thought comes out. A real gift is part of ourselves. The crumbs which fall from our table, the overflowings of our abundance, cannot be gifts. The gift must have in it that which tends to elevate the receiver, to bring him personally closer to us. It must be, as I have said already, a sign; a sign of sympathy, of reverence, of affection; a sign that we recognise the bond by which giver and receiver are held together as men.

As fruits, therefore, our alms will bear the marks of our Faith. That which the Christian gives will carry the impress of self-denial, of singleness, of self-devotion, of thoughtfulness. Of self-denial; Christ Himself comes to us in those who

The Christian Idea of Almsgiving. 199

need our help, and we shall not bring to Him that which costs us nothing. Of singleness; any secondary aim corrupts that purity of intention which is the soul of service. Of self-devotion; our gift, we have seen, is part of ourselves, and must be true-hearted. Of thoughtfulness; care alone can bring that touch of grace which reveals the true purpose of the giver, and guards for the receiver the honour of self-respect.

So, as we pass from point to point, we can recognise in successive traits the idea of Christian almsgiving. And do we not, my friends, as we do this condemn ourselves? Do we not feel how poor and mean and inadequate and unworthy has been our own habitual conception of this fruit of our Christian character? Do we not confess that we have failed to reach the dignity of our stewardship as almoners of GOD?

2. It is not surprising, then, that we often misconceive and underrate the blessings of almsgiving, if we misconceive or overlook its true idea.

For the fruit which St Paul desires for his beloved Philippians is that which aboundeth to their account. The generous deed done in the name of Christ is a fruit, and it is fruitful. *The fruit of the righteous*, in the significant language of Scripture, *is a tree of life.* Each harvest is the seed of still richer return in the time to come. True it is, true beyond all possibility of failure, that 'there can never be one lost good': and, more than this, the good has in it a power of growth. *One soweth* indeed *and another reapeth*, but they *rejoice together* in the end when their labours are revealed and crowned in life eternal.

We cannot in many cases expect to see the issue of our labours, but we can foresee it in faith; and for the present no reward can be more satisfying than to know that another has had benefit through our ministry. It is a reward which stirs to fresh activity. The desire to serve more perfectly, more bountifully, increases with the sense of the joy which comes from each partial effort. The terrible contrasts of life are found to be less perplexing when love is enabled to use them as an opportunity for fresh endeavours after fellowship. If personal wealth has a tendency to encourage selfish indulgence and display, to exaggerate the value of the pleasures which it can command, to occupy and absorb the possessor in sordid cares, the thoughtful use of it, as a responsible trust, deepens the sense of our social dependence, discloses pleasures which do not cloy by continuance, quickens and extends the power of the common life. If the love of money is, as all experience teaches, a root of all evil, the use of money as an instrument of GOD is a spring of divine force.

Under this aspect we can understand the stress which is laid upon generous almsgiving in Scripture. The liberal man has escaped from a material thraldom. He has recognised the ties of human brotherhood. It may be, indeed, that the outward act in many cases comes to be all. It may be that the bounty is no fruit of disciplined love, but a ransom offered by fear. It may be, that according to the false teaching of a corrupt age, wealth is regarded as, in itself, the means of atoning for the sins which it has occasioned. But even so a witness is borne to the master-truth that our goods are not our own to be used arbitrarily for the simple gratification of our desires, but resources placed at our disposal for the service of men. In one way or another, for good or for evil, we must distribute them among others. But that the stewardship may be a blessing to ourselves it must be inspired by that temper which I have endeavoured to indicate. And the temper of self-discipline and self-sacrifice is not born with us. It needs to be quickened and cultivated. And we ministers of Christ may well ask ourselves, not without anxiety, whether in regard to this particular duty we have plainly set out in our teaching the duty of proportionate almsgiving;

whether we have pressed upon all for consideration how far that part of our income which exceeds the right demands of our place is the heritage of the poor entrusted to our use; whether we have endeavoured to apply to our own circumstances the old Jewish laws of first-fruits and tenths; whether we plead that that which is given to God should be a first charge upon our means, and set apart as sacred, and not be found in some chance fragments which remain when every other claim has been met and every fancy gratified. We should not, I believe, find ourselves poorer if we were to place a part of our goods beyond the reach of fortune. I do not fancy that the widow who cast into the treasury of GOD all the living that she had, felt afterwards that she had suffered any loss. Nay, rather there is deep truth in the striking words of Chrysostom, 'If any distress befall thee, straightway give alms; return thanks for the accident, and thou shalt see how great joy follows thereupon. For the spiritual gain, even if it be small, is so great as to obliterate all bodily loss. If thou hast to give to Christ thou art wealthy.'

I cannot, however, pursue these far-reaching questions now. The occasion of our meeting to-day brings before us an urgent problem, which we have not seriously endeavoured to solve. For

The Christian Idea of Almsgiving. 203

clerical distress is an evil which we should aim at remedying, and not only at relieving. Such a work is essentially a lay work. So it was felt to be by the founders of our Society; and once again we must look to laymen to consolidate and complete, at a happier time, an effort which was begun among us in a season of unequalled national division and distress. For the Society was founded in the year of Malplaquet and Sacheverell's sermon; and while a few gentlemen here in the north were loyally seeking to meet the wants of their spiritual teachers, Massillon was vainly trying to rouse the French court with burning eloquence to take pity on their countrymen who 'wandered over the fields to seek food which the earth had not brought forth for man, food which was for them a food of death.'

It is worth while to recall such memories, that we may take heart in face of our own trials. We cannot despair of our commonwealth if we look to the past. Much remains to be done in this field of labour, as in every other.

Much remains to be done, and it will be done. But this is not the place to discuss the details of clerical finance. It must be enough to recognise our duty. Yet, even this is not easy, for in this respect we have suffered from the generosity of our fathers. In many cases no charge is laid upon us for the provision of spiritual ministries, and we forget that to supply them is one of the first privileges of our faith. We must seek to learn the true lesson of our position. We must acknowledge that the greatness of our inheritance is rather the measure of our obligations than the discharge from present responsibility.

But this is not the time to dwell on larger duties which, as I just said, will be fulfilled, as I cannot doubt, when they are rightly seen; we have to-day a very simple work to do. We are required to enable an old and well-tried Society to fulfil its beneficent and yet limited obligations. In view of the requirement, we cannot use the usual pleas for withholding our assistance, the smallness of our resources and the multitude of the needy. Here, at least, we cannot question the value of the service which we are able to render.

I ask, then, that you will not only give your alms generously now in support of the Society, but even more, that you will endeavour by your private efforts and influence to extend its operation. I ask this, not so much for the sake of those who will receive help, as for your sakes who will enjoy the privilege of bestowing it. I ask it not as seeking for the gift so much as seeking for the fruit that increaseth to your account. I ask it that you may apply a simple test to the reality

The Christian Idea of Almsgiving.

and energy of your Christian faith. I ask it as wishing most earnestly that we should bring our belief in the brotherhood of Christians, in the brotherhood of men, to bear upon the common relations of life : that we should draw our loftiest thoughts and hopes from heaven to earth.

A bishop, by the conditions of his work, is in closer and wider connection than any one else can be with men separated as far as possible by place and fortune. He is likely to have had personal experience of great contrasts in his own outward circumstances. He cannot for one moment forget that the estate that he administers is not his own, but that he is for a brief space the steward of a noble heritage. He is enabled, therefore, to say with certain assurance how rapidly cares and not enjoyments multiply with abundance of possessions; how little anything which makes life worth living depends upon worldly goods; how from first to last, with means great or small, joy comes from that completeness of self-surrender in which we offer ourselves with whatever wealth we have, wealth of feeling, or character, or substance, or intellect, for the service of our fellows.

He must, therefore, with whatever force he has, press upon all whom he may hope to influence the lessons of his life, his work, his faith; he must not shrink from claiming what he desires to render; he must repeat without weariness what I will say once more, as I strive now, as I pray that I may always strive, to shew how the generosity of self-devotion is inseparable from the reality of spiritual growth:

"Not that I seek for the gift, but I seek for the fruit that increaseth to your account."

OUR OWN POOR IN INDIA.

*(Sermon on behalf of the Indian Church
Aid Association.)*

Ye also bear witness, because *ye have been with Me from the beginning.*

St John xv. 27.

St James', Piccadilly,
    Sunday after Ascension, 1891.

OUR OWN POOR IN INDIA.

THE occasion and the time of our meeting this afternoon constrain us to think of our duty and our hope as Christians; to ask with more than usual persistence and frankness what our Faith means for us, what obligations and what powers it carries with it, what practical confession of our Creed we make to the world. To-day we stand between the festival of the Ascension and the festival of Pentecost, between the consummation of Christ's earthly life and the birthday of the Christian Church. We bear witness in word and outward form to facts which have a universal significance. The promises which are included in them are not for Englishmen only, or for Europeans, but for men as men. If, then, we have known their strength and their consolation, if we have found them capable of throwing light upon dark riddles of life, if we have experienced their ability to purify and to raise the corrupt and the degraded, if we have recognised how they find an ever growing fulfilment through the services of different races, we shall strive to the utmost range of our opportunities not only to guard, but also to spread them, and so to hasten the coming of the kingdom of God.

And here at once we are brought face to face with the problems presented to us by our commercial supremacy. We hold for good and for evil a unique position in regard to non-Christian nations. We have a burden of responsibility towards them from which we cannot free ourselves. It is through our countrymen in a very great degree that non-Christian nations must receive their impressions of the Gospel, through the sailor and the merchant, as things are, even more than through the clergyman. Every Englishman is an eloquent witness for or against Christ wherever he goes. His life is a proclamation of his creed, easily intelligible, unquestionably sincere, and rapidly effective.

Such reflections are of world-wide application. We cannot pursue them in their widest range; but if we confine our attention to our Indian Empire they may well fill us with anxious questionings. For India England must give account. For India our National Church is the spiritual organ of England. Other communions may do what she has left undone, but they cannot lighten her obligation. And as yet we have not made any serious effort to realise what the obligation is. Meanwhile Western thought is spreading in India immeasurably faster than the Faith of Christ. The ancient bonds of society are loosened, and no stronger spiritual ties take their place. We disintegrate; we destroy; as yet we do not build. Can we wonder at this result? It follows of necessity from the character of the witness which we bear. Our testimony as to material things—the order of the physical universe—is clear and uniform; our testimony as to spiritual things is hesitating and half-suppressed. When we are one we are irresistible; when we are divided, isolated, conflicting, our influence is proportionately diminished.

This state of things demands most earnest consideration, and the more so because we have not, I think, rightly apprehended the conditions of Mission work in India. We speak with just sorrow of the scantiness of our Missionary forces —of a thousand ministers to 200,000,000 people— but we should speak, I believe, with still juster sorrow if the facts were more vividly present to our minds as to the 250,000 unrecognised Missionaries, Missionaries by their name and life, Europeans and Eurasians, who witness too often only to Christian indifference and Christian neglect. If we pass by those of our own blood—and it is calculated that out of this quarter of a million 100,000 belong nominally to our English Church—will not their testimony condemn us? If we are unable to win them to Christian fellowship, must not our failure prejudice our wider claims? These profess to be of us, and we take little heed to strengthen the connection and use the forces of their natural sympathy. The consequences already may justly startle us. The criminals in India from among those who call themselves Christians are relatively nearly three times more than those from Hindoos and nearly twice more than those from Mohammedans. The number of Buddhists and Jains is alone proportionately larger.

It can hardly be otherwise, however terrible the fact may be, until the social Christian feeling is stronger. More than fifty years ago Dr Arnold wrote to a pupil, whose name is dear to Durham, who consulted him on Mission work :— " Whether you go to India or to any other foreign country, the first and great point, I think, is to turn your thoughts to the edification of the Church already in existence—that is, the English or Christian societies as distinct from the Hindoos. Unless the English and the half-caste people can be brought into a good state, how can you get on with the Hindoos?" "Remember," he added a little later, "that the great work to be done is to organise and purify Christian Churches of whites and half-castes." (Letters to H. Fox, *Life*, II., 291 ff.)

The counsel is, I believe, of vital importance, and, in a very large degree, it still waits fulfilment. The fulfilment is, indeed, beset by peculiar difficulties. The Eurasian population presents faults due in part to their constitution and in part to their unhappy position, which it is hard to overcome. But in the vigorous language of Bishop Cotton:—" It is nothing less than a sin to neglect a class who are our fellow-Christians and our fellow-subjects, whose presence in India is due entirely to our occupation of the country." The very existence of the class is a silent reproach to our Faith. If they are uncared for they must become a grave spiritual peril which every year of neglect intensifies.

Meanwhile, the natural course of events in India tends more and more to depress and to degrade them. The spread of education among the Hindus, who are more enduring and more frugal, deprives them of the occupations by which they were formerly supported. Without energy and without self-respect, according to a recent description, which must have touched many of us with shame, they look on labour as a disgrace, and steadily increase in numbers as they deteriorate in character (*Times*, March 6, 1891).

Under such circumstances we can hardly be surprised when we are told that, " Of the whole Eurasian and half-caste population in Calcutta and Howrah, one-fifth are in receipt of charitable relief, a proportion probably without parallel in any other community in the world" (*Times*, l. c.).

And these hereditary paupers—let us dare to face the fact, with all it brings of sorrow and late remorse—are, I repeat, one fruit of English occupation, one presentment to native eyes of our Christian faith.

The Eurasian population offers the most serious problem to the Church in India. But there is also a poor European population which may shortly become scarcely less difficult to deal with. "One-half of the boys of European extraction," I read, "of school-going years are not at present receiving such an education as will enable them to get their living." It is easy to foresee what their future will be unless they can be raised and supported by continuous pastoral care and the sympathetic help of Christian fellowship.

I have no wish to dwell on the dark traits of our Christian work in India, still less to exaggerate them; but we are bound to realise them if we desire to fulfil our duty towards the most splendid empire which GOD ever intrusted to a Christian people to win for Him.

And there are solid grounds for hope. A great Viceroy, who foresaw in the masses of " Indianised English" and Eurasians, "if neglected, a glaring reproach to the Government and to the faith, which it would, however ignorant and vicious, nominally profess," yet added to his words of most solemn warning that "if cared for betimes they would become a source of strength to British rule and of usefulness to India."

To achieve this end we require not merely material but spiritual forces. Material forces can palliate the temporal efforts of evil; spiritual forces alone can remove the evil. We require, in other words, greatly extended provision for education and for pastoral oversight. For education in some places much has been already done. The Bishop of Calcutta thinks that before long there will be sufficient schools in Calcutta itself. I know a little of what has been accomplished in Madras. But pastoral oversight, which is the very soul of education, is everywhere grievously wanting. Three-fifths of the Church of England congregations in India are at the present time without resident clergy.

Still the want is recognised on the spot, though

it is not supplied. Just fifty years ago (1841), before a single railway was constructed in India, Bishop Wilson established an Additional Clergy Fund to meet the necessities of Europeans and Eurasians. But now, when the need is a hundredfold greater, the fund is still apparently little known; for, to furnish one example, twenty-one subscribers in the diocese of Lahore, if I read the Report rightly, can hardly satisfy its legitimate claim upon the generosity of a province.

But I would rather speak of the claims of the fund upon ourselves; and if Churchmen at home, who love India, who are bound to it by ties of commerce or service, who know what it may be and do for Christ in the development of Asia, perceive the momentous issues which are involved in our treatment of the poor white population, the means for dealing with their necessities cannot be long sought in vain.

Perhaps the remedy will be found in the classes where the danger lies. Faults of character are always deepened and sometimes caused by popular disparagement. We tend to become what we are assumed to be. If we look for little we find little. If we ask for much we challenge a response of effort. And it may be that the call to loftier services will awaken dormant powers in those whom we unjustly contemn. Wider education may develop special capacities. It would perhaps be possible to train on the spot teaching brotherhoods, to check vanity by strong leadership, to give dignity to labour by wise association, to sustain weakness of resolve by the community of life and purpose.

Meanwhile much may be done by combining work among the heathen with work among the poorer English and Eurasians. It is the fundamental principle of the Society for the Propagation of the Gospel to approach the native races through our own countrymen; and I believe that we lose greatly by failing to shew openly in this way the universality of our message in its promises, its claims, its consolations. In a far country men will welcome the teaching which separation from home makes dearer. Moved themselves, the English artisans will convey, often unconsciously, the message of life. They will form the nucleus of a Christian society not too far removed from those among whom they work. They will keep the Missionary in touch with the common facts of human nature. They will give a breadth and, if I may so say, a naturalness to his labours. They will take from his ministry every semblance of condescension and reveal it effectually as an office of sympathy. From the trials and sorrows of the poor whose ways he understands, he will turn with fresh power to the poor of strange and alien thoughts.

But while Missionaries can help in the great and new work which the conditions of the time set before us in India, and be helped themselves in helping it, they cannot undertake any substantial part of it, unless, perhaps, in one or two great cities. The work requires its own English agents; and the few facts which I have barely indicated are sufficient to prove the urgency of its requirements. Yet hitherto we have done practically nothing. After ten years the yearly income of the Society for which I ask your alms this afternoon, and the Society stands alone, is little more than £400, a sum which is far less, if I am not mistaken, than that which is gathered in several churches on a single Sunday for the hospitals of London.

I do not wish that the alms offered to our hospitals should be diminished by one penny, but surely the fact condemns the poverty of our imagination. It is a noble thing to alleviate physical suffering; but to care for the moral and spiritual well-being of our own people in India, desolate as they often are, and deprived of the invigorating influences of a Christian atmosphere, is to advance the counsel of GOD, which by the gift of India He has committed to our accomplishment.

Our own Poor in India.

Let us then bear witness here and in India: witness to Divine help and to human wants. Let those who have had direct experience speak what they know. Let them tell of the miserable lot of a large mass of the Eurasian population, shunned alike by both races, on whom they charge their shame, poor in means and more pitiably poor in character, and no effort will seem too great to undo the wrong which we have done. Let them tell of hundreds of bands of Englishmen engaged in our national service, on railways and in factories, who, placed under depressing influences, undefended by the subtle power of high popular morality, are left without the supports of public worship, the chastening and inspiring forces of common prayer and praise, of confession and thanksgiving. Let them tell of the solitary, thriftless workman or soldier, left an outcast in a strange land, and becoming in his utter degradation a mark of the failure of our faith and charity. Let them tell of all these things, of which the faint and distant rumours stir those who love England and our English Church to the depths; and I cannot believe that men or money will be lacking for the fulfilment of a task which lies at the very foundation of our imperial service.

I know something of the difficulties of the task, and I do not wish to dissemble or to disparage them; but the Church of Christ lives by the achievement of that which is impossible with men. We also are witnesses. But there is a Witness which goes before our witness and makes it possible. "*The Spirit of Truth,*" the Lord has said, "*He shall bear witness of Me.*" And then— then with unwavering courage, then unweariedly, then effectually, then only—"*ye also,*" He adds to His disciples, "*bear witness, because ye are with Me from the beginning.*"

The witness of the Spirit is given in the silent pleading of thousands of our fellow-citizens which even now makes itself felt. We cannot but be conscious of our power, of our obligation, of our neglect. And the sense of dissatisfaction is, in the light of the Divine Word, full of hope. It is the first step to self-surrender. And when we cease to measure our endeavours by the standard of our own ability, room is opened for the action of GOD through us.

The spectacle of evils too great for earthly remedies, of burdens too heavy for human strength, forces us to look beyond ourselves. And if our heart fail us, if our heart condemn us, GOD is greater than our heart, and knows better than we can know the depths of our weakness when He sends us to a work with a call which is itself an all-sufficient promise. It is His work, not ours;

His strength, not ours; His command, not our choice.

Oh, my friends, it is the thought of self which puts aside or mars our noblest enterprises. It is the counting of our own resources which brings forgetfulness of the treasury of heaven. It is the straining of our natural vision which keeps the eyes of the soul closed. Our sight is blinded to the realities of the world. We are engrossed by the surface of things. The parable of judgment finds among us a daily application, and we also ask when for a moment the issues of life are disclosed—"*Lord, when saw we Thee an hungered, or athirst, or a stranger, or naked, or sick, or in prison?*" GOD grant that at last we may ask the question in wondering gratitude and not in unavailing consternation.

We know at least that our Saviour is waiting in His least ones for our service of love; and whether we see the fruit of our efforts or not, whether we are allowed to trace dim lineaments of the Divine Image through thick disguises of sin in those to whom we minister or not, whether we are cheered by manifest tokens of GOD's presence with us or not, there can be no endeavour which is made in simplicity for Christ's sake that is lost, no creature who shares the nature which the Son of Man has taken to Himself for whom we may not hope all things, no depth of uttermost darkness in which the believer can find himself alone. The word with which the Lord proclaimed the result of His life of redemptive love, full in the prospect of what appeared to be final defeat, was not "I shall overcome," but "*I have overcome the world.*" In the strength of that assurance it is our part to gather the fruits of His victory.

To-day one way is opened to us along which we may advance towards our goal. The day itself, as I have said, inspires us with great desires. It is the festival of expectation; we too wait for Pentecost.

GOD grant us His Holy Spirit, that we may know our duty and do it. The cause for which I plead concerns our Empire and our Church. It is, I believe, vital to the efficiency of our Missions. It offers to us, even more directly than the social questions of our own land, a test of the reality of our faith.

So may we bear our witness in deed and word, and learn in our own souls, through fresh and glad experiences, the power of the Gospel to answer every cry of man.

SOCIALISM.

CHURCH CONGRESS, HULL.

Oct. 1, 1890.

It is not my intention to discuss in this paper any of the representative types of Socialism—the paternal Socialism of Owen, or the State Socialism of Bismarck, the international Socialism of Marx, or the Christian Socialism of Maurice, or the evolutionary Socialism of the *Fabian Essays*. I wish rather to consider the essential idea which gave, or still gives, vitality and force to these different systems, to indicate the circumstances which invest the idea with paramount importance at the present time, and especially to commend it to the careful study of the younger clergy.

The term Socialism has been discredited by its connection with many extravagant and revolutionary schemes, but it is a term which needs to be claimed for nobler uses. It has no necessary affinity with any forms of violence, or confiscation, or class selfishness, or financial arrangement. I shall therefore venture to employ it apart from its historical associations as describing a theory of life, and not only a theory of economics. In this sense Socialism is the opposite of Individualism, and it is by contrast with Individualism that the true character of Socialism can best be discerned. Individualism and Socialism correspond with opposite views of humanity. Individualism regards humanity as made up of disconnected or warring atoms; Socialism regards it as an organic whole, a vital unity formed by the combination of contributory members mutually interdependent.

It follows that Socialism differs from Individualism both in method and in aim. The method of Socialism is co-operation, the method of Individualism is competition. The one regards man as working with man for a common end, the other regards man as working against man for private gain. The aim of Socialism is the fulfilment of service, the aim of Individualism is the attainment of some personal advantage, riches, or place, or fame. Socialism seeks such an organisation of life as shall secure for every one the most complete development of his powers; Individualism seeks primarily the satisfaction of the particular wants of each one in the hope that the pursuit of private interest will in the end secure public welfare.

If men were perfect, with desires and powers harmoniously balanced, both lines of action would lead to the same end. As it is, however, experience shews that limitations must be placed upon the self-assertion of the single man. The growing sense of dependence as life becomes more and more complex necessarily increases the feeling of personal obligation which constrains us each to look to the circumstances of others. At the same time in the intercourse of a fuller life we learn that our character is impoverished in proportion as we are isolated, and we learn also that evil or wrong in one part of society makes itself felt throughout the whole.

But if we admit the central idea of Socialism, that the goal of human endeavour is the common well-being of all alike, sought through conditions which provide for the fullest culture of each man, as opposed to the special development of a race, or a class, by the sacrifice of others in slavery or serfdom or necessary subjection, it does not follow that the end can be reached only in one way. The powers of men are different, and equal development does not involve equality. Experience will direct and confirm reform, for life is manifold. But the single man will not be sacrificed to the society. He will be enabled to bring it to the offering of his disciplined powers and so to realise his freedom. A common end will hallow individuality for more effective service.

Socialism, as I have defined it, is not, I repeat, committed to any one line of action, but every one who accepts its central thought will recognise certain objects for immediate effort. He will seek to secure that labour shall be acknowledged in its proper dignity as the test of manhood, and that its reward shall be measured, not by the necessities of the indigent, but by its actual value as contributing to the wealth of the community. He will strive to place masses of men who have no reserve of means in a position of stability and to quicken them by generous ideas. He will be bold to proclaim that the evils of luxury and penury cannot be met by palliatives. He will claim that all should confess in action that every power, every endowment, every possession, is not of private use, but a trust to be administered in the name of the Father for their fellow-men.

Such a view of the social destiny of the individual, with all he has, is brought home to us at the present time by the conception which we have gained of the evolution, or rather of the providential ordering of life. There have been, from very early times, dreams of ideal states fashioned by great thinkers who felt how far the world in which they lived fell short of the society for which man was made. They looked within for the laws of their imaginary commonwealths. We have at length a surer guide for our hopes in the records of the past. Studying the course which history has taken, we can forecast the future, for the broad outline of human discipline is clear. In the Old World the ruling thought was the dignity of a race or of a class, to which all beside, in a greater or less degree, were made to minister. In the New World, ushered in by the Advent, the ruling thought has been the dignity of man as man, of men as men, and however imperfectly the great truth revealed in the Incarnation has been grasped and embodied, still it has in some sense been brought home to the West little by little through many lessons.

At first in the middle ages the society was dominant, ordered in a hierarchy of classes: then at the Reformation the individual claimed independence, and the voice of authority was followed by the voice of reason. Now, when the complexity of life baffles purely rational analysis, theoretical freedom has been found to degenerate into anarchy; and we catch sight of a fuller harmony in which the offices of the society and of the citizen, of tradition and conscience, shall be reconciled. Functions which were once combined have been sharply separated as a step towards a more complete union. For here also the law of a higher life has been fulfilled, and the parts of the body have been differentiated, so that their dependence one upon another may be seen in its beneficent operation. In order to deal rightly with these new conditions we must fix our attention on facts and not on words. The permanence of technical terms often tends to mislead. The modern conceptions of capital and trade, for example, or rather isolated facts which foreshadowed them, usury and buying to sell again, were repugnant to mediæval religious feeling; but now that the range of production and distribution has been indefinitely extended we have to face problems which mediæval experience could not anticipate and cannot help us to solve. Even in the last century capitalist, producer, and consumer were not unfrequently united. If each of these three classes has now been sharply distinguished and hitherto kept apart by conflicting material interests, it is, if we may trust the teachings of the past, that they may in due time be brought together again in a full, free, and chosen fellowship. The relations which exist between them at present are modern and transitional. Wage-labour, though it appears to be an inevitable step in the evolution of society, is as little fitted to represent finally or adequately the connection of man with man in the production of wealth as at earlier times slavery or serfdom.

Our position then is one of expectancy and preparation, but we can see the direction of the social movement. We wait for the next stage in the growth of the State when in full and generous co-operation each citizen shall offer to the body the fulness of his own life that he may rejoice in the fulness of the life of the body.

Such an issue may appear to be visionary. It is, I believe, far nearer than we suppose. It is at least the natural outcome of what has gone before. Society has been organised effectively without regard to the individual. The individual has been developed in his independence. It remains to shew how the richest variety of individual differences can be made to fulfil the noblest ideal of the State, when fellow-labourers seek in the whole the revelation of the true meaning of their separate offerings. And nothing has impressed me more during my years of work than the rapidity and power with which the thoughts of dependence and solidarity and brotherhood, of our debt to the past and our responsibility for the future, have spread among our countrymen.

Men have grown familiar with the principle

of combination for limited objects. Such unions are a discipline for a larger fellowship. There is, indeed, enough to sadden us in the selfishness which too often degrades rich and poor alike, but self-respect has grown widely among those who are poor in material wealth. The consciousness of a high calling has quickened to self-denial and a noble activity many who are oppressed with the burden of great possessions. There is on all sides an increasingly glad recognition of duties answering to opportunities; and if education has created or deepened the desire for reasonable leisure, it has opened springs of enjoyment which riches cannot make more healthy or more satisfying.

At the same time our public wealth is quickly accumulating. Buildings, galleries, gardens, bring home to every Englishman that he has an inheritance in the grandeur of his country; and the English family still guards in honour the fundamental types of human communion and fatherhood and brotherhood, which are a sufficient foundation for a kingdom of GOD. All things, indeed, once more are ready, and a clear call is given to us to prove our faith.

Here, then, lies the duty of the Christian teacher. The thoughts of a true Socialism—the thoughts that men are "one man" in Christ, sons of GOD and brethren, suffering and rejoicing together, that each touches all and all touch each with an inevitable influence, that as we live by others we can find no rest till we live for others, are fundamental thoughts of the Law and the Prophets, of the Gospels and the Epistles which he is empowered and bound to make effective under the conditions of modern life.

The result is that reflection and experience have at length made them intelligible. To interpret and embody them in a practical form is the office of believers now. They must shew that Christianity, which has dealt hitherto with the individual, deals also with the State, with classes, with social conditions, and not only with personal character. In the endeavour to fulfil this duty the past will help them by analogy, but not by example. New questions cannot be settled by tradition. There is an order in the accomplishment of the Divine counsel. Even great evils are not met and conquered at once.

Discerning our own work, we shall not condemn or blame our fathers that they did not anticipate it. They did more or less perfectly the work that was prepared for them to do. We are required not to repeat their service, but, enriched and strengthened by what they have won, to bring the doctrine of the Incarnation to bear upon the dealings of man with man and of nation with nation. As we strive to do this we shall come to understand the force of the loftiest truths of theology. We shall find that that which is transcendental is, indeed, practical as a motive, and an inspiration. We alone, I do not scruple to affirm it, we alone, who believe that "The Word became flesh" can keep hope fresh in the face of the sorrows of the world, for we alone know that evil is intrusive and remediable; we alone know that the victory over the world has been won, and that we have to gather with patience the fruits of the victory. Violence can destroy, but it cannot construct. Love destroys the evil when it replaces the evil by the good.

But while we affirm the absolute supremacy of the spiritual and the universal sovereignty of Christ reigning from the Cross, we remember that our work must be done under the conditions of earth, and that it is here on the sordid field of selfish conflicts that we must prepare the kingdom of GOD. At the same time we recognise that the social problem of to-day, the relations of capital and labour, belongs especially to Englishmen, who by their national character have ruled the development of modern industry. As Englishmen have set the problem, so on Englishmen lies the responsibility of solving it. And the position of the English clergy gives them peculiar oppor-

Socialism. 235

tunities for moderating with wise faith discussions which will open the way for the solution. The clergy of the National Church are not a close and isolated caste: they are drawn from every class: they are trained in sympathy with every variety of thought and culture: they are in habitual contact with all forms of experience: they are lifted above the influence of party by the greatness of their work: they are enabled to labour for a distant end by the greatness of the Faith which they proclaim.

I ask then—I ask myself not without sorrowful perplexity—whether we have, in view of the teaching of present facts, considered what GOD'S counsel for men in creation and redemption is? Whether the state of things in our towns and in our villages either answers or tends to answer to the Divine idea? Whether the present distribution of wealth is not perilous alike to those who have and to those who want? Whether we have not accepted the laws of the material order as the laws of all nature? Whether we have pondered over the moral significance of the poor, and whether we have reflected on the wider application of that principle which it is the glory of medicine to have guarded, that every discovery affecting man's well-being is the property of the race, and not of the finder?

I do not enter now on any questions of detail. I desire simply to direct attention to questions which go to the very heart of the Gospel; and I beg the younger clergy, with whatever strength of persuasion I can command, to think over these things; to discuss them with one another reverently and patiently; to seek to understand and not to silence their adversaries; to win for themselves the truth which gives to error what permanence it has; to remember that bold and sweeping statements come more commonly from doubt or ignorance than from just conviction. But I beg them not to improvise hasty judgments. The personal value of an opinion depends for the most part upon the pains which have been spent in forming it. Zeal, enthusiasm, devotion are not enough to guide us in the perplexity of conduct; we need above all things knowledge as the basis of action. We have not yet mastered the elements of the problems of society. Theories have been formed from the examination of groups of isolated phenomena; but life is complex. We must, indeed, see our end before we begin our work; but it may be that different ways will be found to lead to it, and as far as I can judge the social questions of our day will finally receive not one answer, but many. But in one respect all the answers will agree; all will be religious.

Meanwhile, our office as Christian teachers is to proclaim the ideal of the Gospel and to form opinion. And if we do this, if we confess that our mission is to hasten a kingdom of GOD on earth, and if we ourselves move resolutely forward as the Spirit guides us, I believe that we shall find through the common offices of our daily intercourse that peace which springs out of the consciousness of common sacrifice made for one end, and that assurance of strength which comes through new victories of faith.

We cannot doubt that GOD is calling us in this age, through the characteristic teachings of science and of history, to seek a new social application of the Gospel. We cannot doubt, therefore, that it is through our obedience to the call that we shall realise its Divine power. The proof of Christianity which is prepared by GOD, as I believe, for our times, is a Christian society filled with one spirit in two forms—righteousness and love.

EDUCATIONAL VALUE OF
CO-OPERATION.

CO-OPERATIVE EXHIBITION, TYNEMOUTH.

September 3, 1890.

WE have all, I believe, found in our personal experience that a time of success and prosperity is, in an especial sense, a time of trial. Success, though it must of necessity be incomplete, tends to satisfy us. It leads us to substitute a part for the whole, to acquiesce in the less which we have gained, and to forget the greater at which we aimed—perhaps to rest contented with material profit, and to lose the spiritual aspirations which have been, indeed, the very soul of our efforts. It is with societies, also, as it is with men. And in studying the records of co-operation, I cannot but feel that the movement is, in fact, endangered by the great, continuous, growing success of its distributive organization. No one, indeed, can fail to rejoice at the economic and moral results which have been obtained by the stores, retail and wholesale. They have largely confirmed and extended uprightness and trust in small dealings; they have stimulated and they have sustained thrift; they have secured economy in exchange; they have accumulated a large capital, which is available for fresh enterprises; they have influenced trade beneficially beyond their immediate range. They have also gained an opportunity for their directors to shew, on an impressive scale, what the administration of a retail business ought to be for the highest interest of all who are engaged in it, in regard to hours, and participation in surplus profits, and in pensions. The opportunity will, I trust, be wisely and openly used. But, however highly we rate these results, gained already or still to be gained, we must confess that in themselves they do not touch the real problem which lies before co-operators—the problem of our age, the problem of capital and labour. And, therefore, gentlemen, if you pause here and go no further, though you may multiply your gains of this kind a hundredfold, though you may reach the utmost possible limit of cheapness and of purity for the benefit of the consumers, you will have to acknowledge that a great hope has been defeated and a great work has been abandoned. You will have confined yourselves to commerce and exchange, and have left untouched the weightier and more difficult matters of industry and production. You will have ministered abundantly to individual interests, but you will not have effectually quickened the spirit of social service. All that you have done will be capable of being adequately explained from motives of enlightened or even superficial self-interest, and may at last actually increase the spirit of competition, which is most directly opposed to the spirit of co-operation.

I venture, then,—and you will pardon the boldness of an outsider who necessarily regards your mission in its widest range—to ask you to turn once again to the programme of the Rochdale Pioneers, the heroic founders of living co-operation, who clearly foresaw what was involved in the full realisation of the principle which they had grasped. The reform of distribution was for them the first step; and it was, in fact, the only possible step towards the reform of production, the extension of education, the development of the whole man for the service of all men. They recognised, with far-seeing faith, that co-operation— the active association of man with man for truly human ends—embodies an idea of universal application to life, that it is the foundation of a social and not merely of a commercial structure—the watchword of a new order. And the great leaders of co-operation have always guarded this noble tradition. They have had the courage to do the little work which lay before them, and still have kept their eyes steadily fixed upon the distant goal. They have indeed mastered that lesson which is difficult to our half-generous impatience—that that which is permanent must grow slowly; and I trust that they have also abundantly experienced that which is the most enduring joy of man—the realisation in the future, through the energy of faith, of the fruits of their own travail.

At the same time these, your great leaders, have known how to use opportunities. They think—and, as far I can judge, most rightly—that the decisive time has come now, and that you are required to face with resolute energy the problem, not of co-operative distribution only, but of co-operative production. And I am glad that at the beginning of my work in the north I am allowed to take part in this great meeting, which you are resolved "to make memorable in the annals of northern co-operation," and memorable in this particular aspect.

I am well aware of the difficulties which beset the problem of co-operative production. I know something of the failures which have disappointed former leaders. I can measure the immediate sacrifices which will be required of those through whose willing concurrence the effort for which we look must be made. But I have also heard from the lips of one of your most generous representa-

Educational Value of Co-operation. 245

tives, who has made great personal sacrifices for the cause, how the whole character of his work has been transfigured by the new spirit with which co-operation has quickened it; and I have been allowed to read, at least in part, the history of human progress, and I have seen written over all that stirs us with gratitude and enthusiasm in the chequered annals of the past this legend: " Learning through suffering; fruitfulness through sacrifice; life through death." While, then, I do not presume to indicate how the central question of co-operative production will be solved, or whether there will be varied solutions under different circumstances, I do say, without a moment's doubt, that if you accept the duty of solving the problem, the problem will be solved. I do say that you are in a position to claim the prerogative of approaching it with commanding forces, and I will add also, more to encourage than to warn, that the victory will not be won without delays and losses, and that in bearing these you will pay a debt which you owe to your fathers, and leave an endowment for your children.

But that co-operators may be disciplined and inspired to fulfil this office it appears to me that they need an education more thorough, more systematic, more liberal, than they have yet received. Calm, sustained, harmonious action is not directed by sentiment or by instinct, but by resolute choice; and wise choice comes from education. "Education," as Professor Stuart said—and he has been my teacher in this work for twenty years—"is desirable for all mankind, but it is the life's necessity for co-operators." By education I do not mean (and Professor Stuart did not mean) that which enables us to read a journal or to write a business letter or to keep a ledger. I mean that which enables the student to realise the eternal meaning of the world; to follow the laws of personal and social and national development; to distinguish the present lines of salutary action; to gain the power of vision for those revelations of science and art which tend to establish a true proportion between the pleasures of life; to master great ideas in order that we may find an embodiment for them, stable at once and expansive; to see the whole in the part, and so to measure the dignity of all labour; to see the part in the whole, and so to deepen the chastening sense of our own littleness.

It is hard to express in a few words the thoughts which I desire to convey. But let me endeavour to make my meaning a little plainer. Co-operation, as I understand it, and as its founders understood it, deals with the final principles of life. It lays down that the co-operator's

Educational Value of Co-operation.

rule of conduct is not "each for each," but "each for all, and all for each." It lays down that his aim is not in itself personal pleasure or profit, but effective service; that his reward is not wealth, but character. It is a true embodiment of the principle of Socialism, as I understand the word,— a Socialism in which the free initiation of the individual is quickened and guided by the desire to serve the whole body. The educational demands of co-operation will, therefore, necessarily concern the spirit of work and the social relationships of men. There will be an education for co-operation, and there will be an education through co-operation.

There will be, I say, an education for co-operation. True co-operators, to begin with, must be men of faith. They must, I mean, be assured that there is a progress in things, and that they are called to further it; that there is—in the language of the Christian Creed—a divine order and a divine government of the world, and that men are called to be fellow-workers with GOD. To this end they must become familiar with the main facts, the main laws, as we speak, of industrial life and of personal life. And there is, I think, nothing more inspiring than to feel, when we look back over a great space of time, that there are visible even to our eyes sure traces of a purpose fulfilled in spite of—yes, I will venture to say through—social revolutions and individual crimes; though we cannot fail to recognise in the history of nations that successful violence leaves a terrible legacy of retribution. No doubt we find it hard to bear the discipline of delay. But if in moments of depression we are constrained to falter in our proclamation of progress, yet there arises in the heart, at the very moment of denial, the still voice which whispers that "the moral world does move;" that good once gained can never be lost, though it may be transformed; that all things, in the long run, favour orderly advance.

Under such teaching as this, hope can never be extinguished, and patience can never be exhausted. Institutions and ideas, we perceive, have their day, and they cannot long survive the period of their beneficent action. The sun rises in a most true sense every morning upon a fresh world prepared for fresh labours. Each day, each generation, has its peculiar work. We could not, if we would, transplant ourselves into the past. We misinterpret old relations if we endeavour to restore them. Our task is to find out what corresponds to them.

And it is in this sense, you will notice, that co-operation assumes its immediate importance at the present time. Association for good and for

Educational Value of Co-operation.

evil is the characteristic of our age; it needs to be inspired by a moral force, and that need, as we trust, will be supplied. Co-operation, in other words, answers to the position which we have reached in social evolution.

During the last three centuries—in England, at least—there has been the most complete enfranchisement of the individual. And it is now pressed upon us that he cannot stand alone. The man has won his independence and his self-reliance that he may serve the State the better. We have learnt that freedom can only be realised in self-devotion; that the duties of brotherhood are the measure of our common obligations.

Now, he who has been trained by a living study of history to grasp these principles, will be ready to become a true co-operator, and then his education through the work itself will begin. And to take part in a great organisation—in your Wholesale, for example—is an education. To labour for a public cause, to be inspired by wide interests, is ennobling. The duty brings a sense of responsibility in the use of power. It trains in the exercise of authority, and at the same time it reveals the dignity of small things. It shews to us that the wealth of a life does not depend on the abundance of private means. It brings into details the powers of a larger being; it disciplines man in the fulfilment of citizenship through his natural occupation.

And I lay great stress on this fact: the endeavour to embody and extend the spirit of co-operation does not take men from their ordinary work, but gives their ordinary work a new meaning and a new power. And our ordinary work, let us remember, is the staple of our lives. It does not, as we too commonly suppose, furnish the means of living: it is living. And there is no delight comparable to the delight which comes from a sense of doing one's best in one's common duty. No necessary work can be incapable of being made truly human. No doubt there is a great need, in many cases, of improvement in the conditions of labour. But the labour itself offers scope for the exercise of all that is best in man; and when once the common labour is recognised as the mould for character—the character which affects us all together—we shall provide that the conditions shall be worthy of the issues which they influence.

Such lessons as these, I repeat, lie in the path of the co-operator as he goes on his common work. And I emphasise them because I believe they provide for the solution of the problem of co-operative production; for the difficulties by which this problem is beset are moral, and not economical. They

Educational Value of Co-operation. 251

are, as one of your great veteran leaders has pointed out, from within rather than from without; they are due to jealousy, to suspicion, to self-assertion, to want of generous confidence and courageous enthusiasm. But real familiarity with the history of human progress, true insight into the grandeur of present opportunities, the education, that is, for co-operation and the education through co-operation, will bring to the cause the offerings of service and experience, the glad readiness to work for a great, though it may be a distant end, and the clear perception of the next step which is to be taken. And when the leaders are resolved, I cannot for one moment think that the hosts will waver or hang back.

This double education, this education through the past and through the present, this education which interprets our place in the whole course of human life and our immediate office, co-operators are bound to seek, and to prepare, and to pursue, that they may make their partial success a step to higher endeavours, and keep their ideal before them as the call to increasing effort. Something, no doubt, has been done by co-operative societies for education, but those whose judgment cannot be gainsaid deplore the inadequacy of the provision which has yet been made for these higher works. This is the peril which comes from material success, and unless it is met resolutely—let me say it—co-operators will continue to have cheap goods —perhaps they will even have cheaper goods— but they must give up their name. Their end, if they stop short at this point, is seen to be their personal profit secured through others, and not the common profit of all with whom they are united as producers, distributors, consumers. The spirit of self-interest cannot cast out itself. Co-operation will tend to become more and more organised self-seeking. And, as I said before, those who have hoped most will have to mourn over another lost cause, and increased cheapness in distribution may mean only increased suffering in production.

I cannot, however, contemplate final failure. The principle of co-operation—"each for all, and all for each"—is easily grasped. And it is enforced and applied in papers which are accessible to all of you; and a little reflection will shew you all that it demands now a fresh application. And if it be that, for the present, comparatively little will be done by co-operators for co-operative production, yet experience will be gained, confidence will be inspired, and employers and employed will come to understand one another a little better, for they will be members of the same body. Ideals will be brought into common business; the example will spread; and, mark this, new springs of

Educational Value of Co-operation. 253

capital will be available, for there is a strange, silent force of moral pressure towards an enterprise which is seen to be beneficent. There is, I know, an untold eagerness on the part of many to use for common purposes the wealth which they hold, if only it can be shewn that the good which is within their reach will not be outweighed by permanent harm. The union of capital and labour will be accomplished, not in one way, but in many ways; for co-operation is not so much an organisation as a principle, not so much "a state within a state" as a spirit which quickens and moulds every member for the most effective service of the whole body.

Thoughts crowd upon thoughts, and hopes rise beyond hopes, but I must leave them unuttered. I have trespassed too long on your patience with the speculations of a student, and I cannot deal with the details through which they must be made practically effective. But the subject on which I have spoken is one to which I am drawn, not only by the office to which the remnant of my time has been given, not only by the traditions of the See in which I have been called to serve, but even more by the earliest associations of my school life, and by the convictions which have grown firmer through years of busy and varied toil. I have dared to express great aspirations, because I believe more confidently as the years go on that men are moved by lofty motives. For me, co-operation rests upon my Faith. It is the active expression, in terms of our present English life, of the articles of my Creed. Viewed in the light of the facts which I hold to be the central facts in history, I recognise in it an inherent tendency to complete man, to guard the family, to unite the State, to harmonise nations. It is, as I regard it—and you will allow me to speak out my whole heart—man's spontaneous welcome given to the promises of God. It is a proof on the scene of our working world that the Gospel is not an illusion, but an ideal brought into the homes of men. It is—may I not say it? —a special call to England; for, as we have been reminded by one (Prof. Marshall) who two years ago was your president, England led the way in the industrial evolution of modern Europe by free and self-determined energy and will. It is, then, for England to overcome the secondary evils which have arisen in this period of transition by a fresh exertion of the same national characteristics.

I ask you, then, to accept joyfully the part which has been entrusted to you. In order to fulfil its highest possibilities—and I know none higher— you do not need to compass violent changes, you do not need to countenance class animosities, you do not need to call for State intervention, you do not need to lessen one whit the responsibilities of individual men; but you *do* need to be penetrated by the spirit of co-operation, you do need enthusiasm and faith—the enthusiasm which recognises that the highest blessing is realised, not in being ministered unto, but in ministering—the faith which looks far beyond the mountain tops and the clouds which often cover them to that light of heaven from which they draw their transitory glory.

Do I seem to have indulged in dreams? I cannot admit the charge for one moment. I have been taught to pray day by day that the Kingdom of GOD our Father may come on earth. And I believe that He Who enjoined the petition wills its fulfilment through that service of men which He has made possible—a service in which each man with all his powers, all his endowments, all his possessions, recognises that he is the servant of his fellow men, working with them for one end—the reign of righteousness.

THE METHOD, THE AIM, AND THE SANCTION, OF CO-OPERATION.

BLAYDON-ON-TYNE.

November 13, 1891.

THE METHOD, THE AIM, AND THE SANCTION, OF CO-OPERATION.

It would be wholly superfluous for me, in addressing the members of a Society which I have been accustomed to regard as second only to that of Rochdale in the services which it has rendered to the cause of Co-operation, to attempt to trace the different influences, secular, Chartist, socialist, religious, Christian, which contributed to mould the memorable rules of the Rochdale Pioneers, the original Co-operative Charter. Nor do I wish to develop the thoughts which are suggested by the growth and local distribution of Co-operative Stores, though these are full of instruction. Still less do I wish to dwell upon the many failures and disappointments which have accompanied various experiments in Co-operative production. I wish rather to call attention once more to the fundamental principles of the movement, and to consider in the briefest outline their application to our present circumstances.

These principles, as I apprehend them, are found in the method, the aim and the sanction of Co-operation. The method of Co-operation is Association. The aim is, in the language of the Rochdale Rules, the bettering of life domestic and social. The sanction is personal conviction and not public laws. These principles admit of various embodiments according to circumstances of time and place. That which was once impossible may afterwards become easy. Familiarity with an idea tends to find means for fulfilling it. The past is fertile in salutary warnings, but it can fix no limits to human attainment: we learn how to modify conditions most effectively when we have learnt what cannot be modified. A physical discovery, the influence of a great leader, flashes of prophetic thought, disclose unused or unsuspected lessons and powers in things about us and in ourselves. For us the method, the aim, the sanction of Co-operation may mean more than they meant fifty years ago. They may require from us fresh sacrifices and offer to us fresh successes. Let us at least ask ourselves how we regard them.

1. The method of Co-operation is, I say, Association. The co-operator does not use his fellow-man as an instrument for private gain, but as a worker with himself for a common gain. The

the sanction, of Co-operation. 261

simplest association in business rests on an elementary trust in human fellowship which is not everywhere present. I have been told that the trade signs in a street at Delhi shew that this foundation of partnership does not exist in the old capital of the Indian Empire. They bear with few or no exceptions only single names. Where trust exists the impulse to partnership is probably given at first by the hope of increased gain; but soon common counsels, common work, common interests, prove their fitness to call out larger conceptions of dependence, of inheritance, of influence. Then comes a pride in the enterprise itself, a delight in serving it. Thus little by little the thought of a greater life in which we share and to which we minister takes a distinct shape through commercial association. Self-interest yields more or less to social interest. The old maxim 'each for himself' is found not to cover the facts of effort and intercourse. Men recognise that the inexorable law of nature is 'each for all and all for each,' and that this necessity, once understood and welcomed, becomes an inspiration of generous service.

So much we have certainly mastered during the last half century, and especially during the last generation. The method of association has half taken to itself and half revealed a new motive for labour. It has been proved abundantly that workers can be found ready to administer large organisations without thought of any personal gain commensurate with their services for the common good. In this respect the great Friendly Societies and the Trades Unions have confirmed in other spheres the experience and the example of co-operators. Effective agents have been found ready to discharge new duties as occasions have arisen. No doubt the problems have been for the most part definite and simple. But the fact that each claim on forethought and enterprise has been met hitherto offers a reasonable presumption that future claims will not be unanswered.

Thus the forces of association in work are complete in theory. How far then have they been used in practice?

The first enterprise of democratic co-operation, if I may use the phrase, was the Store.

The Store was established for the good of all who were connected with it. It was designed to improve as far as might be 'the domestic and social condition' of consumers and producers alike, and by producers I understand all who in different ways combine to prepare and offer an article for use. The range of the action of the Store was limited both in scope and in direct influence; but it brought invaluable opportunities for education in the highest sense; and as far as the consumers are concerned, it has fulfilled its work perfectly. It has practically extinguished for them 'profit upon price,' by returning what would be 'profit' in a private business in the form of a dividend upon purchases. But this action is necessarily accompanied by serious dangers. The customers are for the most part housewives who naturally judge of the excellence of the store in a great degree by the amount put to their credit. The management seek to satisfy this test in obedience to an intelligible business instinct; and forget that other interests are entrusted to their care. As co-operators they are bound to consider the producers no less than the consumers, and to provide that the producers may be trained and furnished for the fulfilment of their social duties. On this point the leaders of the movement have never wavered; but there is still great need of a more energetic representation of the claims of labour on local Boards.

The first object of the Store, the highest pride of its managers, should be to secure that the conditions under which all who are employed in it, all who contribute to it, should be such as to provide for their highest efficiency, which is in the main their highest well-being, in hours, in wages, in environment, in provision for old age.

Something has been done towards the provision of means of education, of leisure, of recreation, of pension funds, but far more still remains to be done if the Store is to be, as it ought to be, the model of a place of retail trade, in which every shop assistant may find the conditions of his daily occupation not only consistent with but conducive to the healthy exercise of his highest powers. For our life must be in our work and not outside it, and retail business must be the life-work of very many among us.

And more than this, it is the duty of the managers of a Store to ascertain, as far as they are able, not only that the articles which they supply are good, but how they have been produced. The Scotch Wholesale did well when they undertook shirt-making at an initial loss in order to escape complicity with sweating firms. The purchaser at a Store ought to feel assured that cheapness has not been gained by oppression; that every one who has helped to satisfy his wants has been fairly dealt with; that he on his part has done to his fellow-labourer as he would be done by.

In order to satisfy this condition to some extent, Democratic Co-operation has made a further step. The Stores have established the Wholesales; and co-operators taking upon themselves wider responsibilities have developed fresh powers. They have also engaged in a very narrow field in direct production.

And here, though I do not wish to trespass on debated ground, it appears to me that the Wholesales, with their dependent Factories, which are supported by the Stores and not allowed to sell in the open market, are essentially part of the Stores, and that those employed in them must receive advantages of the same kind as other servants of the Stores. At the same time the problems of the social conditions of the workers are here presented on a larger scale and offer opportunities for great experiments.

But Co-operative production, established and supported by the Stores, cannot be permanently confined within its present narrow limits. It must in due time extend to the open market; and in these larger ventures there will be scope for different forms of Co-operation. Thus there appears to me to be ample room for the beneficent activity of 'Individualists' and 'Federalists.' They deal with different conditions and different problems. Each body has its own work; and both works must be faced, if Co-operation is to cover the whole field of industry. The Store and the Wholesale deal with the limited wants of a particular class. By the interchange of their experience waste can be checked. Quality can be guaranteed. Competition can be kept in abeyance. But questions of wider production both for home and for foreign use remain. These must be met by some distinct form of association. I do not presume to decide what the form or forms will be; but it still appears to me that profit-sharing, in one shape or other, is the natural bridge to that which I most desire, the collective ownership of large works by the workmen. I do not indeed disguise from myself the formidable difficulties by which such kinds of Co-operation are beset, or the discouraging results of past experiments. But we learn through failure. And some at least of those who are most competent to judge trust without misgiving the power of artisans to choose the best leaders and to obey them, and calculate that a patient and resolute purpose, which it is not unreasonable to look for, would enable (for example) the workmen in a shipyard to make the shipyard their own in 15 or 20 years. To think otherwise would be, I must hold, to disregard some of the clearest lessons of the last generation.

It is possible that there are some forms of manufacture to which perfect Co-operation will remain finally inapplicable. But even where a business requires a long unremunerative use of capital, or where success depends on the alert watchfulness and fertile energy of a single chief, resources may hereafter be provided to bear the drain and leaders capable of finding their reward in the devoted service which they command.

In other occupations (*e.g.* sea-fishing and perhaps mining) cooperation is the natural arrangement which lends itself to wider combinations. But in every calculation of the probable result of the association of workers, we must remember that the chief end is not larger private gain but the enjoyment and the extension of a nobler life, by partners in a common enterprise. To dwell simply on the prospect of increased material advantage as establishing the claim of Co-operation on general support is to betray its first principle.

One further remark must be made under this head. The Store, which occupies the place of many tradesmen, must accept the duties of the tradesmen whom it has displaced. Tradesmen and especially large tradesmen have in the past given generous support to public works: the Store must assuredly not fall behind their liberality. This obvious obligation does not seem as yet to have received the attention which it deserves, though it is closely related to the aim of Co-operation.

2. For the aim of Co-operation is, as we have seen, the bettering of life domestic and social, and not the accumulation of material wealth. The

Co-operator seeks for himself and for others, wider interests, purer and more permanent enjoyments, a fuller development and a healthy exercise of his powers. His participation in a great business is itself an education and an endowment. Penetrated by a desire for the common good he seeks equally to learn and to teach : he has no business secret, but is anxious to spread as widely as possible his successful methods. Such disciplining and deepening of character is incalculably more valuable than intellectual instruction, however needful this may be; and the spirit tends to spread itself. The whole history of Co-operation is a testimony to the fact. The progress of the cause has been secured not so much by one or two conspicuous leaders as by nameless fellow-helpers who have caught their enthusiasm. Under such influences the worth of a simple life makes itself felt. There is in it enough contact with affairs to give it dignity, and little temptation to seek personal aggrandisement. I shall never forget a conversation which I had with a peasant of Unterwalden as we climbed a hill overlooking the Lake of Lucerne. He expressed his wonder at the restlessness of Englishmen: they seemed to him to fly from peace in the pursuit of new excitement. 'We,' he continued, 'find in our own Canton all we need. We have no wish to go beyond its boundaries. Our civil duties quicken our patriotism. A village office satisfies our ambition, for it brings the praise of those who know us best. Would travelling add anything to the human fulness of our life?' When we reached the hamlet to which he was going, he turned aside into an open Chapel and knelt for a few minutes, and I was thankful to have heard his confession. For is it not true that we for the most part waste the strength of life in seeking for that which if gained we shall be unable to use, and miss the wealth of opportunity rich in common joys which lies about our feet?

Now the Association which engages us in a great business is capable of satisfying our generous desires. It is able to train and occupy not thought alone but feeling and will. As we come to understand our connexion with our neighbours we learn better to recognise what we owe to our fathers. Wisdom, we perceive, was not born with us nor was it born at all full-formed. Placing ourselves in connexion with the past we see that we shall not do our work either by disparaging our heritage, or by resting upon it. We must put it to use. And if an old country has some disadvantages it has ample compensations. We Englishmen can never for a moment suppose that we have created or could have created the treasures which we enjoy. The sense of our debt to those who have gone before us reveals to us that we hold what we have for others. Our Cathedrals, our Churches, our Colleges, are not monuments only but beacons. They light us along the path of fellowship. We enter upon the path, it may be, through very simple duties, but as we see more and more what man is to man we discern with ever-growing clearness what that vast life is in which we are partakers and to which it is our privilege to add the sum of our earthly service.

Such thoughts, if I may for a moment touch on that which is personal, often occupy me at Auckland. The burden of such a place would be well nigh intolerable if I did not feel that in bearing it, as best I may, I am working with those who have gone before me, yes, and with those who will come after me, guarding a trust for our whole people. Everyone who has visited the Chapel, the Chapel of the See, and not the private Chapel of the occupant—and would that every one in the Diocese would visit it—will know what I mean.

So it is that this thought of Co-operation, realised first perhaps as an active principle in little transactions of trade, is found to have the power of rising step by step through the whole range of life, of embracing the widest interests of men, of ennobling the simplest offices of duty, of binding together generation with generation and class with class, and in due time, as we trust, nation with nation, in the acknowledgment of one goal of all true service, where each man finds his own end in the consummation of the race according to the purpose of Creation. Such a thought, born of Co-operation, is able to bring light to the home and glory to each office rendered to a neighbour, bettering in unexpected ways our domestic and social condition. Such a thought, embodied in action, is even able, I believe, to drive out the evil spirits of gambling and drink, which too often seize the empty heart, by the force of new devotion.

3. These loftiest issues of the spirit of Co-operation can only be reached by willing surrender to its influence. No constraint can secure them; and the Co-operator from first to last relies on the force of personal conviction for the effectual sanction of his work. He trusts himself wholly to the fragment of the Divine will which he recognises. The just law may serve to instruct the ignorant and to constrain the unwilling; but if it be as yet against the mass of opinion it is in itself ineffective and even demoralising. It can secure at the most nothing more than outward

conformity. It can check evils. But it cannot create enthusiasm and love. There is a proper sphere for law in social reform. But good laws serve rather to register the right opinion which has prevailed than to produce it. They deal with acts and circumstances and not with character. Now the strength of co-operation lies in strength of character; not in the equality of privilege, which the law can confer, nor in the equality of wisdom or sagacity or force which is unattainable, but in equality of devotion which comes from a true sense of human nature and human destiny.

In this respect we may take heart from the growth of the sense of responsibility within our own memories, on the part of those to whom most has been entrusted: from the general eagerness of all classes to gain a better understanding of the feelings and desires of one another: from the popular acceptance of the conception of brotherhood as a true expression of the relation of man to man: from the very sense of disquiet and discontent which refuses to be satisfied with a standard of life below that which corresponds with the work of man.

There may be in all this much that is sentimental and unreal; but there is much also of sincere belief and generous action. The humblest form of true Co-operation opens to the patient

the sanction, of Co-operation.

worker the vision of an ideal towards which we can all strive and in which we can all find that personal satisfaction which becomes greater when it is shared with more. The smallest act of business may be done in a great spirit. There is opportunity in buying and selling for the discipline of character. Co-operation in the narrowest sense is the first step towards fellowship in labour, fellowship in service. But Co-operators must as a body give more thought to the Stores than they have yet given, as embodying principles, and not simply as serving their interests. It is hard, I know, to remember an ideal when we are busied with little things. But after all little things form the staple of most lives, and it is in these that we must shew of what mind we are.

If then I seem to have wandered far beyond the practical question of Co-operation, I cannot admit that I have really done so. The Store is an embodiment of a vital force which has incalculable capacity for growth. The circumstances of our time enable us to see it as a promise even more than a success. I commend the promise to your keeping, that through your care it may be brought nearer to fulfilment.

THE MANIFOLD REVELATION
OF TRUTH.

πολυμερῶc καὶ πολυτρόπωc.
In many parts and in many fashions.

HEB. i. 1.

CATHEDRAL, NEWCASTLE-ON-TYNE.
Aug. 1, 1893.

Meeting of the British Medical Association.

In many parts and in many fashions. These words describe the Divine method of the education of the world. When we look back over large spaces of time we can see how new lessons have been taught in the past in unexpected ways and added to the treasures of the race. By victories and defeats, by solitary enterprises and national movements, men have learnt from age to age a little more of the power and meaning of life; and the teaching still continues uninterrupted and irresistible.

But there is this difference between the training of the Old World and the training of the New. In pre-Christian times there were two distinct lines of movement : there was on the one side the natural unfolding of human powers, the disclosure of human needs and failures, through the experience of the nations; and on the other side, there was the stern shaping of Israel through repression and chastisement and hope. *In many parts and in many fashions,* as it has been well said, the world was prepared for the Christ and the Christ was prepared for the world. In post-Christian times there is no such division of discipline: the one universal fact, *the Word became flesh,* is offered to all peoples, and still *in many parts and in many fashions,* little by little, the manifold experience of states and men contributes to its interpretation. From the Apostolic age theology has entered into the fulness of life and claimed for its ministry every energy of thought and feeling and will. No element of human activity can be indifferent to the Christian. He seeks a testimony from all the ages. He tries his Creed by the necessities of every class and of every nation. He interrogates with courageous patience Nature and History, and through their answers enlarges his understanding of the Incarnation by which both are invested with a divine meaning.

Meanwhile the problems of thought and life grow more and more complex. We are at the present day contemporaries, as it were, of every stage of civilization, scholars in every school of thought. It is no longer possible for any one student, like the masters of the Renaissance, to occupy the whole field of science. The least fragment is sufficient to interest and to engage a lifetime. We are overpowered by the marvels of

The Manifold Revelation of Truth. 279

detail. We are tempted to be one-sided, and are in constant danger of forgetting the proportion of things. We apply the same sacred name of Truth to conclusions which are wholly different in nature, and then, preoccupied by our own special methods, tacitly claim that tests which are appropriate to the material with which we deal should be applied to all subjects alike.

It becomes therefore increasingly difficult for serious students who are engrossed by definite pursuits and duties to welcome as fellow-labourers those who seem to be outwardly their rivals; to find that different methods of inquiry can converge to one end; to recognise in those who follow not with them equal devotion to the Truth; to acknowledge with the frankness of sincere conviction that various types of intellectual, social, political, opinion can coexist in the unity of one body, and reveal to us *in many parts and in many fashions* fresh aspects of the Counsel of GOD.

Under such circumstances, in an age which is characteristically critical and analytic, we need to use every opportunity—and a great opportunity is given us to-day—for strengthening the sense of spiritual fellowship among representative leaders of thought. There can be no rest while candid and reverent students are kept apart by suspicions and reticences, and hope for the world is clouded by a pessimism which naturally arises when we take the outside of things for the reality. But already we are learning even through

> blank misgivings...
> Fallings from us, vanishings,

that GOD is teaching us *in many parts and in many fashions* and leading us back to Himself.

Life indeed is greater—greater in common joys, greater in lofty promises—than we know. We touch two worlds, the temporal and the eternal. We cannot with impunity identify the phenomenon with that which it suggests to us. After all the burning Bush is the true emblem of Nature[9]. We enter with confidence at every moment into the future and the unseen. We know all things, it is true, in a human way, under the conditions which belong to our present state, but our knowledge is not therefore less valid. It is not the limitation of our knowledge which is perilous, but our tendency to regard the limited as absolute and to treat the part as the whole.

The physician and the theologian are more familiar with these truths than other men from their contrasted and complementary experience. They are bound together by the study of the mysteries of life. They meet in the chamber of death. They know how bodily weakness and suffering reveal unexpected depths of tenderness

The Manifold Revelation of Truth. 281

and heroism. They watch from opposite sides the interdependence of the material and the spiritual, of force and the organ through which it works, of the organism and its environment. They are alike bound to consider that element with which they do not directly deal if they would discharge their office aright. The physician takes account of the action of the 'spirit' when he seeks to restore health to the body. The theologian takes account of the action of the 'body' when he seeks to establish and to develop the health of the soul. In old times—and the practice has found a remarkable revival within the memory of many of us—the offices of priest and physician were united in one person; and it will be a grievous loss to all if those to whom they now are committed separately ever fail to fulfil them with one heart and one soul.

Life, I repeat, is greater than we know. It is strange forgetfulness or still stranger presumption which leads us to think, or to bear ourselves as thinking, either that our senses exhaust the phenomena of the universe; or that the range of our observation is sufficient to give a final view of the course of created being as far as we can observe it. As it is, we ourselves bring from within that which gives validity to our limited apprehensions and invests sequences of phenomena with the force of law. We trust the truth of things. Of necessity *we walk by faith not by sight*—'by faith not by sight,' that is the antithesis of Scripture—and cast ourselves upon the invisible. We unconsciously assume that the order which we can trace for a little distance represents for us the will of One absolutely powerful and loving and righteous. Life justifies the assumption; and at the same time while we study with untiring care that which lies open to us, fresh and unexpected voices come to the patient listener from which the Gospel draws a fuller meaning.

So revelations are made to us now; and I thankfully confess that the conceptions which have brought most light to the Christian Faith during my own time have been drawn from the study of the outward world, the conceptions of continuity and dependence which present the universe to our minds as in some sense a living whole.

The physicist tells us that the earth is as a grain of dust in the systems of space, and the life of man an episode in the history of the earth: the Christian has learnt to recognise that time and space are no measures of the eternal and that it answers to the Divine method in the general ordering of existence that GOD should con-

The Manifold Revelation of Truth. 283

centrate in one point His redemptive work for creation.

The physicist tells us that the last view which we can gain of inorganic substance suggests the thought of life: the Christian welcomes the suggestion as serving to give clearness to the great hope in which he looks for the accomplishment of the Divine purpose to gather up *all things*—and not only all men—in Christ.

The physicist tells us that man cannot separate himself from the world in which he is set: the Christian remembers that from the first page of Scripture to the last the world is associated with man's sin and man's salvation.

Now, not to dwell at length on these illustrations, it is clear that when we study the Gospel under the aspects which are thus opened to us through other studies we are led to feel something at least of its intellectual power and grandeur. For the Gospel deals with the whole sum of existences, and not only with the single soul. It offers subjects for praise as well as for thanksgiving. It claims and it satisfies man's intellect no less than his feelings. It discloses immeasurable depths on every side, through which we can see finite things moving to their consummation.

The thoughts come to us from without, and

the Gospel fills them with transcendent glory. It raises every form of knowledge to a higher power and makes all experience contribute to the completeness of a vision in which we combine the fragmentary promises of a final harmony. We grow wearied with much seeking, and at last the childly heart is proved to be the best interpreter of life.

Even the present sight of failure and suffering ceases to discourage us. We win our souls by patience. If what we see were all, we might indeed be filled with despair; but what we see is not all. Earth-born clouds only hide the light of heaven for a time and do not quench it. As we learn to believe that there cannot be one lost good, so we learn to believe that there cannot be one fruitless pang.

Such beliefs furnish fresh incentives to research. We question, as we have power, every creature of GOD which falls within the range of our intelligence as one of His messengers. We isolate phenomena, and groups of phenomena, for purposes of inquiry, and still everywhere we recognise that that with which we deal is not the whole. The seen becomes for us a Sacrament of the unseen: the known a sign of the unknown. It has been said 'that the religious opinions of 'men rest on their views of Nature[10].' I should

The Manifold Revelation of Truth. 285

invert the sentence, and say 'that our views of 'Nature rest on our religious opinions,' and strive to shew that no man can rival the Christian who is faithful to his Creed, in tenderest regard for "all thinking things, all objects of all thought," because he believes that every observed sequence of phenomena is a disclosure of the divine will, and every least work in the visible creation a fragment which will be gathered up in a final unity in the Son of Man Who is also the Son of GOD.

At the same time this vision of the deeper truths of Nature brings nobility to the commonest offices of life. The Christian is able to receive with a new intelligence the old truth that in GOD *we live and move and have our being. In many parts and in many fashions* he masters the lesson, and *in many parts and in many fashions* he labours to translate it into action. For him every power and opportunity of ministry is a divine endowment. He draws no sharp line between 'natural' and 'supernatural.' He stands everywhere and at all times in the presence of a spiritual power. For him 'gifts of healing' are in the same category as 'miracles' and 'prophecy.' *All these worketh the one and the selfsame Spirit, dividing to each one severally as He will.* For him the exceptional phenomena of the first age are signs through which he realises the full meaning of the memorable words: 'I dress, GOD 'heals.'

It is our privilege then to labour in our several offices as fellow-workers with GOD, inspired by the thought that it is through us He is pleased to reveal and to accomplish His will *in many parts and in many fashions*. Our work, as we welcome it, will be a pledge of fellowship with Him, and through Him of fellowship with all who work beside us. We shall do just that which is prepared for us; and what we do, according to our powers, will become the measure of what we receive. Serving the whole, we shall enjoy the life of the whole; and by such service the highest is brought within the reach of all through equality of devotion.

This issue is of momentous importance. It is in this truest equality of men, this joy of manifold service, this fellowship in the pursuit of the human ideal, that we find the only satisfying solution of the social problems of our time. It is not by a mechanical and material levelling, not by the removal of the severe necessity of a personal labour, not by the obliteration or enfeeblement of individuality through any schemes of collectivism, that we shall reach the end for which we feel that we were made; but by loyal obedience to the spirit of a divine trusteeship in the administration of every gift of wealth or power which has been committed to us; by the generous recognition of the dignity and worth of every form of toil; by the most complete development of personality, not for self-assertion but for common ministry. If the individual is supposed by some to exist for the state, while by some the state is supposed to exist for the individual, we combine the partial truths. It is through the devotion of every endowment to social service that the individual and the state alike reach their end not separately, but together. Thus the highest, as I said, is found to be for all. For the advantages, the pleasures, the rewards, which come through these noblest exercises of man's energy, open to the humblest, are not lessened, like material goods, but indefinitely increased as they are shared by more. Even on earth the true servant enters into the joy of his Lord, and knows the truth of words which express the secret of human happiness: *cum pluribus major erit beatitudo, ubi unusquisque de alio gaudebit sicut de seipso*[11].

And here our inheritance, amassed *in many parts and in many fashions,* is the measure of our obligation and the assurance of our vital unity. When we reflect on what we owe to our fathers, as men, and Englishmen, and, I will venture to add, as Churchmen, on the treasures of knowledge and wisdom, on the privileges and the inspirations of freedom, on the sobering influences of traditional self-respect and self-restraint, on the quiet dominance of a national type of character, patient, upright, resolute, enduring, on the invigorating moral and spiritual forces which are active even through the most sordid tracts of life, we discern our debt to innumerable workers in the past, separated by every kind of difference and even antagonism, who yet worked together and are now united in that better order which they helped to mould.

For it is not only the great sanctuary which is "a temple of reconciliation and peace". The council chamber and the market and the study teach us, through the lessons of a life enriched by the large counsels and wise forethought and penetrative insight of rival masters, how GOD purifies and then unites those whom man puts asunder.

So we come back to the thought which I desire to emphasise that all students of the Truth, as servants of men for Christ's sake through whom He reveals Himself *in many parts and many fashions*, are bound together by ties immeasurably stronger than the forces which tend to separate them; and if only we can realise what the thought is, we shall be enabled to pursue our

The Manifold Revelation of Truth.

several tasks with undistracted zeal, resolved to avoid by strenuous endeavour the waste of isolation, resolved to understand a little better the methods and the objects of those who are placed in fields remote from the plot which we are set to cultivate, resolved at least to strengthen the bonds of sympathy between all liegemen of the Truth and to fortify ourselves with the sense of a great companionship. If we toil in this temper, outward separation will not divide us. No egoisms or jealousies will disturb men who are filled with the greatness of their work. We shall anticipate the judgment of a later age which will see whatever has been worthily done amongst us harmonised in one result; and whether we wander in our investigations through illimitable spaces, or fix our regard on the ultimate forms of life and matter, or enter into the struggles and sorrows of men, we shall, I believe, find GOD everywhere in signs of power and order and beauty and growing purpose, without Whom the thoughts of law and progress are baseless and unintelligible.

For beyond the "many parts and the many fashions" of human education, the many studies and the many methods by which we approach towards the Truth on this side and on that, lies the Truth itself, the Truth which gives reality to thought and word and deed, the Truth in which alone we can find that rest which is harmonious activity untroubled by failure or weariness, the Truth which the Lord has disclosed under the conditions of earth in His Own Person, and brought into the fulness of life.

Slowly indeed and not without suffering we move towards the complete interpretation of the words *I am the Truth*. From age to age we master a little more of their meaning through the discipline of apparent loss. As it is in the experience of our own brief and confined lives, it is in the course of history and in the progress of thought. Opinions, ideals, hopes on which we have set our trust fail us. But if we have not presumptuously identified that which was provisional and preparatory with that to which it witnessed, we shall be enabled to feel when the first pain is over, even when the Lord Himself seems to have left us for a time, that it was expedient for us that He should go away. Such outward losses—losses of the earthly form—leave the spiritual untouched, more open and more glorious.

But in order that we may know this consolation, this enlightening, in our day of trial, we must conquer for our own sake and for the sake of others that irony of thought which dissembles the highest purpose of the student; we must confess with the humblest thankfulness the nobility of our service; we must in all our strivings and attainments look unweariedly to Him Who cannot change; we must believe, and live as believing, that GOD makes His Son—the Word become flesh—known to us *in many parts and in many fashions*, even as in old time He prepared men to receive Him, and that to each one of us He commits the care of some part of His counsel, and speaks in some fashion.

The end for which we look and labour may seem to be far off; but the promise, which has been justified in the past, still remains, that *the Spirit shall take of Christ's and shew it unto us.* For us also the words hold good: *Ye shall know the Truth, and the Truth shall make you free,* free, because it has vanquished for ever the suggestions of caprice and selfishness.

The end may seem to be far off, but each day brings us nearer to it. Men and nations may be defeated, but, it has been truly said, 'humanity never lost a battle.' The loftiest desire which we can frame for the world, the loftiest ideal towards which we can strive, is a faint and imperfect reflection of the will of GOD; and with Him power and righteousness and love are one.

The end may seem to be far off; but to labour for it is to have a foretaste of victory, and to know that the fruits of our service of an hour are garnered in the treasury of GOD, where every difference of small and great is lost in the sameness of love.

In many parts and in many fashions, that is the law of man's learning and teaching: and the purpose of GOD'S good pleasure, which it is our privilege to serve, is, *to sum up all things in Christ, the things in the heavens and the things upon the earth.*

In the prospect of this end learning, teaching, serving, find their inspiration, their support and their reward. May GOD help us to hasten it.

A GOSPEL FOR THE POOR.

The poor have good tidings preached to them.

Sᴛ Mᴀᴛᴛ. xi. 5.

ST ANDREW'S, DEPTFORD.
Third Sunday in Advent, 1891.

Jubilee of the Church.

WHEN I was considering to what subject I could best direct our thoughts this evening, I naturally turned to the Gospel for the day, and in the words which I have just read I seemed to find the lesson which we need. The words, as you will remember, occur in the answer which the Lord returned to John the Baptist, who from his lonely prison had sent disciples to Him to enquire whether He was indeed the promised Deliverer. *Art Thou,* he asked, *He that cometh, or look we for another?* The Lord replied by recounting what He did. His works were his answer. *Go your way,* he said, *and tell John the things which ye do hear and see: the blind receive their sight and the lame walk: the lepers are cleansed and the deaf hear: and the dead are raised up, and the poor have good tidings preached to them.*

The poor have good tidings preached to them. This was the crowning sign by which the herald, desolate, disheartened, abandoned, as it might seem, was to recognise in Jesus of Nazareth the Christ whose Advent he had been commissioned to announce. Greater than the restoration of physical powers, greater than the removal of bodily disease, greater even than the immediate conquest of the grave, was this last miracle of divine power and love, greater, more persuasive, more enduring, the message of a universal Gospel.

It is clear why this always must be the decisive sign of Christ the Saviour of the world. Difficulties may arise as to the reality and significance of isolated phenomena which no evidence can wholly meet. Every event loses its impressiveness by distance. But the Truth which makes itself known to man as man; the Truth which finds us in the changeful labours and sorrows of life, in solitude and in conflict; the Truth which enriches us however poor we are, however slender may be our natural store of moral, intellectual, material endowments; this is its own witness. No time, no distance, no peculiarities of national character, no revolutions of speculative thought, can affect its claims. It appeals to the individual soul: it appeals to the soul of humanity.

Thus the sign by which the divine authority of the Master was to be recognised is the sign by which His Church must vindicate its claims. A great leader—not alas! one of us—wrote forty *for the poor.* 297

years ago, "When any one says to me 'Behold a good man!' I ask 'How many souls has he saved?' When any one says to me, 'Behold a religious people,' I inquire what it has done and suffered to bring humanity to its belief." In like manner we may justly require that a Church when it claims our devotion shall establish in living evidence that it has a Gospel for the poor.

But before we apply the text we must take care not to misunderstand or limit its scope. We must not confine the application of the witness to which the Lord appealed to the simplest and most obvious sense of the words, to the poor as the world counts poverty. Indeed the interpretation which by common consent we give to the term 'poor' reveals and condemns the shallowness of the popular view of life. We speak and think as if they only were poor who are straitened in material resources, who find it hard to provide food and shelter from day to day, who cannot make more than the scantiest provision for times of yet sharper need. But *the life is more than the meat; man liveth not by bread alone.* There is a poverty of heart and soul, sadder and more desolating than poverty of body. There is a poverty which makes itself felt as a crushing load in the palaces of the wealthy and in the schools of the wise.

The least reflection will shew how this is so, and how sorely we need to reflect upon the truth.

For is it not the fact that we ourselves create in a large degree the world in which we live? We give its real value to the abundance or to the penury by which we are surrounded. 'We can,' it has been well said, 'make much of life, if we have much soul'; but if we have little soul, life is dwarfed to our proportions. We see, we feel, no more than we have trained faculties for seeing and feeling. We enjoy that with which we are able to sympathise; and our enjoyment is measured by our sympathy.

Thus the soul which is rich in mental wealth moves about in a poet's paradise. To such a soul

> The meanest flower that blows can give
> Thoughts that do often lie too deep for tears.

Such a soul is joyously conscious of harmonies of sound and colour in the commonest things. It enters into the fulness of being fertile in unceasing variety of beauty. It peoples each familiar scene with heroes of the past. It holds friendly converse with the greatest of all time. The book becomes for it a living voice: the work of art a revelation, a confession of a kindred nature.

The soul again which is rich in moral wealth opens streams of feeling on every side. It is stirred and quickened by the response of hearts touched by its natural warmth. It calls out powers which wait for its bidding to display their activity. It is strong with the strength of multitudes who recognise its sovereignty. If, as we have been taught, love is the measure of life, then no life can be ampler than that which such a soul commands. Gold and silver, purple and fine linen and sumptuous fare, add nothing to the wealth of the soul which makes the whole world its minister.

And what shall we say on the other hand of the poor dull soul? Of the soul which spells out with difficulty the simplest lesson of nature or life, for which the waters have no music and the sky no imagery, for which

> the primrose by the river's brim
> A yellow primrose is..., and nothing more;

for which our great Cathedral, the mother Church of the Diocese, has no lessons in its subtleties of proportion, in its faithfulness to type, in its harmonious combination of work of distant epochs: no message from the fathers on whose manifold inheritance we have entered, from the relics honoured for a thousand years or from the gifts of our own day? Of the soul which is fast confined in its narrow cell, neither understanding nor understood, alone, apart, in the concourse of men: the soul which cannot trust its own impulses, and

A Gospel

cannot interpret them, but which can perhaps feel sadly that it chills and checks the ardour of those with whom it is brought into contact?

Can any outward poverty compare with this inner poverty which touches not the circumstances of life but the powers of life, which leaves the wealthiest beggared in thought in the midst of his splendour, and the wisest destitute of sympathy in the midst of his intellectual triumphs? Oh, brethren, when once we feel what life is, we feel then, and not till then, what poverty is, manifold as the regions of life. And so the power of the Gospel rises before us in its full extent. For in that, in that alone—*the poor*—the poor in means and the poor in faculties, the poor in body and the poor in soul,—*have good tidings preached to them*; and our Church is the faithful herald of the Gospel.

The poor, I say, in the deepest, largest sense, *have good tidings preached to them* in Christ. The power of our Faith is measured only by the wants and weaknesses of men. In this boundless capacity it stands alone. Great thinkers in old times seemed to find for themselves a theory of the universe able to bring peace to a select band of privileged philosophers. But it was peace at the price of isolation. Great observers in the present times seem to find for themselves adequate satisfaction in the multitudinous experiences which they can crowd into the brief space of three score years and ten. But it is the satisfaction of the closet. Such men have no Gospel for the great multitude whose thoughts move in a narrow circle, and whose days are filled with monotonous duties.

And if others again, dazzled by the sight of pleasures which can only be purchased by selfish opulence, are not afraid to offer the luxury of the few as a prize for the labour or the violence of the many, they seem to me to display to a criminal ambition an aim equally illusory and unattainable. For I can see no enduring hope for men in any change of circumstances effected from without. Physical fears and pleasures bring no generous discipline and no unwearying satisfaction. Power carries with it no true sense of dignity, and indulgence leaves no sense of rest. What we need more than any readjustment of the conditions of life, and we grievously need this, is a purer ideal of life, a more prevailing motive of service, a more elevating view of the end of labour. We all of us require to learn, each in the fulfilment of his least office, that we have no rights but duties, and no solitary joy. This Christ teaches still, while He proclaims good tidings to the poor.

Therefore the soul naturally Christian refuses to rest in the partial Gospels of man's invention, which guard their blessings as the prerogative of men of letters or of men of science, as the possession of the rich or of the strong. It turns to the Gospel of Christ, the Word Incarnate, for the revelation and satisfaction of its first and its latest wants, and it does not turn in vain.

The Gospel of Christ the Word Incarnate opens to the meanest, the feeblest, the most desolate in our eyes, a share in that glorified manhood which He has borne to the right hand of GOD. In this *the poor have good tidings preached to them*. Here is the Truth which the most ignorant can grasp for the hallowing of his simplest ordinary work, as he feels that he is an object of the love of GOD, called to fulfil in his measure the purpose of GOD; the Truth which, as the wisest dimly see, has the power not only to occupy but to discipline and invigorate and enlarge every energy of human thought: the Truth, which resting in love teaches us to know that we were made for love, and to find in its exercise our own selves—losing our souls that we may gain them—for

> life with all it brings of joy or woe
> Is just our chance o' the prize of learning love.

The Gospel of Christ the Word Incarnate gives back to every child of earth through the

Atonement his spiritual sovereignty over the world, and˙ shews him how the kingdom over which he is set becomes one great Sacrament of the heavenly Father. Here then is the Truth which establishes on an immovable foundation that devout reverence for the least phenomenon of the outward world which is the glory of physical science: the Truth which witnesses to the reality of a divine presence in things visible which is the inspiration of Art: the Truth which answers to the conviction that the world even as we see it is sacred, the reflection of the Divine Mind which our mind can interpret.

The Gospel of Christ the Word Incarnate declares with a pathetic and irresistible power the unity of mankind, so that we cannot for one moment separate ourselves from any who share with us that nature which He has taken to Himself. Here then is the Truth which consecrates the largest and the least heritage or accumulation of wealth with a social blessing, and constrains each believer to recognise in every gift a talent to be administered for the common good: the Truth which fills the poorest with sympathy for those who have the awful responsibility of great possessions: the Truth which makes it clear—clear in thought as it is clear in experience—that he who would monopolise enjoyment destroys it for himself.

A Gospel

The Gospel of Christ the Word Incarnate, of GOD entering into our life, is indeed good tidings, *good tidings to the poor*, good tidings in its essence to man, simply as man, reaching down to the lowest depths where humanity still lingers, and growing with man's growth to the utmost bound of his possible attainment. Yes, reaching and growing without limit, for if it could be shewn that any forms of man's distress and perplexity are inaccessible to its consolation: that any human powers lie without the range of its benediction: that any facts of nature or history are in conflict with its premises: then I should feel compelled to write against this also the sentence of decay and dissolution and *look for another*. But the Gospel of Christ Incarnate and Ascended is subject to no such condemnation. It shews us that the divine is the foundation of the human and (most overwhelming wonder) that the human is the fulfilment of the divine. It turns our thoughts from what we can do to what GOD has done and is doing. It discloses in the idea of Creation a splendour which communicates its light to all created things. It supplies that which impresses on inevitable change the seal of onward progress. It pierces to the depths of misery and brings back even from their darkness a promise of hope. It transfigures all personal suffering by the thought of a fellowship with GOD in Christ. It is a new, an eternal Covenant in which all things, our utmost hopes, our least efforts, are shewn to be of Him, and through Him, and unto Him.

Here then is the Gospel which we all have to hold and to publish: to hold with a firmer grasp, by publishing with a more personal devotion. Here is the joy which we all are charged to make our own by extending it to others. Here in times of sad perplexity we can find the surest sign that Christ has come. For if in these days of trial—and what days are not days of trial if life is vigorous and sincere?—doubts or questionings as to the Faith rise in the still loneliness of our hearts: if we too ask, in the words of the Baptist, as our eyes fall on some familiar portraiture of the Light of the World in a dark unlovely setting, '*Art Thou He that cometh, or look we for another?*' if we too seek, as the Baptist sought, for tidings sufficient to reassure us, brought directly from the stirring scenes of human activity, we shall not ask and seek in vain. From the Home Mission field and from the Foreign Mission field the same reply comes that now as in the first age, in new distresses, in new forms of civilization, in new races *the poor have good tidings preached to them in Christ.* So you have learnt here in this great town by your own experience during the last fifty years, that while our Church has laboured with fresh-awakened zeal to reach more nearly the masses entrusted to her care, the vision of life has been brightened, the work of life has been quickened, the wounds of sin have been cleansed, the progress of corruption has been stayed by the old—the ever new—tidings of 'Jesus and the Resurrection'; and, above all, that this Gospel has been found by those who have welcomed it to be a Gospel powerful to transform the nature and circumstances of men.

And you have learnt also by the testimony of toilers in heathen lands, that the Gospel of Christ, which our Church bears throughout the world, is able to reach those whom the ordinary forces of civilization leave on one side, forlorn and wounded: able to open the dulled eye to the vision of a Father in heaven: able to stir to noble activity classes paralysed by hereditary bondage: able to call out the response of love by the work of love: able to recover and to reveal the true humanity of the outcast and the savage, disguised and deformed through generations of corruption and violence. What witness to the Apostolic power of our Church could be more eloquent or more prevailing than this transfiguration of men before our eyes wrought through its ministry, whereby the Divine image is seen to flash forth in answer to the Divine call?

Here, then, is the sign, more prevailing than the sad sense of failure and imperfection, that Christ is indeed with us. Here in a word is the proof and the blessing for our own age and our own Church.

Once again the heavens and the earth are being shaken, that things eternal may be seen in perfect beauty. Once again we are learning even through strange teachers that our Faith transcends the limits within which we have been tempted to confine it. Once again we are coming to understand that the message of Christ Born, Crucified, Ascended, brings victorious patience in the stress of conflict. Once again it is witnessed to our souls, and not least powerfully through strife and pain, through the bitterness of controversy and the discipline of failure, that in the Gospel of the Word Incarnate, *the poor*, the poor who feel their poverty, who feel their loneliness in the vast turmoil of life and their littleness before the immensity of Nature, *have good tidings preached to them*.

Brethren, 'it is your Jubilee, therefore it shall be holy unto you,' a time for fresh self-devotion, and fresh endeavours for social ministry, a time when the confession of failure is made the welcoming of a new power of life, a time when every difference of character and endowment becomes an opportunity for personal service to our fellow-men in the light and in the strength of our common Faith.

So may the time be blessed to you, and through you to all among whom you are set to work.

SURSUM CORDA.

LIFT UP YOUR HEARTS.
WE LIFT THEM UP UNTO THE LORD.

SHERBORNE MINSTER.

June 22, 1893.

Commemoration of Sherborne School.

THERE are two necessary elements in a noble life. It must be inspired by reverence, and it must be expressed in devotion. A man who realises in any degree the dignity and the power of human nature must acknowledge something before which he can bow with devout awe, and to which he can bring the tribute of reverent service. In order that he may keep hope fresh, he must recognise the presence of a Power supreme over all the vicissitudes and temptations of transitory circumstances; and in order that he may do his own part, he must welcome as his corresponding duty the obligation of absolute self-surrender to its dominion.

Reverence is in all cases a true measure of our moral worth, and devotion a true measure of our strength. This principle, which holds good universally in its general form, takes a personal shape for the Christian. The Christian knows what man is and what earth is, for he knows that *the Word became flesh*. He can see and serve GOD in man; he can behold heaven about him with the eyes of the heart. The earliest of Greek philosophers held that "all things are full of gods:" the Christian believes, and strives unweariedly to bear himself as believing, that *in GOD we live and move and have our being.*

The thought finds a most touching utterance in words which have held a place in the Communion Office from the earliest times, and the place which they hold in our own office gives them a special force. When we have been encouraged by 'comfortable words,' characteristic of our English Liturgy, to draw near to the Holiest, the voice is addressed to us which has been addressed to more than fifty generations of believers, *Lift up your hearts;* and we dare to reply as our fathers have always replied, feeling in that moment of deep emotion the need and the joy of our heavenly connexion: *We lift them up unto the Lord.*

Ἄνω τὰς καρδίας, *sursum corda, lift up your hearts:* May I not rightly take this phrase to guide our thoughts now when we look to the springs and streams of life? Surely a phrase which has such a history will bring to us victorious sympathy with those on whose conquests we have entered. It is a watchword of Commemoration. It must cling to us. And as we regard it, we shall learn a little more of the force and the promise of the charge with which

Sursum corda.

earlier generations speed us on the work which they have prepared. It reveals to us a continuous motive for reverence. It supports in us an unfailing energy of devotion. It witnesses that all we are and have is capable of consecration, and calls us to place all in the transfiguring light of the Divine Presence. *Sursum corda.*

We look, I say, to-day to the springs of life; and while thoughts of reverence and devotion—of reverence which exalts, and of devotion which assures us—can never be unseasonable, there are places and times which give them a peculiar fitness and power. Can any place give them a fuller meaning than this venerable Minster, which with all its memories of the ancient Church — of catastrophes and restorations — welcomes within its walls a School the firstfruits of a new age? Can any time give them a more direct application than this when we look one with another to the responsibilities which are brought by a great inheritance? Can any congregation entertain them more gladly than a congregation of students, rich in the wealth of youth, united in the fellowship of work, eager for the advent of the day of service? To those who are just beginning to grow conscious of the gifts, of the conditions, of the difficulties of life, the phrase *Sursum corda* must sound, I believe, as the natural, the necessary, the sustaining confession of their faith. It answers to the generous feeling of early years as the spontaneous outcome of high purpose. It answers to the requirements of a patient discipline which needs to be quickened through all its parts with spiritual fire. It answers to the near prospect of labour to be fulfilled in times which are marked by the peculiar trials of a dominant earthliness. It hallows, in a word, the instincts of youth. It sustains the vigour of effort. It opens a heavenly vision which will grow brighter through the stress of life. From stage to stage, under new conditions, it deepens reverence and it kindles devotion.

1. *Sursum corda.* That heavenward look hallows, I say, the instincts of youth. The young are happily drawn by the spirit of enthusiasm and by the spirit of friendship. Enthusiasm is reverence in action. Friendship is devotion in personal intercourse. I ask you then, scholars in Christ's school, to welcome the inspiration and the lessons, which these twin spirits bring, to master them, to make them your own, by reflection, by exercise, by effort.

A youth without enthusiasm means a maturity without faith and an old age without hope. Trust therefore from the first and you will trust throughout the noblest thoughts for the world and for yourselves which GOD gives you. They are the truest thoughts which man can have, even if their fulfilment lingers. We cannot wish anything better for the universe than GOD'S will. Just as we regard all things in Him, 'the Creator and Preserver,' we find a solid ground for confidence in our highest desires, and in our humblest endeavours. The world is for us as we ourselves are. Nothing is easier than to mark the trail of the serpent on the withered leaves, but shall we therefore refuse to see the rich beauty of the wide landscape and the splendour of the overarching sky?

Trust then, I say, the noblest thoughts which GOD gives you and translate them into action. They are for use. They are not sent to us as an idle adornment of life or a source of beautiful dreams, but to make great deeds possible. Our Christian Faith is nothing if it is not practical. The enthusiasm which it fires is akin to the love *which beareth all things, believeth all things, hopeth all things*, and, I would fain add, doeth all things. Such enthusiasm is effective in each sphere of human effort. It brings to reason the loftiest working hypothesis on which our intellectual powers can find the fullest play. It brings to feeling the widest range and the most prevailing motive, and gathers into one the scattered or conflicting tendencies to self-devoted service. It brings to will the resolute fervour which comes from that vision of the eternal which is able to overpower the distracting influences of the present. It is at first the spontaneous expression of half-unconscious reverence, and then as it gives little by little distinctness and force to the feeling from which it rose, we learn to move with a holy fear, through a world which is found to be for us a revelation of GOD.

In purifying and deepening enthusiasm you will discover the value of the second endowment of youth of which I spoke, the spirit of friendship. Friendship, like enthusiasm, rests on reverence, on the discernment of that which we can honour with unquestioning trust. In later years we must often look in vain for those to whom we can open our joys and our griefs: the plans which have survived disappointment: the memories which are still eloquent with hope. As time goes on it becomes harder to speak out of the fulness of the heart. But at school it is not frankness but silence which is strange. At school the revelation of the meaning of life comes to most of us, the parting of the ways, the crisis of choice, the solemn endowment for service in Confirmation. At school in the exercise of high responsibility fellow-labourers, fellow-believers, grow strong by the interchange of kindly counsels, by the acknowledgment of high ambitions, by the confession of sad misgivings. At school it is possible to make provision for the lonely hours of solitary labour which will follow through that intercourse of soul with soul which reveals the underlying depths of our common manhood. At school we learn that we are strong by fellowship, and school friendships open the way to larger sympathy, and the devotion of personal intercourse discloses the joy of devotion to social service.

2. For at school we must look beyond school. The spirit of enthusiasm and devotion has a wider field of exercise. It is not enough to welcome generous impulses, to yield ourselves to their influence, to embody them as they arise. If we offer ourselves without reserve to do GOD'S work and feel the grandeur of the call, we must also consider, as in His sight, how we can best do it. This obligation of preparing for the future is laid upon the young. And again I say, *Sursum corda.* That heavenward look, which kindles reverence, sustains the fullest energy of devotion. The elder among you have already gained sufficient experience to realise the secret of life, to work, that is, as knowing that you were born not to enjoy but to serve: to strive with the aspiration of unsatisfied desire and not to rest in any personal attainment: to aim not at quick returns but at a harvest

which will gladden those who come after us. You can discern by this time how large a part the past occupies in every life, and you know its lesson. It is not the easy victory, it is not the individual gain, it is not the transitory if innocent indulgence, which becomes in us a spring of strength and joy, when we look back upon it, but the vigorous effort in which we thought only of our duty and not of the issue: the hidden ministry of love which no one could repay or recognise: the failures which become witnesses to us and prophecies, witnesses that we have found the end for which we were made, prophecies that GOD, in His good time, will grant us grace to reach it.

Taught then by the experience of your little world, in which the problems of after-life are presented openly to minds not dulled by custom, you will take courage to look forward. Life is far too solemn to be lived at random. No one can safely improvise in action, and it is by action we prove our manhood. Our early plans may perhaps find no outward accomplishment; but none the less we shall be trained to do that which is given us to do by the discipline of that self-examination and calm resolve in which they were fashioned. We are all of us visited by great hopes; and happy are we if, in the flush of youth, we do not allow them to float vaguely about us, but patiently

Sursum corda. 319

bring them to inquiry, and wisely order them, and then, if it may be, seek our work in pursuing them to fulfilment. A purpose, a plan, in life, indeed, is not everything, however wisely it may be shaped, and however exactly it may correspond with our circumstances. Mechanical action is scarcely less perilous than improvised action. But still a plan is helpful. If it does no more, it preserves for us precious memories and keeps that which is best in our past as a present power.

As you look forward then to the field of labour opening before your eyes, as you choose within the limits which have been providentially marked out for you the lines of your activity, as you exercise your prerogative of creative energy with which GOD has endowed man formed in His own image, listen to the call, *Sursum corda*. Dwell on no vision, admit no project, press no endeavour, which will not bear the invocation of that heavenly destiny. Cherish the noblest ideals, for none can reach the truth of our Faith. Do not suppose that any estimate of that which is essentially eternal can be too high. Great thoughts go best with common duties. Whatever therefore may be your office regard it as a fragment in an immeasurable ministry of love. Think nobly of human life which GOD has taken to Himself in Christ. It will never disappoint those who remember that the Word became flesh, and that the Father has sent the Holy Spirit to us in His Name. *Sursum corda*: the voice which rises to utterance, like a fountain springing to light, in the joyousness of young strength: the voice which directs us to the glory of creation veiled but not destroyed: the voice which stays the wayward inconstancy of wandering fancies and gives a settled purpose to the promptings of duty: is able to sustain every great hope in the believer under the heaviest perplexities of our state.

3. For yet once again, this heavenward look will open a vision of spiritual glory which will grow brighter in the stress of life. And you, the men of the next generation, will need the light. It is idle to attempt to compare the intensity of human trials at different times. An age of torpor is as perilous as an age of revolution. Life is always mysterious, awful, full of unsolved difficulties. But, as it seems to me, that which gives a peculiar character to your coming trial, that of which you will do well to take account—if for a moment I may go beyond the lessons of the place—lies not so much in the nature of the evils which you will have to face as in the nature of the remedies which are popularly accepted as adequate to heal them.

There has never been in England more widespread or more candid acknowledgment of the social and personal wrongs which claim patient consideration and redress; never a more generous or more universal desire to deal with them; never a more ready or larger army of self-denying labourers in the cause of humanity; and at the same time there has, I fear, never been less real trust in a present, living, speaking GOD, accessible and sovereign, as the one Helper from Whom we can gain the solace and guidance and strength which we require. We are tempted to worship with conventional service a GOD Who has withdrawn Himself from the world which He has made or a GOD Whom we can localise. We seem to exhaust ourselves in seeking material relief for spiritual maladies. We are overwhelmed by the pressure of things which can be seen and handled. Almost unconsciously we enthrone wealth as supreme by assuming that that which wealth can provide would itself cure our sorrows. We forget that the life is more than the meat. We forget that in times far sadder than our own prophets, apostles, evangelists, saw GOD, and through the revelation of His Presence gave life to a dying age. The vision of GOD is indeed the transfiguration of the world: communion with GOD is the inspiration of life. That vision, that communion, Christ by His coming has made our abiding inheritance. As often as the Christian touches heaven, the heaven which lies about us though our eyes are holden that we should not see it, touches it with the heart and not with the hand, he is again filled with the powers of the world to come. Then reverence finds its perfect satisfaction, then devotion finds its invincible strength.

So once more we are brought back to the great invitation which meets us in the new joys and in the grave counsels and in the stern riddles of life. *Lift up your hearts,* not locally but spiritually, lift them not away from earth, but to earth as GOD has made it—*Sursum corda. Lift up your hearts:* lift them, I say, not away from earth, but to earth: earth is higher than we see. We are not bidden to deny or to dissemble or to extenuate the evils and sorrows by which we are surrounded. We are bidden to look through them and to look beyond them. We are bidden to look to the Paraclete Who knows every secret of our souls. We are bidden to look to the sovereign counsel of GOD, and to win peace in the contemplation of its certain progress, the peace of Christ, which is not insensibility to the sufferings of wandering and wounded men: not ease in the midst of fierce struggles for right and truth: not rest while the day still offers opportunities for labour; but the trust which casts out fear, the calm assurance that we have a Father in heaven in Whose hand are we and our works, and not we and our works only, but all that He has made. If He is invisible the blank is due to our blindness and not to His absence. He shews Himself indeed in many forms, but each revelation remains an abiding light for the days to come.

Nothing, be sure, is lost in the progress of the life of Faith; and nothing is found incapable of ennobling change. Keep then all of you with grateful affection the simple trust of childhood when heaven seems nearest: keep the brightest hopes of youth when the prospect of labour is most inspiriting; keep every thought through which you have at any time known GOD'S Presence; so the force of mature years will not be dissipated in aimless occupation or selfish indulgence; and at last the weariness of age will not be uncheered even in the retrospect of disappointment. *Sursum corda.*

Perhaps I may seem to some to have wandered in what I have said beyond the range of school interests. But my own experience leads me to believe that I have not done so. If sympathy can give insight I may claim some knowledge of the young. Greater victories than Waterloo, doubt not, are won in the schoolroom and in the playground. Claim then, young soldiers of Christ, your share in these conquests of service. Justify your position as sons of one of the firstborn

Schools of our reformed Faith. Every School is dear to me, but here of necessity in the work of this School I seem to have the happiness of living again and of seeing my old faults corrected, my old negligences repaired, my old hopes fulfilled. I too have a part in the blessing of the motto which has been given you: *They shall prosper that love thee.* And in my love I have offered you—it is the best I can offer—the surest lesson which I have learnt in long years of strenuous work: *Sursum corda.*

Life must be hard—you will not complain of the necessity—hard to the end; but it will be enough if, as often as the voice of GOD comes to you—comes through the blessing of great cares, through some unexpected happiness or grief, through some occasion for fruitful service, through some sad discomfiture, through some crushing difficulty, through the sight of the wilful and unloving, through the memory of the righteous dead—saying *Lift up your hearts,* grace be given you to reply with a reverence which has been deepened by thought and a devotion which has been quickened by experience, *We lift them up unto the Lord.*

Sursum corda.
Habemus ad Dominum.

A QUIET LIFE: ITS JOY AND POWER.

AUCKLAND CASTLE, 1891.

Address to the Young Men's Christian Association.

THERE is a remarkable scene at the close of Plato's "Republic," in which the disembodied souls, now ready to return again to earth, are represented as choosing in order the lives which they shall lead in their next mortal existence. The last turn of all falls to the soul of Ulysses. Touched by the remembrance of its former toils, the soul of the illustrious hero goes about for a long time in search of the life of a quiet, private man, and when at last it finds it lying neglected by all others, chooses it gladly, and says that it would have done the same if its turn had come first.

The fiction expresses a truth worth pondering, and I will venture now, even in this chapel filled with many stirring memories, to say a few words on the blessings and the powers of a simple, quiet life. The fabled experience of Ulysses, gained in wars and wanderings, may have a meaning for ourselves in the final lesson which it taught. For we need, I think, to learn this lesson of calm and silent work, the lesson of the deep tide, "too full for noise or foam." We live in an age of transition. We are advancing ever nearer to the social conditions of a democracy, and we cling to the external forms of life which belong to an earlier order. The powers and the opportunities of individual men are tending more and more to equality; and at the same time effort is directed towards the attainment of those conspicuous outward signs of pre-eminence which were natural or necessary when authority belonged to a privileged few.

Hence, in part at least, come the struggles of commercial competition, the restless strivings for material wealth, the acceptance of visible standards of success. We waste a large part of our energy, even to our last years, in seeking for new conditions of action. There are on all sides unflagging endeavours to obtain the means of living, but very little thought of life. We seem to be too busy to live. We are practically forgetting that "the life is more than the meat:" that life itself is immeasurably greater than the circumstances under which it is fulfilled: that a life the least eventful and the least conspicuous is a poem, a revelation of things infinite and eternal.

A Quiet Life: its Joy and Power. 329

Now I will venture to maintain that to forget these truths is to lose the power of overcoming the sorrows and sadnesses which overshadow the world. For, as long as our primary aim is fixed in material well-being, there can be no peace and no satisfaction. There can be no peace, because competition must grow keener as rivals grow more numerous and better furnished for the contest. In the enjoyment of perishable treasures "companionship is one with loss." There can be no satisfaction, because the soul of man—because man—needs that which outward riches cannot give. The words are true, true in the experience of the wealthiest and the poorest, that man's *life consists not in abundance,* in the overflowing store of resources at his command: nor does it spring *from the things which he possesses.*

We turn then from the restless turmoil of unsatisfied activity to the quietude of settled work, from self-centred to social aims, from the material to the spiritual. And here at once we find ourselves in the presence of a force which is infinite, which is sovereign, which increases in energy of blessing as it is spread more widely. A spiritual force which is of GOD has the character of Him from Whom it flows—as spirit, light, love—penetrating, purifying, quickening, uniting all with which it comes in contact. In the presence of this animating force we feel at last what life is: we feel how we all, the humblest and weakest, as living, share in the wealth of the one life, with its full potency and promise, and can find in our simplest duties that which serves mankind and fulfils the divine will, and makes us "friends of GOD," than which no destiny can be greater. A sense of the whole brings dignity to the least part: and the least part is welcomed as essential to the perfection of the whole.

Resting on this conviction, we discern how the claims of individualism and patriotism, of the man and the State, are harmonised. The complete satisfaction of our personal being is found— is found only—in social service. We are born for the commonwealth. We cannot seek our own good apart from the good of our fellows. The simplest ministries of love are doubly blest. And through the manifold discipline of imperfect devotion we recognise the truth of the poet's judgment that

> Life, with all it yields of joy and woe
> And hope and fear,
> Is just our chance o' the prize of learning love,
> How love might be, hath been indeed, and is.

In learning this supreme lesson we learn at the same time that "the commonest is the most precious." That which is most universal is richest in capacity of blessing for each one. The affections of home, the open glories of earth and water and sky, the inexhaustible problems of daily intercourse, offer to the heart and eye and intellect enough to exercise their noblest powers. So it is also with the works of man. That which is greatest in literature and art speaks to man as man in a common human language, and not in a technical dialect. The keenest delight in the living effect is wholly independent of the power of analysing its conditions and elements.

"Money," it has been well said, "is not re-"quired to buy one necessity of the soul;" and I appeal to the experience of everyone to justify the statement. The joys which have been deepest and most lasting are those through which we have been brought into a closer fellowship with nature or man or GOD, through which we have lost our separate selves to find our truer selves, for the words of the Lord hold good as a rule for the guidance of our daily conduct: *Whosoever will save his life shall lose it: and whosoever will lose his life for My sake shall find it.*

The words hold good in things which we call small and great; and we know that they hold good; for the capacity of man as man answers to the grandeur of his natural inheritance. He is

born to seek GOD, to entertain the loftiest ideals,
to reach out to the Divine likeness. But he is
disturbed, distracted, hindered in the search by
nearer and more obvious objects.

> Earth fills her lap with pleasures of her own. . . .
> The homely Nurse doth all she can
> To make her foster-child, her inmate, Man,
> Forget the glories he hath known. . . .

We need therefore to cultivate that generous
ambition of which St Paul speaks, that we may
not only keep fresh the childly spirit of wonder
and trust and self-surrender, but use it to mould
a constant temper of reverence and faith and
tenderness. Three times, as some of you may
remember, St Paul speaks of the Christian's
ambition. *Be ambitious,* he says, *to be quiet. We
are ambitious to be well pleasing to the Lord. I
am ambitious to preach the Gospel to those who
have not heard it.* The sequence answers to the
growth of character. First we must strive for
that calm in which we can dwell upon the Divine
vision: then for the energy by which thought is
turned to deed: then for the devotion which
constrains us to bring to others what we have
found.

Such ambition is the moving force and the
joy of the quiet, simple life—the life that is
within the reach of everyone, which I desire to

A Quiet Life: its Joy and Power.

commend. For, as I said before, "the commonest is the most precious"—the commonest in pleasures and in occupations and in opportunities. The average man is the staple and the hope of a nation. The most irresistible influence is the influence of personal conviction and personal character. The changes which we need, and for which we confidently look, will come not through violence, not through the formative power of legislation, but through that solid and intelligent opinion which it is the duty of everyone to help to form by act rather than by words: by act, I say, rather than by word, for our worst evils only yield to the patient efforts of individual service. Such service, by revealing friendship, calls out independence and self-respect, even in the outcast, and opens sources of common joy. By improving the character of men it improves their circumstances; and I know no other sure hope of improvement, for to increase the means of men and to increase their leisure is worse than vain till they have learnt how to use them. On the other hand, man has the power, to a large extent, of fashioning his surroundings after the likeness of himself.

Such service—watchful and tender, full of forbearance and sympathy—we all can render wherever we may be placed. It is the peculiar prerogative of the quiet life, where the loving eye is ready to mark each opportunity undisturbed. But, that we may so serve, we must resolutely keep seasons for reflection, we must guard ourselves against the prevailing hurry of thought and action, we must ponder the central truths of our Faith.

We must keep, I say, seasons for reflection. At the very time when we are beginning to think lightly of our tranquil Sunday, continental writers are discovering its value. A French Roman Catholic traveller lately expressed his admiration of our Australasian colonies. "What is the "cause," he asks, "which renders the population "so rational and practical? In my opinion we "must attribute it principally to the habitual "reading and deep knowledge of the Holy "Scriptures. . . . The repose of Sunday is "consecrated to the study of the Bible." We may wish indeed that the statement were more absolutely true; but at least the weekly break in common work, the stillness, the spiritual atmosphere, the sacred memories, the encircling presence of Divine thoughts which our 'Rest day of the Resurrection' brings to Englishmen, has done much to make them what they are. "The "observance of Sunday rest," wrote Mr Gladstone to an International Conference on the subject held less than two years ago at Paris, "has rooted " itself deeply in the convictions, as well as in the " habits, of the great majority of my countrymen. " . . . Personally I have always endeav- " oured . . . to avail myself of this privilege; " and now that I have arrived near the goal of a " laborious public career of near on fifty-seven " years, I attribute in great part to this practice " the prolonging of my life and the preservation " of my faculties." Another distinguished living statesman, I have been told, was speaking of the long hours of his professional labour. " But you " have had your vacations," was the answer. " No," he replied, " I worked as hard then as in " Term time: but I had my Sundays."

So let me beg you, my friends, most earnestly to keep your Sundays apart from other days for the hallowing of your quiet life. Keep them free for the welcoming of heavenly thoughts, for childly communings with a loving Father, for the unimpeded play of those subtle influences which reveal something of our eternal destiny, for the teachings of 'a wise passiveness.' Keep your Sundays holy, and GOD will make them blest.

I will go further. I will ask you to keep also, as far as you can, those few other days which long custom has set apart out of our working time for meditation on the central mysteries of human life, the personal union of manhood with GOD on Christmas Day, the final revelation of man's sin and GOD's love on Good Friday, the assumption of all that belongs to the perfection of man's nature and man's life to the Father's throne on Ascension Day, and, I would gladly add, the glimpse which is given to us of what GOD had prepared for the close of sinless service in the Transfiguration. To reflect on such facts, such truths, calmly, resolutely, patiently, is to learn, as far as we can yet learn, what man is, what GOD is, what life is, what the world is:

> O world, as GOD has made it, all is beauty,
> And knowing this is love, and love is duty.

No one can question that we need to learn the lessons which are thus brought home to us, and they cannot be learnt in the hurry of business. They can be applied at all times, but they must be learnt in silence. And one who has learnt them in any degree will no longer dare to say, as has been said, that "prophets and "redeemers have rather consoled the fears than "confirmed the hopes of men."

He who believes "in GOD the Father who made him and all the world," will know that "all objects of all thought" speak to him of Divine wisdom and Divine love, and bear himself with noble reverence in the presence of every created thing.

He who believes "in GOD the Son Who redeemed him and all mankind," will know that he is bound to everyone who shares his nature by a fellowship in comparison with which every difference of race, or class, or position, or character, or possessions, is as nothing.

He who believes "in GOD the Holy Ghost "Who sanctifies him and all the elect people of "God," will know that every circumstance of his daily state is capable of receiving and reflecting the Divine glory, and that he need seek no happier conditions of service than those which his actual state supplies.

So it is that our Faith supports, extends, ennobles the highest desires by which we are visited, and brings peace while it stimulates endeavour; for it calls on all alike to be fellow-labourers with GOD.

Do you, my friends, obey the call with glad hearts. For youth the ways of life are still open. For youth enthusiasm kindles hope, and custom has not yet barred enterprise. The future is with you, and you can see what GOD would have it to be through your labour. Hold and hallow the place which is committed to you. Offer yourselves to the fulfilment of the least duties without misgiving, but accept no rest which leaves you without service. Be concentrated in the energy of personal action. Be diffusive in the unity of spiritual sympathy.

Already there are, I think, clear signs of a truer understanding, a deeper communion, between men and classes and nations than the world has yet seen, an understanding, a communion, which find their spring and their consummation in the Gospel. GOD bids you forward their advent according to your power. Can any office be nobler, any command more inspiring?

One of the greatest of German teachers said some years ago: "I see before my countrymen a "deep abyss, but above it shines a bright light. "Is it the dawn or is it the evening twilight?"

Shall we hesitate as to our answer now?

The light has grown brighter since Neander put the question, and in that light may we work as it grows onward to the perfect day.

OUR DUTY TO POSTERITY.

Not unto themselves, but unto you.
1 PETER i. 12.

PETERBOROUGH CATHEDRAL,
June 2, 1892.

Not unto themselves, but unto you: such is the Divine interpretation of the prophet's work. St Peter has described the earnest strivings with which the heralds of GOD sought to enter into the full meaning of the chequered message which they were charged to deliver, to give distinctness to the prospect of promised grace, to harmonise the conflicting images of suffering and glory which the Spirit brought before them, to fashion the portraiture of the Christ Who should endure and conquer death. And in answer to their anxious and fruitless questionings it was revealed to them—for the lesson is strange to human impatience—that their ministry was not for themselves, but for a later age; that they must bear the burden of perplexity and disappointment, of hope deferred and doubts unresolved, in the sure confidence that others would enter into their labours. And, indeed, such confidence brings all the light which we need for courageous endurance. The crown of service is to know that the service, barren, perhaps, for the moment, will bear fruit in after-time.

Thus the words of the Apostle are a voice of encouragement to all who catch a distant and interrupted vision of the later fulfilment of GOD'S will. The student and the seer may not be able to piece together the many fragments on which they look, but they can recognise that they belong to a glorious whole; they can gladly undertake labours which are directed to gain blessings not for themselves, but for their children; they can enter on the fruition of the larger life by confessing hopes which are beyond their attainment, and preparing for achievements of love which will be the joy of a later generation.

Not unto themselves, but unto you: this is the judgment which history addresses to us in recording the toils and aims of those to whom we owe our splendid inheritance in our National Church. They gave their best in thought and deed to the cause of GOD, and left the using to His wisdom. And while we, on our part, gladly acknowledge our debt to them by generosity proportioned to our means and our opportunities, GOD in His great love makes known to us that the works of a later time may bring blessing to those who have gone before. Through the salvation wrought in the fulness of the ages, it is His good pleasure still, as we believe, in the language of the *Benedictus*—most mysterious sign of the unity of our being—"to shew mercy towards our fathers."

The occasion for which we are gathered together constrains us to recall these far-reaching thoughts of inspiring obligation and active gratitude. Every work of loving faith is a spring of inspiration for those to whose care it is intrusted. We know what this Minster has been to many in the past. We know how it has borne for centuries an intelligible message to waiting hearts by the peculiar features of its structure; how it has symbolised the wide welcome of the faith by the amplitude of its unique portal; how it has expressed the self-devotion of service in the unity of the long nave, guarded through changing styles; how it has shown in the western porch that an urgent peril may be made the occasion of a fresh beauty; how it speaks to us in the southern spire of the loyal skill with which a master crowns the unfinished design of another with a work of matchless grace.

Thus the mediæval builders wrote their thoughts in their temples for our learning; and the lesson has not been unheeded here or unfruitful. Among the memories of this Minster none is dearer, I think, to those who love it, than that in troublous times, when in the judgment of sober men we seemed to be on the verge of a revolution, its guardians accomplished on a noble scale the work of restoration, which as a sign and a call has since quickened corporate Church life throughout our land. That work trained on the spot a school of artists and craftsmen of whom the city may be proud. To-day children complete the work of their fathers, and hand on the great tradition which they have received, shewing in new forms that faithfulness, life, hope are the unchangeable attributes of true art.

So it is that everything about us speaks of tender reverence for the work of our fathers and of confident trust in the work of our children. Here, in a peculiar sense, old and new meet together. And it is as shrines guarding the offerings of every generation that our great churches do their work, and bind age to age with natural piety, sacraments to us in a most true sense " of the grace of life," active in many parts and in many fashions. If we forget the past in the most generous and thankful enthusiasm for that which GOD has shewn to us, we shall not wisely serve the future. But in this Minster such forgetfulness is impossible. Change follows change, but all changes are harmonised by one unchanging life. The legend of Oswald, which connects Peterborough with my northern home, tells us in a noble parable how simplicity of devotion clothes the corruptible with incorruption. The arm hallowed by deeds of love can never decay. The fashion of this world passeth away, but he who doeth the will of GOD—who strives only to express His glory by thought and work—abideth for ever.

Such thoughts carry us forward. When it was my happy privilege to minister here, I was glad to speak once and again of our debt to the past. Now I wish to speak of our debt to the future. It is but another aspect of the same truth. For, as we contemplate our gathered treasures, we cannot but ask to what use we shall put them, and so we pass on to the wider question of the office which we are called to fulfil for our children.

The question needs to be pondered. The progress of human life imposes the duty of large forethought on each succeeding generation with ever-increasing force. Thought advances with accelerated motion. The expression of truth, the interpretation of life, must change with broadening experience. And this change is partly a growth and partly a shaping. Both processes are recognised in the Apostolic portraiture of the development of the Christian society. It is a body and it is a temple. It is the manifestation of an inner power of life. It is the result of calculated effort. We can distinguish, but we cannot separate, the parts of the twofold action. The body is built up and the temple grows. We may check or we may further the expression of the vital energy. We may, by wilful and impatient self-assertion, delay the end which even in our ignorance we desire; or we may by wise humility become in perfect devotion fellow-workers with GOD.

Under this aspect the work of the Church is prophetic. Its ministers are set to provide that under every change of circumstance the Divine idea of life shall be presented in conformity with the conditions under which it must be realised; to watch with dispassionate regard the currents of popular thought that they may prepare a natural welcome for fresh voices of the Spirit; to guard, to cherish, to develop that which in the Divine order will be the ruling idea of the next generation. They can—nay, if they are faithful, if they indeed believe that the society which they serve is the living organ of the living Spirit, they must do so. And just so far as they proclaim unweariedly the fact of the Incarnation they offer the interpretation not only of one phase of life, but of all being. In the discharge of this ministry there can be no idolatry of the past, and no presumptuous pride in the present. But there will be thankfulness for growth, and for the unexhausted power of growth. Yes, for the power of growth; for if humanity is, as Pascal said, a man who lives and learns for ever, the Church is the teacher of this undying man. The National Church is for us the teacher of the nation. And hitherto, however sadly we may reckon up its failures and faithlessnesses, it has never disowned its solemn responsibility; it has never ceased, consciously or unconsciously, in some measure to fulfil it.

The National Church has guarded among us in the past, in good report and in evil report, the true aim of education, the training of men, and not the training of industrial combatants, the formation of character, and not the accumulation of wealth.

It has brought from time to time the aspirations of the multitude to the test of the conscience and illuminated their concordance by fresh light from the source of all light.

It has reaped and garnered the harvests of every age, and kept them without preference for use in due season. It has shewn us the strength and the grandeur of corporate life in the Middle Ages; it has shewn us the awful prerogatives of the single soul in the individualism of the Reformation;

and now it is striving through all perplexities and divisions towards a fuller truth, towards the apprehension of the highest unity in which the indestructible fact of personal responsibility shall be combined with the adoring recognition of one life in Him in Whom all things are reconciled and summed up.

Nor will the striving be vain. We, indeed, shall not see how it will prevail, but we can in patience prepare the way for the crowning victory of faith which our children will win. And, even now, we dimly discern how this last idea of unity embraces "all objects of all thought;" how it extends to nature, to society, to mankind; how it fashions our view of creation; how it directs our mode of action; how it encourages us with the conviction that there can be no final loss, and leads us to recognise more and more that we are called to be fellow-workers one with another and all with GOD.

1. There is, I say, already among us a final perception of the unity of creation which it will be the health of our children to realise, a unity in Christ. Many of us have watched from the beginning the progress of the physical conceptions of the conservation and transformation of energy. We have apprehended with increasing clearness that nothing in the universe is isolated, and that

we ourselves enter into all of which we are conscious. We move falteringly, from point to point, to the deepest and the highest; and at last roused, elevated, baffled, we bring back the conviction, which Whichcote was never weary of affirming, that the mark of man is action, and not thought. The lesson is precious, both for guidance and for quickening. It saves the pursuit of knowledge from becoming selfish curiosity; and it saves the attainment of knowledge from becoming passive contemplation.

2. There is again among us a growing acknowledgment of the unity of society which it will be the strength of our children to realise, a unity in Christ. Every one speaks of the present tendency towards democracy. But there is a danger lest the outward political interpretation of the phrase should obscure its deeper spiritual meaning. The idea of democracy is not, if we look below the surface, so much a form of government as a confession of human brotherhood. It is the equal recognition of mutual obligations. It is the confession of common duties, common aims, common responsibilities. True democracy—and in this lies its abiding strength—substitutes duties for rights. This substitution changes the centre of gravity of our whole social system, and brings the promise of stable peace. It is not our work,

but the way in which we regard our work, which makes the difference between man and man. It is not the slave's task which makes the slave, but the slave's thought. Till the workman is proud of his work, till he sees and welcomes it as a social service, there can be no rest. But he will be proud of it, he will see its dignity, when he learns that as a member of Christ he serves the whole body in his least function, and shares the one life according to his capacity.

3. There is yet more among us a feeling after a unity of humanity, a vaster, fuller, enduring human life, which it will be the joy of our children to realise, a unity in Christ. It is not possible to regard the attitude of nations now one to another, even if Europe is an armed camp, without recognising that new forces are at work which make for a better understanding between them, which place in a clearer light their complementary endowments and offices for the enrichment of the race, which tend at least to subordinate temporary material interests to the common good, to control the political by the spiritual. The end, indeed, for which we have just prayed, "peace, unity, and concord among all nations," will not be reached at once, but slowly, step by step, with many relapses, it may be, and many falls. But it is in sight, and it is seen. The recognition of the

variety and the interdependence of forms of national life as contributory to the fulness of Christ is a new thing. If the Stoics spoke of the "members" of the race, it was without that sense of the One Head in Whom we are coming to see the spring and the support of the widest fellowship of mankind.

Such thoughts as these of an unrealised unity felt to be attainable, felt to correspond with the idea of creation given back to us in redemption, answer to the spirit of the age. They are in the air. They foreshew, that is, the truths which in the fulfilment of the Divine order are offered to us by the Holy Spirit. They convey the assurance of a living confirmation of the faith drawn from the deepening sense of the one thought fulfilled before our eyes in all nature and all history, of which the Christian creed is the final expression. They shew us how we can each in our measure hasten the time when the fulness of life shall be the common inheritance and the common joy of all. They point forward to the day when the kings of the earth shall bring their honour and glory into the city of GOD, a city which is the true Holy of holies. It is for the Church in the fulfilment of its prophetic office, even with imperfect and troubled knowledge, to welcome them, to give them shape, and to transmit them to the next age for the guidance and inspiration of its work.

The truths lie, as I have said, in the Gospel of the Incarnation. The urgent problems, the very dangers which rise before us, disclose in the central fact of all life—the Word became flesh—new depths of wisdom and consolation. We ponder the fact, in its unlimited range of influence, and the unity towards which we look in nature, society, mankind appears in a new light. We correct the false analysis that leaves GOD and the soul as the final elements in religion, and give to the world—to creation—its due place as the revelation of GOD'S working and the field of the soul's activity. We learn to rejoice more and more in the sense of dependence as bringing nobility to every labour, and in the devotion of service as checking all selfish ambition—

> Too great for haste, too high for rivalry.

We watch the instinct of sympathy passing from the class to the nation, from the nation to the race, for the completing of the fulness of the body of Christ. We discern that time belongs only to the human apprehension of the course of events, and in the disappointments of delay catch something of the patience of Him with Whom a thousand years are as one day. We do not yet

Our Duty to Posterity. 353

know the end—we have no power to know it—but we know the way—even Christ, Who is able to subdue all things unto Himself.

In that Presence we confess that the world is not a factory, or a warehouse, or a paradise of delights, but a sanctuary in which GOD'S glory can be recognised and His voice still heard.

It is not a factory in which every energy is to be absorbed in providing overflowing abundance of material supplies; for Christ bids us meditate on the abiding lesson of Nature—"Consider the lilies of the field, how they grow; they toil not, neither do they spin."

It is not a warehouse in which we can innocently pile up perishable treasures to feed pride and flatter the foolish heart with the hope of pleasures that will not be realised; for He sounds in our ears the inexorable warning—"This night"—when the darkness is felt—"thy soul is required of thee."

It is not a paradise of thoughtless delights while there are sick untended, strangers unwelcomed, prisoners unvisited on every side; for His judgment is addressed to us—"Inasmuch as ye did it not to one of these least ye did it not unto Me."

But in spite of every burden of toil, of ignorance, of weariness, of suffering laid on sinful man, it is a sanctuary, full of the glory of GOD, in which each believer offers the worship of life and the sacrifice of his whole being; for the Son of Man still fulfils His promise in this latest time while He says to His people by signs which faith can read, " Lo, I am with you all the days to the end of the age."

Oh! my friends, heaven is not so much another world as another view of this world, seen in the light of GOD, which through the Incarnation falls about us still. For the Incarnation enables us to trust the impressions which we receive, and fills them with a larger meaning. The Incarnation is the solid foundation—I know no other—of that knowledge which rises within the veil, and brings to things transitory an eternal splendour.

This light, this larger significance of things, this heavenly splendour of earth, this sense of opportunity, is even now borne in upon us on many sides, and it is the prophetic office of the Church to discern the signs of the fresh dayspring from on high, and prepare her sons to use the lessons of the new order.

It will be said that such ideas are mere dreams. If they are, I reply that it was one appointed sign of the outpouring of the Spirit in the last days that old men should dream dreams.

Our Duty to Posterity.

I reply that the ideas of one age are the laws of the next. Look back a hundred years, and you will feel the reality and the limitations of this truth. Great thoughts reveal to us our own capacity. We need them for the support of our spiritual life, as they come still ever fresh from the spring of all life; and, so far as they are truly embodied, man, made in GOD'S image, acknowledges that they correspond with his needs and with his aspirations. The highest *is*; we do not make it. The life *is*; we simply receive it, realise it, shew it forth in our measure. He who believes in GOD—Father, Son, and Spirit —can hope all things. He can look forward and know, and declare his knowledge, that through every seeming loss—and all progress must be through loss—the counsel of GOD moves on to its appointed end. And what an end—such as in some way we can call up before us by a contrast. The discipline of the old world issued in the fulness of time in the august fabric of the Roman Empire, the peace of man; the discipline of the new world, under which we are fashioned and labour, will issue in the kingdom of our Father, the peace of GOD, which it is our privilege to hasten.

In this sure trust we join with one heart in thanking GOD for all the gifts which His servants have gladly offered to-day for the service of His sanctuary. And the thanksgiving passes into a prayer that the material fabric in its renewed stateliness and beauty may help us better to worship in spirit and in truth.

Happy shall we be if those who come after us and see our works and ponder our thoughts shall say, "They who so wrought and thought in a season of sore trial strove to guard and cherish each germ of new life, to keep open each inlet of fresh light, to translate their faith into act, to use their resources in the endeavour to provide that the conditions of a true human life should be within the reach of every man, to rest in no attainment which left outside the pale of hope and fellowship one brother for whom Christ died. They could not, indeed, see the issues which they prepared; they could not interpret the perplexing signs of suffering and glory which marked the prospect of the future towards which they strained their gaze; but they trusted Him Whom they knew to be a living and a speaking GOD; they acknowledged their duty even when they deplored their failures; they scattered good seed often in tears, while we bring home in gladness the sheaves of their harvest; not unto themselves, but unto us did they minister thoughts of far-reaching hope, which we have seen fulfilled, and works of watchful sympathy, which have been for us the foundation of lasting fellowship."

Even so, O Lord, that in the great day he that soweth and he that reapeth may rejoice together.

APPENDIX I.

1. WALKING BY FAITH, NOT BY SIGHT.
2. THE CONDITIONS OF PROGRESSIVE REVELATION.

I.

WALKING BY FAITH, NOT BY SIGHT.

We walk by faith, not by sight.
2 Cor. v. 7.

ST MARY'S, CAMBRIDGE.

Ascension Day, 1880.

WE have grown accustomed through popular use to assume that there is a natural, a necessary, contrast between faith and reason, a contrast which many exaggerate into an antagonism. There is, however, in Scripture no foundation for such an opposition. In Scripture faith is opposed, not to reason but to sight, and reflection enables us to realise the importance of this contrast, which brings before us the essential conditions of our human life.

We walk by faith, not by sight. The fact and the phenomenon of the Ascension bring the truth vividly before us. The Life of Christ as it was fulfilled under the conditions of earth was necessarily limited. Even the Risen Christ, in His compassionate tenderness, revealed Himself to His disciples under the forms of time and space that they might be assured that nothing was lost in that glorious transfiguration by which He had entered on a new order. During the great forty days this lesson was taught and learnt through many significant signs, till the time came when *it was expedient that Christ should go away* and establish with His people a connexion not local but spiritual, not earthly but heavenly. In that interval of preparation the company of believers was trained to bear the last trial of leaving which is often the prerequisite of a closer presence. Then the Revelation of the Risen Lord was consummated by the final sign of a new life. The Life of the Word was with GOD before the world began, and by the Ascension the Incarnate Word bore the life of humanity to its goal with GOD. Thus the

Ascension was, so to speak, a loftier Resurrection. This was the fact of the Ascension; and the phenomenon in which it was presented was an eloquent symbol of the truth. There can of course be no higher or lower to Him who fills all things. The Fathers insisted on this while still they held the earth to be a level plain covered by the vault of heaven. The right hand of GOD, they said, is everywhere, *dextra Dei est ubique.* Yet to human eyes that bearing aloft, that intercepting cloud, spoke a message which the soul could interpret. Thenceforward the disciples were enabled to realise *a Christ not after the flesh*: to feel that as their Lord had lived through death, so this power of His life reached them wherever they were: to feel that the unseen is no strange realm, but the home of Him in Whom they are: to feel that an element of eternal meaning is added to each circumstance of our visible being: to feel that men are greater than they know, strong by touching the heaven which lies about them, sharers by the will of GOD in a present divine life.

And we too in this later age must take the blessing to ourselves. *We* too, as St Paul says, so far as we enter into the teaching of the Ascension, *we too walk by faith, not by sight.* Our thoughts, our efforts, our actions, that is, are guided, sustained, inspired, not by the superficial appearance of things, but by that which we are enabled to see beneath it with *the eyes of the heart.* The great phrase which has been repeated in the Christian Liturgies for seventeen or eighteen hundred years, *Sursum corda,* is a call, not to any local elevation of thought, but to deeper vision through which we can rest where the Spirit of GOD rests.

We walk by faith, not by sight. The context in which the phrase stands brings it into close relation with the Festival of to-day. The apostle is speaking of the outward trials by which he was beset, of the inevitable end to which he looked, of the continual processes of loss and decay which represent what we call life, of the supreme change of death by which we are separated from that transitory organization which we are tempted to identify with ourselves. There is, he shews, an abiding reality underlying this perpetual dying: there is a transfiguration of glory in that last falling away. The body is given us to be, not 'the tomb of the soul,' but the organ of its discipline, the promise, the sign of its eternal energy. To rest in the earthly body as the final expression of our powers is to miss the very end of our being. This body is the expression under present conditions of that which is striving towards a larger fulfilment. The sense of this nobler destiny gives meaning to the transitory shows of the world and reveals the joy which is born of sorrow. Therefore when we turn to the Christ in His glory we can be of good courage; we can keep hope fresh in the prospect of suffering which 'bids not sit, nor stand, but go,' in the prospect of dissolution which admits us to a new order, as knowing that *while we are at home in the body*, looking for nothing beyond, occupied and absorbed and satisfied with that which can have no continuance, *we are absent from the Lord, for we walk by faith, not by sight*.

But the words which thus refer primarily to the most momentous issues of our sojourn here have a wider, a universal application. They describe, as I have said, the conditions of all life. From first to last, from the dawning of personal consciousness to the richest triumphs of scientific imagination, in the interpretation of nature and in the intercourse of society, *we walk by faith, not by sight*. Faith is not the peculiar foundation of religion, but the absolute foundation of life. As soon as we move beyond our own consciousness, and the limitations under which its activity is realised, we are supported by faith. All life is directed by some view of the unseen and the future; and we enter the unseen, we anticipate the future by faith, and by faith only. The immediate impressions of sense are a starting-point, a suggestion, but no more. What we use, what we live by, is the meaning which, through long discipline, we have learnt to give to the symbols which we observe. We read, as it were, a vast book, determining with unwearied patience the value of each character, spelling out the complex message, but the thoughts which rise in the soul, as the words are slowly deciphered, are more than the writing which stirs them. And it is by these thoughts which we trust, by these thoughts which, when they have been tried according to our powers, we are made to trust, that we gain some image of the invisible, and test the fabric of our aspirations.

We walk, I repeat, not in religion only but in all life, *by faith, not by sight*. The statement is true of that which we know most directly of our own selves. No mystery can be greater to a man than his own person. He gathers unto himself the results of an immeasurable past and the hopes of an immeasurable future ; and all these he holds in a present which has no stay. He is indeed a riddle insoluble, in our present state, and there is not one of us, I suppose, who has not paused from time to time, startled and perplexed, to ask if all be not a dream. No doubt we put the question by at once, but it is only because we have faith, because we are so constituted that we cast ourselves upon the truth of things as those who know only in part, and who recognise the conditions of partial knowledge. So, as soon as we begin to think, the contradictions in our nature point us to some fuller form of being, and to this we reach forward by faith.

Thus it is when we look within ; and the conviction that the appearance is the occasion and not the object or the measure of knowledge is brought home to us still more clearly when we look without, to nature or to society.

Walking by Faith, not by Sight. 367

However much the truth may be overlooked, physical science is occupied with the invisible. It is the revelation of the invisible. That with which the student of nature deals is not the phenomenon, the appearance, but the fact which he is led to infer from it. He constructs the universe with atoms which no eye has seen or ever can see, and we rejoice in the vision of unimagined order which is laid open to us. He detects the presence of movements of exquisite sensibility in the inorganic masses which seem to us to be dead matter, and we rejoice in the presence of a life immeasurably vaster than we had known. He carries backward the lessons which he reads to-day, and 'the everlasting hills' unfold a record of progress which enlarges and ennobles our conception of the Divine counsel and of the Divine working. He carries these forward, and in doing so He teaches us with solemn emphasis that the earthly order which we can trace and follow is a limited episode in the order of existence, of which the end can be fixed in the scale of years. '*By faith not by sight*' is, in a word, the phrase which must be written over the most splendid achievements of the physicist.

Nor is it otherwise when we pass from nature to society. Here also *we walk by faith, not by sight.* How do we gain the sustaining, invigorating thoughts of patriotism, of friendship, of love? How scantly the appearance in itself justifies the devotion which we feel for country, for friend, for father or wife or child. We see a little and the soul uses in faith what it sees as the vantage ground for its own generous activity. It turns itself from nothing and it interprets, it transforms, all things. It dares to regard the strifes and the selfishnesses of classes and parties, and to look through them to that common enthusiasm which lies still and deep, drawn from long ages and ready for service in time of need. It dares to take account of the weaknesses and imperfections, and faults of those by whose fellowship it is strong. It dares to acknowledge the misunderstandings, the coldnesses, the failures of sympathy, the frailties of self-will, which cloud the sunshine of the family. It dares, in a word, to rest on faith and not on sight: to realise not by any creative energy but by a true power of divination that to which the appearance most imperfectly witnesses.

Yes, *we walk by faith, and not by sight,* in the face of nature and in the ordinary conduct of life. And shall we stop here? Shall we suppose that a power which has served us so far can avail us no more? If I endeavour to give distinctness to the vast realms of space crowded with worlds to which the astronomer directs me; shall I think of them as void, desolate, untenanted? shall I think of man as the only rational creature? shall I isolate him, as a solitary exile, on his lonely earth? If I follow the indications, which are pointed out now with growing clearness on every side, of vital energies active in all things about us; shall I picture to myself a world alive in all its parts and yet sharer in no common life?

Nay rather, in such measure as I am loyal to the principle which has guided me hitherto, I must welcome these largest facts as signs which in turn must be interpreted: I must reach forward to a spiritual sympathy coextensive with creation: I must feel after a life of which I can at the most acknowledge the reality without attempting to define the conditions: I must look with unwearied intensity of devotion to Christ who *ascended far above all the heavens that He might fill all things.* Nothing, it appears, can be less reasonable than to confine to humanity the intelligent apprehension of the universe, or to confine to men the sympathetic communing over its mysteries. Every discovery which extends our conception of material being in vastness, in variety, in beauty, is fitted no less to stir us with corresponding thoughts of spiritual existences. So we listen for the still small voice, the voice of life to life, when the turmoil of the elements is brought to rest.

Nor do we listen in vain; for here our Christian Creed meets us with the assurances which we need. Looking at it in the light of new thoughts we find that our uttermost aspirations are satisfied by its promises: we find that man is not alone in the universe; that he is not separated from the kingdom over which he is set: we find that the Incarnation, which was fulfilled historically on one narrow scene in a few short years, reaches in effect to all things *upon the earth or in the heavens*, we find that *all creation groaneth and travaileth in pain together* in no idle anguish but waiting for a new birth at *the manifestation of the Sons of GOD:* we find that we are come to the heavenly Jerusalem with all its hosts of angels and spirits of just men made perfect; we find that for us the veil which in old times hid the Divine Presence from the worshipper is rent asunder and that through the way of Christ's flesh we can enter into the holiest and gaze upon the glory of GOD: we find, that is, that when we have mastered the last lesson of nature, the last lesson of life, the Gospel bids us use them that we may enter a little further into the fulness of its teaching, and rejoice that every victory of imagination and reason is crowned with a divine blessing.

Here then, I believe, lies our characteristic duty to whom GOD has given the opportunities of intellectual culture. We are charged, we are encouraged, to *walk* and to shew that we *walk by faith, and not by sight*, to trust the thoughts which arise, I will say, naturally from what has been made known to us in our latest age, to bring them to the test of experience, to prove their power in the stress of action, to strain forward, rising in hope above the barriers of space by which we are separated one from another and from the objects to which our minds are turned.

And to this end we are not required to cast aside or to disparage any earthly endowments. St Paul's desire is not to *be unclothed* but to *be clothed upon*. He would not, that is to say, be divested of one imperfect faculty, of one fragmentary result of personal effort and conflict, of one portion of the long inheritance of the race; but he would have all completed, illuminated, harmonised, by some new power which belongs to the new order. The emancipation, the fulfilment, of the soul lies not in stripping it of the instruments through which it works, as Plotinus thought, who thanked God that he was not tied to an immortal body, but in adding that to its resources which reveals what is still wanting to complete the harmony of their results.

For we have not yet exhausted the conditions of human existence. The thought is a most helpful one, and I will venture to say it is most practical. We commonly assume, or rather we unconsciously imply, that our present powers are an adequate measure of being, that that which is insoluble by us now is finally insoluble, and so we are tempted to dissemble the difficulties which are really watchwords of faith. But for one moment let us in St Paul's image 'unclothe' ourselves. Let us realise if touch were our only sense, what our world would be. If to touch sight were added we should still be limited to our own experience: the gift of hearing first makes us heirs of the experience of our fellows. And shall we suppose that the wealth of GOD's blessings is exhausted by this endowment? As we ask the question our thoughts turn once again to the Revelation of the Risen and Ascended Christ, and in that we find the living signs which shew our true manhood, raised above its present conditions, the same and yet gloriously transfigured. We learn that the work of Christ, the Son of Man and the Son of GOD, was not redemption only but the inbreathing of that fulness of life, which man was created to attain.

Walking by Faith, not by Sight

In the prospect of this revelation we can therefore as Christians bear without anxious fears

> those obstinate questionings
> Of sense and outward things,
> Fallings from us, vanishings,
> Blank misgivings of a creature
> Moving about in worlds not realised,

and at last find in them

> the fountain-light of all our day.

For in some sense we all come to know a little of this last lesson of the Ascension, the passage from the seen to the unseen, from that which we can, as it were, touch and grasp to that which lies beyond the reach of sense. We have perhaps ourselves known Christ very near to us within the little range of our personal interests and thoughts according to our narrow vision, and then, when wider views are opened which claim to be considered, we lose, or rather we think for a moment that we lose that familiar companionship. We strain our eyes to heaven to catch some glimpse still of that which seems to have been taken from us, and Divine messengers turn our thoughts back to earth, to the Divine which lies about us. We look to this last manifestation of our Lord and Saviour, and once again we have to *walk by faith, not by sight*: to recognise that which may be handled and seen as a transitory sign of the eternal.

And the power of the Ascension reaches yet further. That revelation of the unimagined glory of human life enables us to rest in hope when at present the work of GOD is not made clear: to feel that behind every unnoticed sorrow and every passionate outburst of evil lies the Divine righteousness and the Divine love: to know that the moral difficulties by which we are most sorely perplexed come from the substitution of the appearance for the truth to which we have not yet reached:

to add to all things human that element of infinity which brings the Gospel into the very heart of life : to remember that when the Christ was parted from the disciples and from the world His hands were raised to bless, and that that blessing still rests over the scene of His redeeming work.

It is this conviction which we need above all to make our own. We need to see life as GOD made it, not as we have made it, to bring to light its spiritual side, to shew it in connexion with the unseen. That which is poor and sordid and trivial is changed when the light of heaven falls upon it. Such a blessing, the blessing of Christ, Born, Crucified, Risen, Ascended, is as universal as the sunshine if we will give it entrance, if we will find it entrance. And to give the entrance, to find the entrance, is our work, our work by the grace of GOD for ourselves and for others, as those who *walk by faith, not by sight*.

Brethren, I have ventured to touch on great thoughts : thoughts strange perhaps and in part obscure, but yet thoughts which concern us most nearly in our daily life. Great thoughts are more than thoughts. They are witnesses to us of that greater life to which I have pointed, that greater life of which the Ascension is the sign and pledge. They are not of our creation. They are the gift of GOD, and man can take them to himself and live by them because he was made in GOD's image.

As often then as the old words fall upon our ears, words which bring the power of the Ascension to our own failures, trials, thoughts, works, may the answer be ready by the Divine help. *Sursum corda*; that is the voice of Christ : *Habemus ad Dominum*; that is the voice of the believer which He makes possible.

II.

THE CONDITIONS
OF PROGRESSIVE REVELATION.

It is expedient for you that I go away; for if I go not away, the Comforter will not come unto you; but if I go, I will send Him unto you.

St John xiv. 7.

WESTMINSTER ABBEY.

8th Sunday after Trinity, 1888.

IT is expedient—it is profitable—for you that I go away.
No words could have been more unexpected or strange to
the apostles who had followed the Lord on His last journey
to Jerusalem, full of wondering hope, and faith, and love.
If He had said to them 'It is inevitable' or 'It is necessary' they might perhaps have schooled their stricken
hearts to submit to an irresistible force or to an inscrutable
counsel of GOD; but how could they understand that it
was '*expedient for them*' to lose a Presence which they
had known to be their stay, their light, their life? expedient that they should be left alone to face perils which
they had at least learnt to recognise? expedient that that
most blessed of all conceivable companionships, which
seemed little by little to bring them into a Divine fellowship, should be interrupted? expedient that they should
hear no more the voice which interpreted to them the
deepest thoughts of their souls and stirred them with a
generous passion of devoted service? The Christ whom
they beheld, and to whom they clung with reverent affection, had already taught them to know GOD as He had
never been known before, as the Father not only of a
world or a race, but of each childly soul: to know men as
men, as their true fellows not in death only but in life:
and could they without grievous loss be separated from a
Master Who had not yet completed their training?

So they must have reasoned; and indeed it would
have been easy to combat the Lord's assertion by the
surest results of ordinary human experience; but the
Divine method takes us beyond our common selves. For

us the importunate urgency of the present overpowers alike the past and the future. 'The world is too much with us' to leave free scope for the action of the invisible. We are swayed by that which is nearest. All life is a witness to the fact. We should naturally have supposed that the Gospel which meets man's needs would have found a universal welcome : that the duties which we acknowledge would at once have been embodied in act : that the certainty of death with its incalculable issues would have exercised a continuous and sensible influence over the whole conduct of life. As it is we know how passion, and prejudice, and momentary pleasure cloud the vision of the heart : how wide a chasm separates conviction and practice : how ineffective is the distant and the uncertain to sway and sustain our noblest resolves. So GOD trains us to realise the unseen. He offers us types of truth and duty by loving hands and then He leaves us to incorporate in our hearts what were before outward images and to change commands into principles. He interprets to us the perils and the remedies of our self-will. He takes from us helps which if continued might create presumption or paralyse endeavour. He enables us, if we trust Him, not only to endure but even to look for present disappointments, to confess that the way of sorrow leads to Him, to accept, not as an inevitable necessity but as a salutary discipline, that *we must through many tribulations enter into the kingdom of heaven*, that we are to *strive*—strive with the energy of unflagging effort—*to enter in through the narrow door*, through which an indolent and late desire finds no passage, that *he that loveth his life loseth it, and he that hateth his life in this world shall keep* (guard) *it unto life eternal.*

In this general sense we are prepared to find the explanation of the Lord's words ; and if we consider their exact form we shall be brought nearer to it. *It is expedient*, He says, *for you that I*—and the emphasis lies

Progressive Revelation.

upon the pronoun—*I* whom you have followed, *I* whom you think that you have known—*go away; for if I go not away*—here the emphasis is changed—if the separation, that is, is not outwardly complete—*the Comforter*, the Advocate, Who pleads your cause with prevailing power—*will not come to you; but if I go*—'go' to the Father on a Mission of love to fulfil My Work, and not only 'go away'—*I will send Him to you.* He will not only 'come,' but He will be my representative, and fulfil that which I have still to do.

Looking back with our fuller knowledge we can now perceive the literal truth of the startling paradox. It was expedient for the disciples that the Lord should go away. As long as He was with them in the flesh, they could only know Him under the limitations of earth. As long as death was unvanquished, and humanity unglorified, they could not have in Him that communion with GOD for which He was preparing them. As long as the Spirit was unsent by Him, the Divine word could not (may we not dare to say?) move the hearts of men with that completeness of sympathy which it has when it comes from Him who can *be touched with the feeling of our infirmities.* By going to the Father Christ substituted a spiritual for a local Presence. By offering Himself upon the Cross He maintained even through death the fellowship of humanity with GOD, and opened a way for believers to the innermost sanctuary in His own Blood. By taking His seat as Son of man, Priest at once and King, upon the Divine Throne, He gave validity to our human thoughts of spiritual things, and united the visible to the invisible in a sacramental union.

The Christ Whom the Apostles had known and Whom, like the eager Magdalene, they wished to keep, was subject to narrow bounds of place and time and form. How could He have been with them all when they were scattered throughout the world? how could He have continued to later generations the immediate teaching which He had given to them? how could He, Whose bodily Presence seemed to fill the capacity of man's devotion, have been recognised in His Divine Majesty? When the fire fell from heaven, they knew that it was expedient that He should go away. Thenceforward none could say in the loneliness of bereavement *Lord, if Thou hadst been here.* He was withdrawn from the cognisance of the senses that He might be *with them all the days*, and be seen in *the glory which He had with the Father before the foundation of the world.*

For the Christ whom the Apostles had known was not yet glorified. He had taken to Himself the infirmities of men. He had shewn weariness and grief and anger, and brought Himself closer to loving hearts by bearing the sorrows which He removed. Twice within the last few days His disciples had wondered at His tears by the grave of the friend whom He called back to life, and over the city which He committed to an irrevocable doom. There were still clouds, disharmonies, distresses unremoved. He went away, and then first His victory was found to be complete. His Cross was seen to be an altar and a throne. The preachers of the universal Gospel felt the full meaning of the words with which He heralded the Passion : *I, if I be lifted up from the earth, will draw all men unto Myself.*

The Christ whom the Apostles had known had spoken with direct and winning authority. Even His adversaries confessed that *Never man so spake.* Every word came to His hearers with such power of persuasiveness that they were constrained to obey Him Whom they reverenced for every grace of a perfect humanity. Thus there was danger lest they should be contented simply to receive what they were required to make their own by intelligent thought. He returned to the Father, and there they were enabled to realise within what had come to them before from without : to know that as a power of personal life which had been an overmastering influence: to win for themselves in spirit and in truth the fulness of devotion which had been in their earlier intercourse the response of earthly affection.

By following such reflections we can perceive that it was expedient for those who loved most that their Lord should go away. The very perfectness of His limited Presence hindered them from seeing or striving to see what was beneath and beyond. He went away, and nothing was permanently lost by that departure, though all was transfigured. The past grew luminous in the fresh light. The very sharpness of the pain of the Apostles, the intensity of their immediate distress, became a measure of their final gain. *Ye therefore*, the Lord said shortly after—'therefore' because through you a new order is to be born—*Ye therefore now have sorrow, but I will see you again, and your heart shall rejoice, and your joy no one taketh from you.* As the world is now, a season of anguish is the condition of the new life. So it was for the Christ: so it was also for the disciples. It was expedient for them that He should go away, that they might fulfil their glorious office and conscious of His inspiring Presence (*I will see you*) proclaim to the world the Risen and Ascended Lord.

It is expedient for you that I go away. The lesson of the words is not exhausted by their first and deepest fulfilment. They express a universal law. We have ourselves felt its action in our own experience: we can trace it in the education of the world. Again and again we have all found in the progress of years that we must surrender some belief which has been a stay to us, some thought which has been a beacon to our steps, some sweet fancies of life, and heaven, and GOD. We have seen, as we think, glories pass from the earth. But we know that it was expedient for us that they should go away. If we are true-hearted we shall confess that every loss has been the occasion for a nobler gain; that the one delight has faded away because it has faded into a more embracing joy: that friends, feelings, hopes, which are no longer with us as in the time of old are still present, with a purer and more habitual influence, if our days are duly 'bound each to each by natural piety': that the light which first made the solitary mountain peak a torch of dawn is the same light which floods the whole earth with the splendour of noon-day.

And as it is with individual life so is it also with the larger life of nations and churches.

The history of Israel is, under one aspect the history of the withdrawal of GOD from man. It is enough to mark three stages. *The LORD, we read, spake to Moses face to face, as a man speaketh unto his friend.* To the prophets again *He made Himself known more remotely in visions and spake unto them in dreams.* Then came the period of lonely growth in conflict with the nations when the psalmist sadly confessed that his countrymen *saw not their signs, and there was no more any prophet.* But still in each stage of the training of the people it was expedient for them that their King should, as it were, go away from them. The fact of a Divine Communion was first given as the inspiration of their growth; and then the glory on which Moses had desired to look was afterwards foreshewn *in many parts and in many fashions* through promises and chastisements, through victories and defeats, through exile and dispersion, through heroic achievements of faith and still more heroic and more effective sufferings, till in the fulness of time *the Word became flesh.*

Thus it was with Judaism; nor has it been otherwise in the growth of Christianity. The last question which the disciples are recorded to have put to their Risen Lord was *Dost Thou at this time restore the kingdom to Israel?* The answer came to them in the desolation of the Holy City; but from the ruins which entombed their first hope rose a Catholic Church. Once and again in later ages it seemed that the Faith would gain the sovereignty of the world and in each case what appeared to be disastrous failure became the occasion for an advance towards the Divine consummation. When the Roman Empire became Christian, the hosts of barbarian invaders overwhelmed it, and the faithful carried the treasures of the old civilisation into religious strongholds from which they shortly issued to win the new races to the Gospel. The advance of Islam filled Europe with one desire to regain for Christ by force of arms all that had been lost. The Crusaders, baffled and beaten back, gained through defeat rich fruits of conflict, and learnt to acknowledge the worth of men as men. The Bishop of Rome claimed to exercise more than Imperial power, and when his claim grew near acceptance the awakening of national life brought into play the independent factors which must contribute their mature differences to the harmonious fulfilment of humanity.

In the overthrow of the Empire, in the failure of the Crusades, in the dismemberment of Christendom, great hopes were shattered: great ideals were frustrated: great sorrows and anguish of disappointment were endured; and yet we know that it was expedient that the bitterness of apparent loss should be endured for the coming of a greater good.

But the trial is sorest when long-cherished opinions fail us: when that which our fathers have held to be truth, that by which the popular Creed has been shaped, can no longer be maintained. Then indeed GOD is teaching us some great lesson; and the simplest trust in Him, the most complete forgetfulness of ourselves, can alone enable us to bear it.

It is difficult for us to understand now how terrible was the shock to religious belief in the xvith Century when it became clear that the earth was not the centre of our System but a little planet revolving round the Sun.

It seemed in every sense as if the foundations of the world were fatally shaken. But we know that such fears were vain: we know that it was expedient for men that wider views of the vastness of the material universe should prepare them for a deeper perception of the work of GOD in Redemption: that they should be brought to see how He gathers up into one representative part, small in our eyes, the life, the destiny of the whole.

We have ourselves known something of the distress of pious minds when the records of the rocks were proved to extend the chronology of the earth immeasurably beyond the point at which the current interpretation of the Bible had fixed its beginning. It seemed as if the very Word of GOD had deserted us. But we know—do I not say what many here have felt?—that the spectacle of that slow fulfilment as we observe it, of the one thought of the Creator through the long ages supports us, as perhaps nothing else could support us, when we look upon what we deem to be the lingering progress of His counsel of love, and men ask us mockingly *Where is the promise of His Coming?*

And even now GOD is leading us to bear with more than patience what many feel to be another departure of a Sacred Presence from among us. Hitherto, and more especially in modern times, the Holy Scriptures in their literary, and not only in their spiritual, aspect have been isolated from all other books. They have been regarded as sudden creations, so to speak, without ancestry and without kindred, removed from the scope of historical criticism and guarded from the action of those forces which disturb the transmission of secular literature.

It is not surprising therefore that those who have not been specially led to study the problems of Biblical inquiry should be startled when they are told abruptly how many points of contact in form and substance our Scriptures have with other writings, how fragmentary they are, how intensely human in their structure and characteristics

Progressive Revelation. 383

how we can see them, as it were, built up out of different parts, witnessing to different sources, reflecting natural influences. It is not surprising that many devout believers should by admitting such conclusions seem to lose a Divine Presence in the light of which they have lived. Yet here also the Power, which they have clothed for themselves in a vesture of man's device, says with a voice of tender warning, *It is expedient for you that I go away;* and already we are coming to know the blessing which the withdrawal of old opinions discloses : to know, as we have never known before, that the Bible is a living Book, one in many parts springing directly in external form out of the manifold fulness of that human life to which it still speaks : to know that it offers the past to us not as a dead thing but as a clear mirror of eternal Truth : to know that in that record of the divine, marked in some sense with the traces of our infirmities, we can find the interpretation of GOD's present dealings with the world : to know that treasures painfully won in many and strange scenes of labour come in due time into His treasury : to know that in His sight nothing is futile and transitory, and that the least word which He addresses to us through men, is, if we will but let it tell its full message, able to give to us

Thoughts that do often lie too deep for tears.

For you will have noticed that in each departure on which we have touched, the departure was of that which was outward only. The spirit which those transitory forms embodied for a time remained unchanged. The Son of man is not farther from us, since He 'went away,' less tenderly compassionate, less presently helpful, but closer with an inward power. The vision of the kingdom of GOD has not grown dimmer or more uncertain because the shapes in which it was prematurely imaged have vanished, but it has been opened to us through defeats and revolutions with a larger and a deeper scope. The facts of the Gospel have not seemed less natural to men since we have learnt the position of our globe in the material universe, but fuller of meaning when we ponder the purpose of the Father *to sum up all things in Christ, the things in the heavens and the things upon the earth*. The course of Providence has not been made less intelligible, since we have been enabled to trace it back through incalculable periods of time, but rather enlightened by the same revelation of a continuity of progress in which slowness is no discouragement. The Bible has not lost one least fragment of its Divine authority since it has been placed in all its parts in vital connexion with the experiences and aspirations of growing humanity, but nearer to us and dearer with a sympathetic voice which answers to our own hearts.

In each case the Divine Message which said, It is expedient that this outward form in which men found a perfect or partial expression of religious feeling, according to the fashion of earth, should go away, has been justified. In each case the immediate sorrow has been the travail-pang of a nobler birth. In each case the present loss has been the opportunity at least of a greater gain, the transfiguration of the external into the spiritual. In each case men have been enabled to rise a little higher towards their goal, a little nearer to the last benediction of the Gospel, the benediction of the Risen Christ, the benediction of the later Church; the benediction which I pray GOD in His love to give to us, *Blessed are they that have not seen and yet have believed.*

Days of trial are days of insight. The darkness of great depths or of the night reveals the immeasurable glories of heaven which the sunlight hides. We welcome the lesson: and when some splendid vision on which we have rested passes from us, we endure with unshaken trust as *seeing the Invisible* to which it pointed, and say with trembling and expectant hearts: 'Yea, Lord, it is expedient that Thou shouldest go away: for so Thou wilt send the Comforter to us, to guide us into larger regions of the Truth.'

APPENDIX II.

1. LETTER TO THE ARCHDEACONS OF THE DIOCESE.
2. LETTER TO THE CLERGY AND LAITY.
3. LETTERS TO THE CLERGY.
4. WEARMOUTH DEANERY OF CHURCH WORKERS.

I.

AUCKLAND CASTLE, BISHOP AUCKLAND,
Advent, 1890.

MY DEAR ARCHDEACONS,

During the last six months I have endeavoured to use to the best of my power the many opportunities which I have had of becoming acquainted with the main outlines at least of Church work in the Diocese, and perhaps I may be allowed at this season to ask you to bring before the Clergy some points to which I wish to direct their attention, and on which I hope to have their counsel, if it may be, at some future opportunity.

But, before touching on other subjects, I cannot but express once again my heartfelt gratitude to GOD for the splendid inheritance of loyal devotion and spiritual unity in the Diocese which my predecessor has left for me to administer. May I be enabled through the help of all my fellow-workers to transmit it unimpaired to him who shall come after me.

The occasion of our Conference early in the Autumn led me to consider very carefully the ruridecanal organisation of the Diocese. Some improvements will, I trust, be made in the assignment of parishes to the several Deaneries, but I cannot express too strongly my sense of the value of the Deanery as an element in our Diocesan life. The Ruridecanal Chapters and Conferences serve effectively already, and they may be made, I believe, to serve still more effectively, to consolidate and inspire with energy every form of Church work. They are sufficiently large to include representative types of opinion and experience, and not too large to offer adequate scope for fresh thought and enthusiasm. Their deliberations can hardly fail to bring home to all who take part in them the vital importance of a full recognition in every parish of the manifold obligations of the National Church, while they leave each worker free to act according to the conditions of his own charge.

In this respect, I venture to express the hope that the Rural Deans will take such steps as they think best to secure that in every parish some provision may be made whereby the people may be encouraged to assist in

1. Foreign Mission work.
2. Home Mission work.
3. Religious Education.
4. Social Progress (Temperance, Purity, Recreation).

Contributions to Diocesan work under the second and third heads may be made most conveniently through the Diocesan Fund.

Circumstances will determine in each particular case the relative importance of special objects, and the central society through which they can best be sought. But the healthy vigour of the Christian life requires that all four groups of work should find some place in our scheme of common service, and the comparison of different methods of action gives to all the workers a larger vision and a more intelligent sympathy.

One thing, however, is necessary that our work in each region should be done distinctly as the expression of our Faith and on the lines of the National Church. In this way we shall be, I believe, best able to advance the great causes of truth, purity, and righteousness, in which we welcome as fellow-labourers those who are not included in our own Communion, and to profit ourselves by the spiritual force which they embody.

In each department which I have marked much re-

of Diocesan work. 389

mains to be done before we have even apprehended our duty as English Churchmen. I will mention a few details under the several heads which suggest materials for reflection.

1. There are still forty-four parishes (out of about two hundred and forty) from which, so far as appears, no contributions are offered for the support of Foreign Missions; and the whole amount which is contributed to the Mission cause is (may I not say?) confessedly inadequate to the resources of our own Diocese, even if the sum be judged by the standard of other Dioceses. But I should be unwilling to acquiesce in such a standard. We have not as a Church realised at present, in any practical sense, our duty towards India and the native populations of our own Colonies. On these fields no other Christian society can share our responsibility, however generously they may labour to advance the cause of Christ throughout the world. It might be said, not without truth, that our most prominent missionaries are our sailors, and how little we have yet done to prepare and discipline them for their inevitable office.

2. The peculiar circumstances of the Diocese secure for us an unusually large supply of Clergy in proportion to the population. This provision, which is due to no efforts of our own, imposes upon us the obligation of helping less favoured districts; but hitherto the claims of the Home Mission Societies have not received among us that cordial acceptance which they deserve.

At the same time, as far as I can judge, the character of our population, both in the densely crowded colliery villages and in the dales, requires a large development of lay work, and especially of voluntary lay helpers. The scheme of Lay Evangelists which was most happily framed by my predecessor, is as yet established only in four Deaneries. It will, I trust, be soon extended throughout the Diocese; and I specially commend this subject to the consideration of the Ruridecanal Conferences. Cases of temporary failure in the past will suggest important lessons in remodelling the work; and here even more than elsewhere enthusiasm is essential for a leader. The election of lay representatives to the Conferences next Easter will give a favourable opportunity for securing for a considerable period the services of those who are best able to contribute most effectively to the furthering of this and other forms of lay work.

3. In addition to the provision which is already made for directing and testing the religious instruction given in Elementary Schools, some provision ought also to be made for the higher religious education of those who have left school. The lectures of Canon Talbot in part supply this want, and their educational value will be greatly increased if classes for private study in connexion with his syllabus are formed at each lecture centre. A series of lectures on the general Outlines of English Church History might be drawn up with very great benefit. Nothing would furnish a more natural and effective element in Church Defence. Accurate positive instruction given in quiet times is a better safeguard than the most brilliant controversial efforts made in seasons of excitement. Our aim must be to give knowledge and conviction of the truth and not simply to silence an opponent. There is also a want among us, as far as I can ascertain, of connected instruction in the elements of Christian Doctrine. For this purpose use might be made of catechising in church. It would be possible to draw up a brief summary which would ensure the proportionate treatment of different topics, and guide the class in their preparation. Above all care should be taken in making arrangements in every parish for a wide and continuous study of Holy Scripture. Teachers and taught alike will learn most surely from the prophets and apostles to win their souls in patience.

It may seem strange if I place open churches among

the instruments of religious education; but I do so with a deep conviction of the power of their influence. An open church is a school of reverence, an impressive lesson on the Divine Presence. The lesson will need, indeed, some illustration and enforcement from the parish priest, but it can, I am sure, be made effective to the simplest worshipper, and I do not know where a poor man can elsewhere find a quiet meeting place with GOD fenced round with solemn memorials and guarded from external distraction. We have not, indeed, ourselves yet learned to use our churches habitually as places for brief meditation and refreshment, but the hurry of work is forcing us to recognise the need which they satisfy; and before long, as I trust, we shall be eager to make known to others, whose need is greater than our own, what we have found in the silence of the House of GOD through private thought and prayer.

4. The experience of a long and busy life has pressed upon me the urgent necessity of approaching social questions from the spiritual side. It is the business of the clergy to indicate to their people the Christian ideal. The duty was never more paramount than at present when power is being more and more widely extended. We do wrong to our Faith when we seek to limit its application. Nothing lies beyond the scope of its beneficent application. It points us to the highest aim, and inspires us with patience in the effort to approach it. We can bear delay if we know that we are moving towards our true end. I ask, therefore, that our Clergy should endeavour to lead their hearers, by appeals to reason rather than to feeling, to extend to the relations of nations and classes the principles which are universally admitted now in the relations of men to men. Arrogance, self-assertion, cupidity, do not become virtues when they are displayed on a vast scale. Perhaps we have yet to learn that for nations, as for men, the way of duty is the way of service.

To descend to humbler questions. Popular amusements open a wide field for inquiry which we are bound to examine. Cruel sports, gambling, and the like, are perversions of instincts which must be disciplined and satisfied; and I hope to learn, through the experience of others, how far music, gardening, gymnastics, &c., are severally fitted to supply that healthy recreation which corresponds with the conditions of labour among us. More especially I desire to know how best we can guard and strengthen the ties of family life. Many things at present threaten the sanctities of home where they still have a place. Our part must be, in trust on the Gospel which is committed to us, to establish them where they seem to be excluded.

The varied activities to which these reflections point call for much greater resources in the form of Libraries, Institutes, Mission Rooms, &c., than we possess at present. The sense of the want brings into prominence a forgotten duty. As a Church we have neglected the principle of proportionate almsgiving. We have grown accustomed to trust to the generosity of the rich to supply that which ought to represent the effort of the whole body. In this respect we have fallen far behind other religious societies among us. We have received from our fathers great gifts, but their liberality is an example to us, their children, and not a final absolution from all sacrifice. If we all were to set aside a tenth of our income as not our own, we should not, I believe, find ourselves in fact poorer.

But our Faith demands an offering not only of our substance but also of our labour. Every true Churchman must be a Church-worker. There is room for all and there is need of all. All will not be fitted intellectually or spiritually for the same work, but every member will have some office in the body. To fulfil this he must be carefully prepared. Meanwhile whole groups of workers are as yet unused: we have not made it a rule to commit

of Diocesan work. 393

to men of business the details of parochial finance, in which they can find exercise for their trained experience. We have not secured the help which our artisans can give in factories, and shipyards, and pits, and mines. Here they can do a work which no others can do ; and we must by every means claim the service from them. For the energy of Church life we need, in other words, on every side a much wider combination of servants of Christ than we have yet formed. As this grows, the sense of cooperation will bring enthusiasm, and it will bring also the discipline and the strength of fellowship.

What I have said will mark, I think, sufficiently clearly the different directions in which I desire to obtain, as time goes on, the counsel and active help of all those for whom and with whom I am set to work. The contemplation of the facts of life and of the facts of our Faith will teach us forbearance ; and, more than this, they will inspire us with sympathy. If we quietly consider in the sight of GOD, as the Ember days come round, our promises and our commission : if we gather together in each Deanery at least once a year to meditate on our aims, our failures, our needs, our opportunities, on all that GOD has wrought through us, and to offer ourselves again for our Master's use ; we may hope for a continuance of His blessing. When I came to the Diocese, it was my joy to be assured that the clergy were of one heart and soul ; my prayer is, to repeat what I have said, that I may be enabled to guard that unity for my successor strengthened by a continuous fellowship of service.

Believe me to be,
My dear Archdeacons,
Yours most faithfully,
B. F. DUNELM.

The Venerable
  The Archdeacon of Durham.
  The Archdeacon of Auckland.

II.

TO THE CLERGY AND LAITY OF THE DIOCESE OF DURHAM.

My dear Friends,

The great seasons of our Christian year seem to invite from time to time the expression of thoughts which, however familiar, yet require open acknowledgment if they are to work their full effect among us. While therefore it is impossible for me to meet face to face everyone over whom spiritual oversight has been given to me, I gladly use the opportunity of the approach of Lent to seek such spiritual intercourse as is possible with those to whose service I have been set apart, that we may labour together with one heart and one soul in evergrowing zeal and charity for the promotion of the glory of GOD and the edifying of His people.

In Advent 1890 I called attention to some forms of Diocesan work in which there appeared to me to be room for closer and wider fellowship amongst us, and I acknowledge most gratefully the generous and thoughtful spirit in which the suggestions which I then made have been received. A Diocesan Mothers' Union and a Diocesan Missionary Union promise to make experience and enthusiasm wherever they exist among us available for approaching urgent problems of Christian duty at home and abroad with concentrated force; and I cannot but

Lent Thoughts. 395

hope that the Union of Church workers in the Rural Deanery of Wearmouth will shew how Churchmen can fulfil, through active co-operation, without waste and without uncertainty, the services which they owe to the nation.

I do not wish to dwell on any of these topics now. I wish rather to touch on some simple truths affecting our spiritual growth, to which I think that our thoughts may profitably be directed during the coming weeks—Retirement, Meditation, Family Prayer, the Confession of our Faith, the Presence of the Holy Spirit. We all need to reflect on these things. May GOD bless our reflections to ourselves and to all those whom we influence.

(1) Everyone feels and in word deplores the hurry of modern life. The days are crowded with engagements; and we seek to fill with excitement whatever intervals of leisure may be left to us. We are afraid to be alone, to be silent, to be ourselves. "The world is too much with us." Under the pressure of constant occupation we borrow our opinions, our arguments, our standards, our rules of conduct. We have no time, so we think, to place ourselves, calm and receptive, in the presence of the unseen realities which lie behind the transitory phenomena of life. We shrink from the solitude in which GOD speaks. And still our faculties, our opportunities, our difficulties, our temptations, are ours alone. The responsibility of dealing with them is ours. We cannot live our proper life either at random or by tradition. All alike need to look to the eternal in quiet moments with the eyes of their heart in order that they may see what their life is. And all can command the inspiring vision. Time is no measure of spiritual effort, or of spiritual experience. The discipline and the blessing of retirement can, if it must be so, be found in the crowd. But there are few of us who are unable to command brief occasions when we may listen in the still church—for our churches, I rejoice to know, are

more and more commonly left open throughout the day—
or under the clear sky, for voices which the waiting soul
will not fail to hear. Is it not possible for us to use such
occasions in the coming Lent with more definite and steady
resolution?

(2) Retirement—self-withdrawal from earthly anxieties—calls out meditation. Life is not easy. It appears
to be a Divine law that the difficulty of a duty increases
with its importance. The sense of the importance of the
issue, when it is once realised, sustains the vigour of
endeavour. But we must see our own duty first for ourselves as in the presence of GOD, and then seek the power
to fulfil it. Our chief dangers lie not in gross sins but in
things relatively wrong, things which for us are not "of
faith." What we require to know is not the Divine will
generally, but the Divine will for us. This knowledge will
not be gained all at once. Each attainment brings the
promise of a larger view. The question, What is life for
us? will receive an answer always new and always old.
Life is in every part an offering to GOD and to men in
Him. The application of this truth is the one test of
Christian labour and Christian recreation. If we abide by
it we have within our reach a power of devotion, of supplication, of thanksgiving, of praise, which grows through
use. We have the consciousness of a living faith. But
we may never with impunity cease to ask ourselves "What
our intention is?" On this point at least we cannot be in
doubt. Do we sincerely "desire to please GOD in all
things?" or do we acquiesce in imperfection? Our common
business is the staple of our life. This, and not anything
added to it, is our appointed sacrifice.

(3) Under this aspect Family Prayer is revealed in a
new light. It brings most solemnly before us the fact
that whatever is highest in the Christian hope is for all.
It affirms and consecrates the social foundation of life.
It teaches us to find the bond of fellowship in that which

is wider than ties of blood, or natural affection, or kindred tastes, or like offices. It claims as the one prevailing force for the discharge of common duties, "*in the name of the Lord Jesus.*" It claims as the one dominant end of the most ordinary acts, "*to the glory of God.*" Such thoughts, if we ponder them, are even startling in their far-reaching consequences. And yet we see at once that they are included in our Faith, and that we are bound to ponder them. They are the foundation on which a Christian household rests. And if, as I believe, it is through the family that we must look for the ennobling of our national life, for the quickening of the spirit of brotherhood, by the recognition of the paramount obligations of mutual services, they demand our attention now with impressive power.

(4) The social confession of our Faith, so far as it is sincere, passes into a personal, continuous confession. St John, we shall remember, finds the proof of the presence of the Spirit not in mere belief in Christ, but in the open acknowledgment of Him. The review of a day or of a week may well lead us to ask, not without sad misgivings, "How would men know that we are Christians?" Is there anything in our tone or temper or aims or conduct which constrains those who do not share our Faith to recognise that it is a power over us and in us? If it has not given us new convictions as to our relations to our fellow-men, as to the use of our possessions, moral, intellectual, material, can we be said to really hold it? If it exercises no restraint, if it supplies no guidance, if it kindles no aspirations, if it supports no endurance, if it brings no strength, what does it mean for us? We cannot be Christians in fragments. Christianity finds expression in a Christian life, and not simply in Christian acts. There is an infinite difference between failure and acquiescence in failure. It is not humility but indolence which accepts a low standard. If we deliberately live below our calling it is sin. We shrink in-

stinctively from hypocrisy; but it is no less hypocrisy to dissemble the good desires by which we are possessed than to affect devotion which we do not feel. Our Faith—we must dare to say it, with whatever shame it may be—lays upon us great obligations and offers us great resources. The Lord says to us, if we are His disciples, " *Ye are the light of the world; ye are the salt of the earth.*" Such a commission constrains us to inquire importunately, till our souls return some answer, What have we done, what are we doing, to scatter the heavy clouds of selfish materialism which hide the dignity of life? What have we done, what are we doing, to bring home to men the Gospel of the Risen Christ, by which things transitory and corruptible are invested with an eternal glory?

(5) We think of ourselves, and our hearts fail us. We look round and find no help adequate to our needs. We do not—this is the secret of every failure—believe in the Holy Ghost. Our controversies, our perplexities, our restless searchings in the past, our timorousness, all combine to condemn us of want of faith in a living, acting, speaking GOD. There is much religiousness among us; there is a widespread and effective reverence for holy things; there is a vague confidence in a Providential government of the world; but there is little of the courage of a Divine fellowship. Yet the Paraclete abides with us, and is in us. These also are "times of Christ." GOD was never nearer to men than now. Our fuller knowledge of the general laws of His working tend at first to make us pause short of Himself. It fills us with wonder and submission. But when we reflect we find that wonder and submission bring us to Him with humbler confidence when He calls us to be His fellow-workers. "Physical science itself," as it has been admirably said, "becomes to us a Jacob's ladder, whose foot indeed rests upon earth, but the angels of GOD are ascending and descending upon it, and the Lord GOD stands at its summit." "Heaven

lies about us" still, and as we turn heavenward light falls on our darkness, and weakness becomes strength. This then is the truth which I commend above all others to the patient, resolute, open contemplation of all who desire to fulfil the vows of their baptism, the Presence among us of a living Spirit. He is, we profess, "the Lord, the Giver of life"; and He is this not in some remote sphere but here and now. Do we then from day to day, in our work and in our rest, look to Him, offer ourselves to Him, listen for His voice, withdraw nothing from His purifying influence, and confide in complete self-surrender upon His unfailing grace?

If by the help of GOD we are enabled during the coming weeks to ponder in due succession such thoughts as I have indicated, to realise their meaning for ourselves, to turn their lessons, as we may have opportunity, into deeds, to sound the depths of our needs and of our Faith, then Easter, I cannot doubt, will dawn upon us with a new fulness of hope.

So may *the GOD of hope fill you with all joy and peace in believing that ye may abound in hope, in the power of the Holy Ghost.*

Your most faithful Servant and Pastor,

B. F. DUNELM.

AUCKLAND CASTLE,
  Septuagesima, 1892.

III.

TO THE CLERGY OF THE DIOCESE.

AUCKLAND CASTLE, BISHOP AUCKLAND,
March 3rd, 1892.

(1) MY DEAR SIR,

You will, I think, agree with me in thinking that it is our duty in the present time of great anxiety, when our chief industry is threatened by serious dangers, to request the prayers of our congregations that it may please GOD to grant to all on whom rests the responsibility of counsel or action in regard to the matters now in dispute such a spirit of forbearance and considerate wisdom as may avert the national calamity which hangs over us.

As Christians, we know and confess that one class cannot gain by the loss of another. The true gain of one must in the end be the gain of all: the loss of one the loss of all.

If we meditate on these unquestionable truths in the presence of GOD, I cannot doubt that the Holy Spirit will teach us how we may each do something to give practical effect to them at the present crisis.

I have not, as far as I can learn, any authority to issue a prayer for general use. But if the request be made publicly, our Common Prayers will furnish abundant opportunities for fulfilling it.

May the GOD of love and peace answer the prayer of faith for the blessing of us all.

Yours most faithfully,
B. F. DUNELM.

(2) MY DEAR SIR,

The continuance of the strike during these weeks which are set apart for solemn reflection cannot but have given a special character to our self-examination, and have led us to consider how far we, each, in our several positions of authority or dependence, through what we have done or left undone, have contributed to bring about the state of mutual distrust which makes our unhappy divisions possible.

The Services of Good Friday seem to me to invite us to give a united expression to the feelings which have thus been stirred in our minds; and I hope that you will request your congregation to join in them with a devout remembrance of our present anxiety and distress.

The season constrains us, while we refrain from judging our neighbours, to judge ourselves with keen sincerity. So looking into our lives we shall all, I believe, without distinction of rank or place or occupation, find reason to confess before GOD

- Our forgetfulness or disregard of the peculiar infirmities and temptations and trials of classes of men different from ourselves;
- Our neglect of habitual intercession, as masters or servants, workmen or employers, one for another;
- Our self-seeking and self-assertion in taking undue advantage of our superior strength or knowledge in dealing with those relatively weak or ignorant;

Our want of charity and patience in thought and word in judging the plans and motives of others.

Conscious of these widespread sins of omission and of act, we shall pray for

A more effectual sense of kinsmanship between the children of one Father in heaven;

A present sympathy with those who share with us the blessing of one Redemption;

A readiness, if need be, to suffer for others, and to honour all men for their work's sake.

And at the same time we shall add to our confessions and prayers, thanksgiving to GOD for the blessings which He has given to us during the last fifty years:

For the improvement in the material and moral conditions of labour;

For the opportunities of education open to all;

For the large increase in the provision for pastoral care and worship;

For the general respect for law and order amongst us.

It may be that while we thus regard, humbly and patiently, in the light of the Cross, what GOD wills for us and what He has already done, we shall be enabled to learn, even through our present sorrows and disappointments, a little more of the mystery of our fellowship in One Body, and to gain a fuller confidence one in another, as workers together for the establishment of the kingdom of GOD on earth. To acknowledge this fellowship and this common mission is to find the source and the support of lasting peace and concord.

Your faithful fellow-servant,

B. F. DUNELM.

AUCKLAND CASTLE,
Fifth Week in Lent, 1892.

AUCKLAND CASTLE,
June 2nd, 1892.

(3) REVEREND AND DEAR BROTHER,

I shall, I am sure, give expression to your own desire in requesting you to ask your parishioners to offer their humble and hearty thanks to GOD for our happy deliverance from the strife by which the Diocese has been long afflicted ; and to pray that we may all hereafter be enabled through His help to set forward more effectually than before the cause of brotherhood and love, by which we are taught that Christians should be known.

Yours most faithfully,

B. F. DUNELM.

IV.

(1) LETTER TO THE CHURCH PEOPLE OF SUN-
DERLAND ON THE RECENT MISSION.

> AUCKLAND CASTLE, BISHOP AUCKLAND,
> *Nov.* 21*st*, 1890.

MY DEAR FRIENDS AND FELLOW-WORKERS,

The great Meeting at which I was allowed to be present last night shewed clearly that you have been deeply moved by the Mission which has now been completed. But a Mission is a beginning and not an end; and, in proportion as you have felt in the past year and in the past week the power of tender human influence and the reality of Divine help, you will be anxious to extend to your fellow-townsmen the fruits of your own experience. Your thankfulness will naturally seek some outward expression. You have discovered, if you did not know before, that service is a necessary element in the fulness of Christian life. You will ask therefore what you can do; for every Churchman must be, according to the measure of his opportunities, a Church worker. I will not attempt to answer the question directly. Your appointed Ministers will advise you from their knowledge of your character and position as to the special duties which you can severally best fulfil. I only ask that you should place some part of your time and endowments at their disposal. State simply what you can offer, and leave with them the arrangement of your task.

It may be that very many of you can spare only a little thought or labour for direct service. Bring then that little gladly, as knowing that the greatest effects are produced by the accumulation of small actions. You are severally members of Christ. Nothing more is required of anyone than the fulfilment of his peculiar function, however humble; but that is required for the healthy energy of the whole Body.

The office of the Church we must remember is social no less than individual, to prepare and to hasten the Kingdom of GOD. Nothing that concerns the true life of men lies without the scope of its spiritual activity. As the Body of Christ it aims by the inspiration of the Holy Spirit at continuing the furtherance of His work Who *went about doing good.* For this end the active ministry of every part is requisite.

But while I ask for some special service from every Churchman, in order that the whole society may discharge its duty towards the world, I ask for no more than each one can render naturally and certainly. Enthusiasm often prompts a fresh labourer to undertake more than his proper duty; and before long, failure brings lasting discouragement. Let each one then be quietly assured as to his ability before he undertakes his work; and in this case he may hope that capacity for service will be increased by exercise.

Some special offering is claimed for the consecration of each life; but beyond this there is also the spontaneous confession of Christ in and through life. Every occupation offers occasions for witnessing naturally to what we know, and using our Faith as an influence to check open manifestations of evil in word or act. In this respect we greatly underrate, unless I am mistaken, both our obligations and our power. A simple and unostentatious affirmation of the claims of purity, temperance, and righteousness calls out a sympathetic response which, as far as my experience goes, surprises him who has the courage to make it.

Above all I venture to press upon every Church-worker the duty of deepening both the spirit and the signs of fellowship with all who are devoted to the same service. Association not only increases but multiplies our resources; and at the same time it enlarges our spiritual vision, and brings that peace in the midst of our superficial diversities which flows from the sense of Christ's Presence with all our fellow-workers.

It is more than twenty years since I pleaded at Harrow for some simple fellowship of "brethren and sisters of the common hope." When from time to time I have pleaded for it since, it has seemed to me on each occasion to be nearer attainment. As I looked on your Hall, full from floor to roof, I could not but feel that it might perhaps be GOD's will that it should be formed within the limits of your own town for a victorious conflict with the evils which you see around you in the strength which you have lately felt.

But, however the Divine counsel shall be accomplished, I ask your prayers that I may be guided and supported in my heavy charge, *being confident* at the same time *that He which began a good work in you will perfect it until the day of Jesus Christ.*

Your most faithful Servant in our Common Faith,

B. F. DUNELM.

Union of Church Workers. 407

(2) SPEECH IN CO-OPERATIVE HALL, SUNDERLAND, JUNE 9, 1891.

MY FELLOW-WORKERS,

I have to thank you from my heart for the opportunity you have given me this evening, of addressing this large meeting on a subject, which has been in my mind since I came first to the diocese; and I can honestly say, that to be allowed to be face to face with such a body of Church Workers, as I meet to-night, is an ample reward for a year of anxious labour.

The day and the place of meeting alike offer us good omens for our work. The day, as some of you may remember, is St Columba's Day, the anniversary of the day on which I was allowed last year to complete one fragment of the work of my predecessor, and consecrate the great Church on the other side of the river. Our place of meeting again is the Co-operative Hall, and co-operation seems to me to represent in economics a great and universal principle—a principle which we trust to carry this evening into a new region and wider applications—the principle of social sympathy. We trust to be guided to do our Church Work through the truest, the fullest, and the most energetic co-operation.

This lesson of social sympathy is, I fancy, one of the chief lessons which you learned in the late great Mission, and it is the lesson to which we wish to give a practical shape to-night. In that Mission you learned, as perhaps you had not learned before, what is the inspiring power of the principle of social sympathy. You felt what it could do then for a time, and you were led to ask why it should not be equally energetic abidingly, and that is what we wish to make it now. The enthusiasm which was stirred then quickened a spirit which has brought to us a great opportunity, and we must try, GOD helping us, to use the opportunity to the uttermost.

As Christian co-operators in this highest sense, we are brought to the very central thought of our Faith. The fact of the Incarnation, which is the life of our Creed, places us very close one to another in all that is highest, however much we may be separated by the more trivial circumstances of life. In virtue of that fact our Faith is social. We can feel then, at once, when we come to reflect, that service is a necessary element in every Christian life. It is through service rendered to others that we can secure—that we can alone secure—our own personal growth. And, this being so, my friends, surely it must strike us with wonder to see the overwhelming disproportion between the number of those who bear the name of Christ, and the number of avowed Christian workers. I speak, of course, only of our own Communion; but certainly at present we have not, in our great National Church, claimed from every Churchman the fulfilment of his own proper work. We must claim it. We cannot rightly rest till every Churchman—as I have said again and again, and I will not be ashamed to repeat the words as long as I am allowed to labour among you—till every Churchman is a Church Worker.

We need then some fellowship which shall bind together all workers of all classes, all men and women, in their endeavours to do, in the words of our Communion Office, "all such good works as our Father has prepared for us to walk in." Yes, my friends, let us notice that phrase: "The good works which our Father has prepared for us to walk in." The work is not of our creating or choosing; it is of our heavenly Father's preparing. All that is required of us, that we on our part may accomplish it, is, that we offer ourselves, our souls and bodies—and not some fragment of our substance only—for the doing of it. And therefore those to whom, in different degrees, the oversight of the Church is given, cannot be satisfied till all Church workers, in whatever position

Union of Church Workers. 409

they may be placed, are recognised as ministers of the Church.

The citizen, we have either learnt or are rapidly learning, is the servant of the State, and is bound to use all his endowments for the common good. How much more, then, is the Christian bound to yield that which GOD has committed to him—position, or wealth, or intellect, or influence, or character—for the good of the Church, the living Body of which he is a member? There is a difference, of course, between the work of the layman and the work of the clergyman; but there is not this difference, that the one works and the other does no work. The layman, let us remember, has received his own proper ordination, when in Confirmation the Bishop's hand was laid upon him. He has been solemnly set apart—appointed in GOD'S own way—to discharge his office in the Church; and as we humbly trust, GOD has in this ordinance pledged to him the strength to accomplish that which it is his duty and his privilege to do. Laymen and laywomen are bound to work. And in our experience of life, we all know by this time, how much we need the counsel, the experience, the support, the enthusiasm of all. The life of the whole is shewn at each point of the living body, and, if the Church is to fulfil its true mission to the world, we cannot dispense with the Church-wide witness of life. The Apostle St Paul could appeal to his Corinthian converts, who had only lately received the Faith, as declaring openly in the eyes of men as a living "letter" what the Faith was; and dare we, to whom the office of proclaiming the Gospel is committed, dare we stake the truth of our Gospel upon the lives of those who profess to have accepted it?

The circumstances of the time, as I have already often said, make this witness of the whole Christian body of vital importance. At present the currents of opinion shew the urgent need of approaching social questions from the Christian side. We *can* so approach them. Nothing that belongs to men lies outside the scope of the Gospel. We *ought* so to approach them: what is required of us is, not simply silent, inward faith, but open, courageous confession. I know how hard it is to make such a confession. I know, how many generous feelings—feelings of our own utter unworthiness—check the words of confession as they rise to our lips. But in spite of this, if we do believe, we *must* have boldness to *say* that we believe. If we are silent, we dishonour our faith.

But then, many may say—many here are saying now—"I have so little power; so little time; so few and fleeting opportunities; that the little I can bring would make no difference to the final result." But, my friends, in such questions as these, there is no consideration of great and little. What GOD requires of us is simply what we have to offer—what we are. He requires no more, but He requires no less. And we are very poor judges in spiritual things of what is great and what is little. Our joy is to remember that GOD has tempered the whole body together, and it may be that its efficiency, its life, depends upon the right action of some part which we can hardly discern. We know by our own experience that vigour and strength come in living things, from the harmonious combination of many small forces. So too it is in that greatest of all living bodies—the Church—which is the Body of Christ.

Now, to gather all these small forces together, to provide for their effective action, we must avoid waste, and we must provide scope for each. We must, that is, have a sufficiently large area in which to combine our forces together, in order to secure both agents and fields for activity; and, on the other hand, we must regard each part of Church work in relation to other parts, and have, so to speak, a kind of rough plan of the whole field before we choose our path.

And here, I think, some one will meet me with an

Union of Church Workers. 411

objection which I have constantly heard, "Ah, this sounds very well, but we all know what are the evils of over-organisation." Well, my friends, I too know the dangers of mechanical, vicarious, formal service. I know pretty well by this time, from a Bishop's experience, something of the multiplication of meetings which do not *always* seem to be fruitful. And if, in order to marshal our forces for the more adequate fulfilment of the manifold duties which are laid upon us, it were necessary in any way to destroy or even to impair the sense of personal effort, or personal responsibility, then, at whatever cost, I should give up the endeavour to marshal them. But without the least doubt, I say that these evils which are foreseen are not real. Let us remember the figure which is so constantly used in Scripture, which tells us of our warfare; tells us of the army set in battle array; tells us of the conflict which we must wage, duly armed and fitly drawn up, against ignorance, suffering, and sin. And perhaps we have already found that there are some things which can be better done by an impersonal committee; whilst there are, as we know, many things which can only be done by the action of a friend. Our work is social, and therefore it must be organised: we are called upon to prepare and hasten the Kingdom of GOD.

Many, perhaps most, claims upon Churchmen have been already met in different ways; but what I feel is, that these different works have been done by separate societies, distinct in some measure in their organisation, and even in their spirit, from the one Society. And in such a case, there is always, as we know, a great tendency to disproportion. You may have met—as I have met—many who, for example, in their righteous zeal for temperance, have almost forgotten other duties; as if (I am speaking of a case which came before me) total abstinence were the sum of all the obligations of the Gospel. Now we must, as members of the Catholic Church, try to shew how the most different forms of activity—of Christian activity—are only so many different aspects of the manifold activity of the one Body of Christ.

So far therefore from developing over-organisation, such a scheme as I desire to recommend to you tends to simplify, to unite, and instead of isolating, to bring together those who have the most varied experience; to deepen sympathy between those who are engaged in different works; to join in the fellowship of one service those who stand apart in the execution of their offices; and, as I said before, we need the witness of one Society; one Divine Society, which claims and gathers into one all human efforts; which deals with, and is able to deal effectually with, everything which concerns man's welfare, in the power of a common faith; for if in any degree we can realise this thought, we may hope to move the world, when it sees men of every type combining together to offer up their best; and this is the charge which the Lord has left to His Church.

The *first thing*, I said, that we need, in order to secure such a Union *is an adequate field for labour*. We require an area which will provide opportunities of close connection; and also secure stability and continuity of action. Now when we consider the ecclesiastical divisions of our National Church, which we have received as part of our inheritance from the past, we feel that the *Diocese* is too large for such a Union, at least at the beginning. It is too wide to allow constant and familiar intercourse between Members of the Union. The *Parish*, again, depends upon a single man, by whose removal the working of the place may be changed in a day. We may therefore, in our search for a field for a Union of Church-workers, set aside the Diocese as not giving us the element of close connection: and the Parish as not being able to furnish us with the element of stability. We take next the intermediate division, the *Rural Deanery*, and that, I think, exactly meets the necessities of the case. It is not too large for frequent and full discussion among its representatives of the various questions which are brought before them, nor for a real co-operation between clergy and laity. On the other hand, it is sufficiently large to offer, what I may call, an average of life, of character, of opinions, of problems, of forms of work; and therefore to secure a substantial continuity in methods of action. The deficiencies of one parish, in this arrangement, may be met by the resources of another. One parish—I seem to see it in your own great town—wants workers; another parish wants variety of fields of work. In some parishes there is a waste of organisation. In others—I know how sad it is—there is a feeling of isolation and loneliness. In others, again, there is a tendency to narrowness, and to congregationalism. And so, in order that we may do our work as Christian co-operators, with healthy vigour, we need to look beyond our neighbourhood, to look from the parish to the Rural Deanery, from the Rural Deanery to the Diocese, and then from the Diocese to the whole breadth of the Church. The gain is obvious, and I know how many of you, in this Rural Deanery, have already felt the advantage of wider interests; some in the clerical Association, and many more in the Association of Sunday School Teachers.

So much then for the *area* which our Union shall cover. Having fixed this, we have to consider what are the *subjects* with which the Union shall deal. And here we must strive to get a general view of what Church work is. At once we feel, if our eyes are opened, that every true human work is also a Church work. But from our point of view the work falls into two great Divisions. There is the *aggressive* or *restorative* work of the Church, and there is the *educational*, or *expressive* work of the Church.

There is first the *aggressive* work of the Church. We have to deal with suffering, and neglect; with sin; and with all the problems which these bring before us. We must take an account of visiting; of nursing; of the administration of relief; of the poor outcasts with whom some of our streets are thronged; and of the terrible conditions of life, which seem physically to make a true Christian life all but impossible. And then we have to consider how we can best wage a successful conflict with the manifold forms of sin : intemperance, impurity, vicious and excessive amusements. Under this head, too, we must consider the case of prisoners brought to our police courts for the first time, and the case of those who are discharged. Looking beyond our own country there is also a work in which we all alike are interested,—Foreign Missions.

Now we shall see that such subjects as these involve questions of the greatest difficulty, and in order that we may deal with them at all satisfactorily, we require knowledge, for zeal alone is perilous. Someone has said, very cynically, and yet not without truth, that a great part of the wisdom of the wise is consumed in counteracting the folly of the good. We require then, that we may escape the application of such a charge to ourselves, to bring together, to classify, to question facts. We require for the fulfilment of our work, means for conference, for discussion, and for the comparison of our several experiences. We require in each case knowledge of the particular circumstances; of the special temptations to which those whom we wish to win are exposed. We require, in other words, what can only be given by the combined assistance of a multitude of devoted fellow-workers. And I will add, that in order to cope successfully with such evils as surround us on every side, we must meet them by local knowledge and zeal, and not by any distant central organisation. What we want is not to gain successes in a few brilliant skirmishes, but to win a vast campaign.

Union of Church Workers. 415

From aggressive Church work we go on next to the different forms of constructive Church work—education, intellectual, moral, spiritual. How much good may be done by a Church worker who is manager of an Elementary School if he shews the keen interest which he feels in the Bible lesson ! And it is a satisfaction to me to know that in this the largest town in the Diocese a good system of Bible instruction has been established in the Board Schools; so that those of you who are School managers can make the children feel the paramount importance which you attach to the words of Scripture.

Then again, Night Schools—I don't know whether at present you have Saturday classes, which have been followed with most abundant blessing in London—and Sunday Schools offer a fruitful field for the labour of Church workers. There is also later teaching—all that is included in Bible classes; in lectures for those who are engaged in special occupations; in Church Reading Societies; in libraries. And there is beyond this, the whole question of clubs and recreations; and that which seems to me to be the very key to our Christian position, the maturer training of the fathers and mothers of England. For it is to the family that we must look for the surest hope of the future. And I think that in the past we have looked too little to the family. The good mother makes the good son and the good daughter. And nothing, here let me speak frankly, has given me so much pain, and caused me so much misgiving, in looking to the future, as the general decay, I had almost said in many cases the total absence, of parental authority in the North. The children among us, even from their infant years, seem to feel none of that natural respect, that due reverence, for mother or father, which is the one foundation of the Christian character.

It is a natural transition from the home to the Church, from the reverence of parents to the worship of God. And here how much has been done; how much may be done, by the churchwardens and sidesmen! I rejoice to know how highly these offices are esteemed, and with what generous pride laymen regard the important duties which they carry with them. Then there are the duties of the choir, and of the bell-ringers, which require to be placed in their true religious dignity. And to go outside direct Church work, there is room for important services in connection with Friendly Societies in which Churchmen may yet take a keener interest than they have hitherto done.

With these manifold branches of Church work opening out before us, we can feel how much scope there is for powers and endowments of every kind. And when such services are felt to be part of the one offering to God in His Church, many will be united in the closest and holiest sympathy, who at present are hardly conscious of any bond to hold them together. The whole body of churchmen will come to know something of that feeling which characterised the first Church, when all were of one heart and one soul, when to be a Christian was to find the assurance of a friend in everyone who bore the same most holy Name.

This being so, you will feel at once that it is of vital importance to our Union of Church Workers that we should secure an adequate representation of every class, as well of women as of men. What work (for example) which no one else can do, may be done by vigorous and devoted foremen in our shipyards, and in our great factories? They alone can do what their position places in their power. They can do what no minister can do. They can spread about them an atmosphere of purity under which evil must die.

In all that I have said I have assumed what experience has, I am sure, already shewn us, that such Church work as I have described must be done on a religious basis. In this respect, as members of the National Church, we are

Union of Church Workers. 417

bound, in all humility, with all confession of our failures, to recognise what our responsibility is. We must remember that no other Communion, however devoted, can lessen even in the least degree *our* responsibility. Every man may take away something from the weight of our burden, but to the last the inexhaustible responsibility rests with us. Yet while we recognise this overwhelming charge, we shall welcome to the uttermost, help which comes to us from others who are not included in our own Communion; and in the sketch which I have given of the different forms of Church work, there are many works in which others who love Christ, no less sincerely than ourselves, can join with us. So far, then, I say, let us welcome their help, and join with them in shewing the strength of the Name by which we are called; and so far let us work with them, while we hold unfalteringly and loyally to our own confession. And I myself believe that it is through fellowship under these conditions that fuller outward fellowship in GOD's good time will come to us.

Meanwhile, for ourselves, we shall endeavour to give a deeper spiritual life to our Union by common prayer; by simple social gatherings, in which all Church-workers will meet in the strength of their common faith; and by periodic services. And just as I charge our younger clergy to study again and again the counsels and the promises given to them in the Ordination service, so I would ask our laity to study again and again, when their zeal grows cold, the services for Baptism and Confirmation. Taught and sustained by such words, we shall do in patience, in confidence, in quietness, whatever we do together; and that which is so done and brought to GOD, assuredly He will bless.

While I give this counsel, I can say naturally that I am glad that this idea of a Union of Church Workers which I have watched now, and not without anxiety, for some six months, has been carefully considered and well weighed, before it has even been conditionally adopted. I am glad that it was not accepted at once through an outburst of enthusiasm. The difficulties by which it is beset have been pondered. That which begins its life under such conditions as these, promises a continual and a stable growth, and we may trust that in GOD's time it will bear fruit. But let me bid you not be anxious about results. Results are not for us. We know our work : GOD will give the issue as He sees good. We look back over the past history of the world and we see that GOD waits ; and perhaps we can see, even with our feeble vision and poor judgement, that it was well He waited. Where He waits we can wait too. As we wait, if it be so, in the fulfilment of our work we shall recognise that we all have an appointed office prepared for us by GOD. We shall offer the fulfilment of that office to Him in His Body the Church ; offer it in His strength, and for His glory, that is, that we may make Him a little better known. So working and so waiting, we shall gain from day to day and from year to year, strength for ourselves ; and GOD helping us, we shall make our Christian faith a little better known to those without; and we shall also make the splendid inheritance which we have received in our own loved Church a little better known to those who at present often misunderstand it.

In this hope, my friends and fellow-workers, I commend the idea of the Union most heartily, most confidently, to your thoughts, to your actions, and to your prayers.

Before I conclude, may I offer you an outline of the scheme as it presented itself to my own mind, that you may feel that what I wish to propose is nothing fanciful, nothing extravagant, nothing which cannot, in a very short time be made a fact. I propose—

(1) That the Ruridecanal Conference which already exists, shall be as it were a General Committee of the Union.

Union of Church Workers. 419

(2) That the Conference shall hold at least two meetings in the year for this work.

(3) That the Conference—many of you know its constitution—shall appoint a certain number of Committees—I have marked down six—to take charge of the different subjects which I have rapidly enumerated, consisting of an equal number of laymen and clergymen, with power to co-opt into their number others who are not members of the Ruridecanal Conference. You will see what is my meaning in this proposal. There are many Committees on which the services of ladies would be invaluable.

According to my plan, the *first* Committee would deal with visiting, including nursing, relief, sanitary inspection, and the like.

The *second* Committee would deal with evangelistic work, including all action with regard to temperance, purity, gambling, and profanity.

The *third* Committee would deal with foreign missions.

The *fourth* Committee would deal with one group of educational subjects—elementary, night, Saturday, and Sunday schools.

The *fifth* is a second educational Committee, dealing with Bible classes, Lectures, Lectures on Church History, and the like.

The *sixth* and last Committee would deal with Clubs, Friendly Societies, and Amusements.

Such six Committees would be able, I think, to deal with the whole range of subjects which I have sketched out.

When the Committees are formed, offers of work should be invited in every parish. A list of volunteers should be drawn up by the Parish Clergyman, with a description of the work already done or promised by each. Existing organisations would, of course, be welcomed, and brought at once into their proper place in the whole scheme. These lists would be sent to the Rural Dean, and lists of workers, in every department, would be sent to the corresponding Committees.

The Committees, having got the lists of the workers in the Union, would endeavour to cover the whole field of work with workers, not necessarily taken from the Parish to which they are assigned. I lay stress upon this ; and as I was coming here I heard to my great satisfaction that in an important parish in Newcastle every worker comes from other parishes.

As time goes on, if our work prospers, I hope that each Committee, gathering the varied experiences of different workers, will be able to suggest general lines of work in the particular department with which it is charged, not as obligatory but for general instruction and guidance. And we shall have men and women, masters in their several services, who will be able to give counsel to those who will afterwards carry forward their labours.

Each member of the Union should receive a card of membership, signed by the Chairman of the Committee dealing with the subject of his work, and signed also by the Clergyman of his Parish.

The card should exhibit the rules of the Union, which ought to be very simple.

(1) Each member should be a regular communicant.

(2) He (or she) should undertake to do some definite work distinctly assigned to him (or her).

(3) He should strive to the uttermost of his power to realise his fellowship with all those who are engaged in like work with himself, and use daily the prayer of the Union.

After some time of probation, workers in different departments should receive a formal appointment from the Bishop—just as at present Readers and Evangelists have a formal appointment—as Visitors, or Teachers, or Helpers.

Well, there is my scheme, and you will see, I think, that it is at any rate simple and practical. I commend it to your attention, and hope that you will do anything you like with it. If it fails to meet your approval, then substitute for it a better one.

NOTES.

1. p. 12. Service for the *Consecration of Bishops: The Archbishop.* Will you shew yourself gentle, and be merciful for Christ's sake to poor and needy people, and to all strangers destitute of help?

Answer. I will so shew myself, by GOD's help.

The corresponding Question and Answer in the Roman Pontifical are:

Vis pauperibus et peregrinis omnibusque indigentibus esse propter nomen Domini affabilis et misericors? Volo.

2. p. 21. A set of the Reports of the Society (1798 [fifth edition 1811], 1800 [fifth edition 1811], 1802, 1805, 1808, 1815) which is, I believe, complete, has been given to the See by Canon Tristram. The chief founder and most active member of the Society was Mr (afterwards Sir Thomas) Bernard, who was appointed Chancellor of the Diocese of Durham in 1801. He died in 1818, and the Society does not appear to have continued its activity afterwards. Mr Baker in his life of Sir T. Bernard gives an interesting account of the origin of the Society; and Mr Bernard's contributions to the Reports are of permanent value. His 'Introductory Letters' to the third volume addressed to the Lord Bishop of Durham [Bar-

rington]; to the fourth volume addressed to the Right Honourable Henry Addington; to the fifth volume addressed to William Wilberforce Esq., M.P.; his 'Prefatory introduction to the second volume,' and his 'Preliminary address to the Public' prefixed to the first volume are masterly papers, and fully deserve the praise given to the last by Mr G. J. Holyoake that 'it would 'be difficult to find to-day in any modern quarterly, 'a more discriminating or better-written paper, or one 'more advanced in conception' (*Self help a hundred years ago*, p. 30).

The scope of the Society is described in the following paragraphs of the original memorandum of its establishment:

The following are selected as 'the subjects of informa-'tion (*sic*), upon which the society is desirous of obtaining 'and circulating information:

'PARISH RELIEF—how it may be best directed for the 'benefit of the poor.

'FRIENDLY SOCIETIES—their good effects, and how they 'may be best encouraged.

'PARISH WORKHOUSES—the amendment of them.

'COTTAGES—the increasing the comfort and neatness 'of them.

'COTTAGE GARDENS—and the means of enabling the 'cottager to keep a cow, or of supplying him with milk.

'PARISH MILLS for corn; and parish ovens.

'VILLAGE SHOPS, for better supplying the poor with 'the necessaries of life.

'VILLAGE KITCHENS, and soup-shops.

'COTTAGE FIREPLACES and chimnies—the improvement 'of them.

'FUEL—how the poor may be better supplied with it.

'APPRENTICES to manufacturers, and all parish ap-
'prentices.

'COUNTY JAILS—the means and effects of reforming
'them.

'BEGGARS—the least exceptionable modes of assisting
'them.

'PUBLIC ROOMS for the resort of the industrious poor
'in cold weather.'

The thirty-nine articles in the first volume deal with some aspects of nearly all these questions, and the later volumes give abundant illustrations of the zeal with which clergy and laity endeavoured to meet ignorance and distress. Mr Holyoake has given many extracts from the Reports in the work above quoted. I have, I may add, been unable to find the copy of the first volume of the Reports (dated 1797) which Mr Holyoake sent 'duly bound in ecclesiastical morocco' to Bishop Lightfoot in memory of his Presidency at the Co-operation Congress at Newcastle in 1884.

3. p. 105. May I be allowed to quote once again words which give their full message only in the original?

In lectulo [Columba] residet pernox; ubi pro stramine nudam habebat petram, et pro pulvillo lapidem,...Ibidem itaque residens, ultima ad fratres mandata, solo audiente ministro, commendat, inquiens, 'Hæc vobis, o filioli, no-
'vissima commendo verba, ut inter vos mutuam et non
'fictam habeatis caritatem, cum pace: et si ita, juxta
'sanctorum exempla patrum, observaveritis, Deus, con-
'fortator bonorum, vobis auxiliabitur, et ego, cum ipso
'manens, pro vobis interpellabo; et non tantum præsentis
'vitæ necessaria ab eo sufficienter administrabuntur, sed
'etiam æternalium bonorum præmia, divinorum observa-
'toribus præparata, tribuentur.'

Notes. 425

The account of Columba's death which follows must be added:

Sanctus, necdum egrediente anima, apertis sursum oculis, ad utrumque latus cum mira vultus hilaritate et lætitia circumspiciebat, sanctos scilicet obvios intuens angelos. Diormitius tum sanctam sublevat ad benedicendum sancti monachorum chorum dexteram manum. Sed et ipse venerabilis pater, in quantum poterat, simul suam movebat manum, ut videlicet quod voce in egressu non valebat animæ, etiam motu manus fratres videretur benedicere. Et, post sanctam benedictionem taliter significatam, continuo spiritum exhalavit (Adamnan, III. 23).

Circa galli cantum [Hilda] percepto viatico sacrosanctæ communionis, cum, arcessitis ancillis Christi quæ erant in eodem monasterio, de servanda eas invicem, immo cum omnibus, pace evangelica admoneret, inter verba exhortationis læta mortem vidit, immo, ut verbis Domini loquar, de morte transivit ad vitam (Bede, *Hist. Eccles.* iii. 23).

4. p. 106. The answers to Bp Barrington's Primary Visitation in 1792 are preserved at Auckland, and give a most vivid and instructive picture of the religious life of the Diocese.

The Methodists, as a general rule, attended Church. They are habitually distinguished from 'Dissenters.' Thus the following answers are found:

'There are some Methodists, but no Dissenters.'

'The Methodists regularly attend Divine Service, and 'are very seldom absent at the Communion.'

'We have no Methodists but what come to Church.'

'There is a Meeting attended by some of the common 'people...who disperse at the Bell's ringing for the last 'time for Church, and many attend the Service of the 'Church afterwards.'

W. C.

In a few cases there was Daily Service. Holy Communion was administered commonly five times a year, and in a few cases every month, and on the Great Festivals.

There were a fair number of Sunday Schools, and some returns of Catechising in Church in Lent and in Summer.

About one fourth of the Clergy were non-resident.

The stipends of Curates, often in sole charge, range from £15 to £50 (in one case £80). One Curate received £6 'which' he writes 'I refused to take for some time but 'in time necessity compelled me to take it.'

5. p. 113. Acts xvi. 7. The reading τὸ πνεῦμα Ἰησοῦ is supported by overwhelming authority. The phrase is unique. Compare Phil. i. 19 τὸ πνεῦμα Ἰησοῦ Χριστοῦ Rom. viii. 9, (1 Pe. i. 11) πνεῦμα Χριστοῦ.

Τὸ πνεῦμα occurs absolutely in the Acts: ii. 4; viii. 18, 29; x. 19; xi. 12 (28); (xxi. 4).

6. p. 120. The Collect used at the opening of Convocation is of singular beauty. It was used at the Convocation of Canterbury in 1562 when Abp Parker said prayers in Latin, 'with the usual Collects and a new Prayer proper 'to be said in a Provincial Synod' (Strype *Parker* i. 241).

Domine Deus, Pater luminum et fons omnis sapientiæ! nos, ad scabellum pedum tuorum provoluti, humiles tui et indigni famuli, Te rogamus, ut, qui in Nomine tuo, sub auspiciis clementissimi Regis N., hic convenimus, gratia tua cælitus adjuti, ea omnia investigare, meditari, tractare, et discernere valeamus, quæ honorem tuum et gloriam promoveant, et in Ecclesiæ cedant profectum. Concede igitur, ut Spiritus tuus, qui Concilio olim Apostolico, huic nostro etiam nunc insideat, ducatque nos in omnem veritatem quae est secundum pietatem: ut, qui, ad amussim sanctæ Reformationis nostræ, errores, corruptelas, et superstitiones olim hic grassantes, tyrannidemque Papalem, merito et serio repudiavimus, Fidem Apostolicam et vere

Catholicam firmiter et constanter teneamus omnes; tibique rite puro cultu intrepidi serviamus, per Jesum Christum, Dominum et Servatorem nostrum. Amen.

7. p. 135. 'An analysis of the elements of happiness 'would hardly be in place here, but it may be remarked 'that neither poverty nor wealth have much part in it. 'The main conditions of human happiness I believe to be 'work and affection, and he who works for those he loves 'fulfils these conditions most easily' (C. Booth, *Labour and Life of the People: East London* i. p. 131 note).

8. p. 147. This saying, which Mazzini quotes more than once, comes from Pascal, (*Préface sur le traité du vide*, i. p. 98 ed. Faugère) ...la même chose arrive dans la succession des hommes que dans les âges différents d'un particulier. De sorte que la suite des hommes, pendant le cours de tant de siècles, doit être considérée comme un même homme qui subsiste toujours et qui apprend continuellement. Pascal then develops the thought which Bacon brought into prominence: *antiquitas seculi juventus mundi*.

9. p. 280. There is I think, a higher aspect of Nature which combines the two aspects described by Browning in the prologue to *Asolando*. First

'natural objects seem to stand
Palpably fire-clothed,
...like the Bush
Burning but unconsumed.'

Then

The lambent flame is—where?
Lost from the naked world: Italia's rare
O'errunning beauty crowds the eye—
But flame? The bush is bare.

We may feel truly that GOD not only 'transcends,' but

is immanent, and makes Himself known through all that we come to know of the world. The Divine light is seen in and through and not around the objects of sense.

10. p. 284. Steffens quoted by Emerson in his Address on the Progress of Culture.

11. p. 287. Herveius Burgidolensis (sæc. xii.) on Hebr. xii. 23.

www.ingramcontent.com/pod-product-compliance
Lightning Source LLC
Chambersburg PA
CBHW071434300426
44114CB00013B/1436